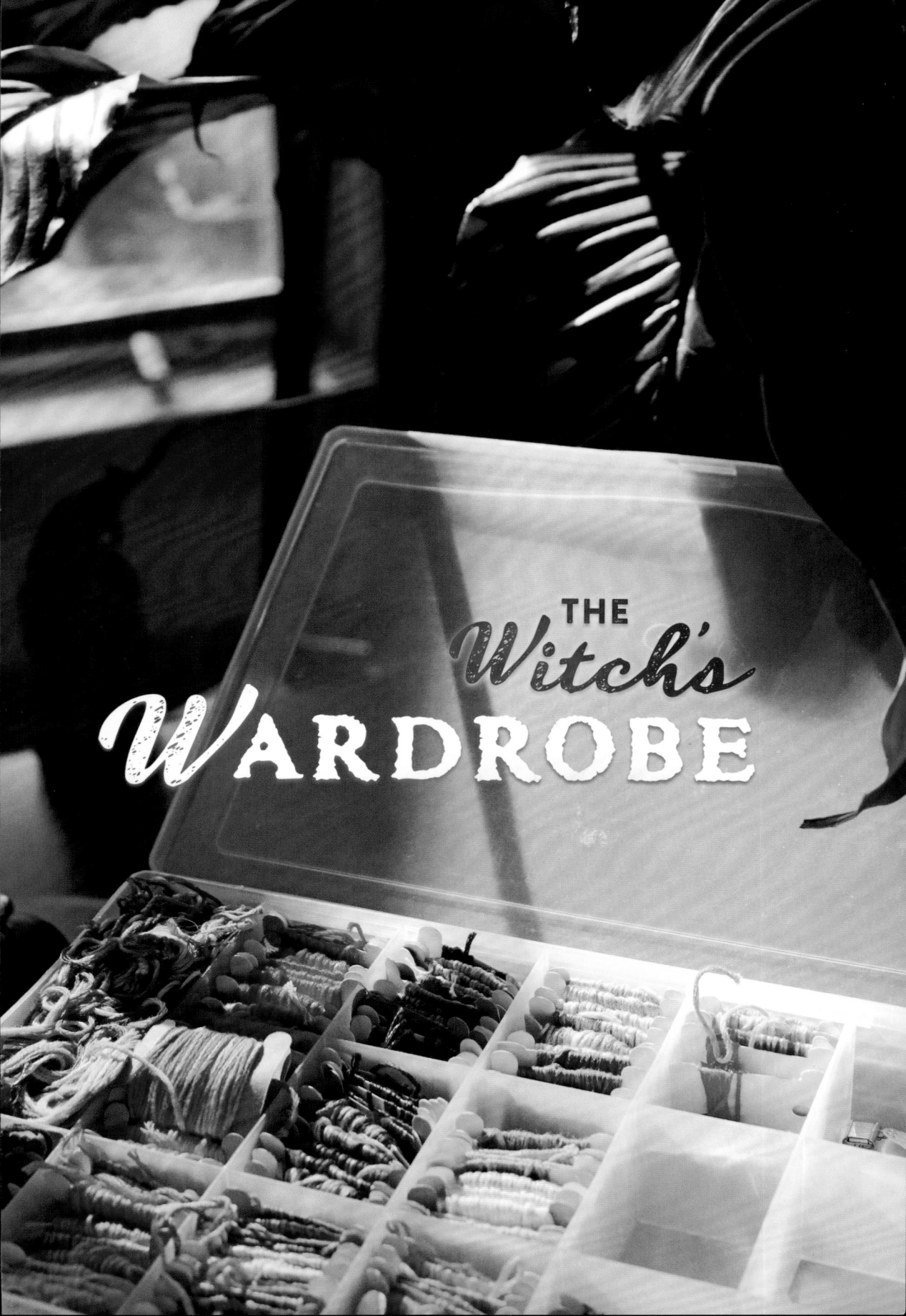

© Teresa Gugerty

ABOUT THE AUTHOR

Raechel Henderson is a Pagan and witch, following an eclectic and independent path. She currently works with Hestia and Turtle in her magical practice. She contributes articles to Llewellyn's almanacs and calendars, and she blogs about magic, creativity, and living by your own patterns. Raechel is a dual-class seamstress/shieldmaiden and has been sewing professionally since 2008. She is also the author of *Sew Witchy*, *The Scent of Lemon & Rosemary*, and *The Natural Home Wheel of the Year*. Visit her on Instagram: @idiorhythmic.

THE
Witch's
WARDROBE
sew your own
WITCHCORE WEAR

RAECHEL HENDERSON

LLEWELLYN
WOODBURY, MINNESOTA

The Witch's Wardrobe: Sew Your Own Witchcore Wear Copyright © 2024 by Raechel Henderson. All rights reserved. No part of this book may be used or reproduced in any manner whatsoever, including internet usage, without written permission from Llewellyn Worldwide Ltd., except in the case of brief quotations embodied in critical articles and reviews.

FIRST EDITION
First Printing, 2024

Book design by Lauryn Heineman
Cover design by Shira Atakpu
Cover photo by Tara Schueller
Interior illustrations by Llewellyn Art Department, except on pages 15, 73, 86, 99, 111, 119, 139, and 145
Photos on pages 46, 87, 120, 125, 126, 133, 149, 150, 159, and 166 by Raechel Henderson
Photos on pages iii, vii, viii, x, 11, 16, 22, 28, 32, 36–37, 38, 44, 50–51, 52, 56, 58, 63, 64, 74, 80, 88, 94, 98, 100, 105, 106, 108, 112, 116, 134, 140, 146, 152, 160, 164, 168, 170, and 172 by Llewellyn Art Department

Photography is used for illustrative purposes only. The persons depicted may not endorse or represent the book's subject. All participating familiars were rewarded with treats.

Llewellyn Publications is a registered trademark of Llewellyn Worldwide Ltd.

Library of Congress Cataloging-in-Publication Data (Pending)
ISBN: 978-0-7387-7709-2

Llewellyn Worldwide Ltd. does not participate in, endorse, or have any authority or responsibility concerning private business transactions between our authors and the public.

All mail addressed to the author is forwarded, but the publisher cannot, unless specifically instructed by the author, give out an address or phone number.

Any internet references contained in this work are current at publication time, but the publisher cannot guarantee that a specific location will continue to be maintained. Please refer to the publisher's website for links to authors' websites and other sources.

Llewellyn Publications
A Division of Llewellyn Worldwide Ltd.
2143 Wooddale Drive
Woodbury, MN 55125-2989
www.llewellyn.com

Printed in China

MIX
Paper | Supporting responsible forestry
FSC™ C007683

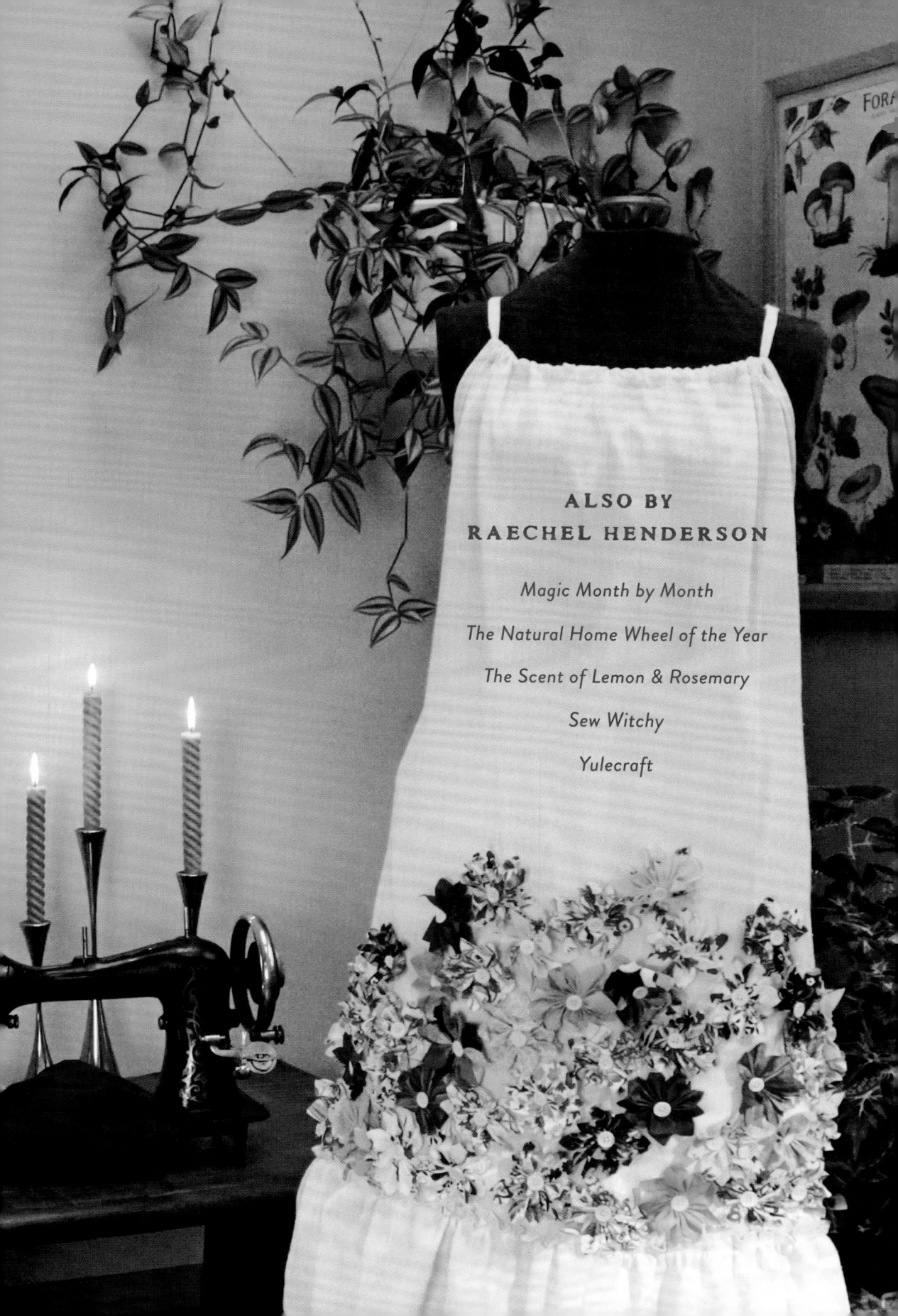

ALSO BY
RAECHEL HENDERSON

Magic Month by Month

The Natural Home Wheel of the Year

The Scent of Lemon & Rosemary

Sew Witchy

Yulecraft

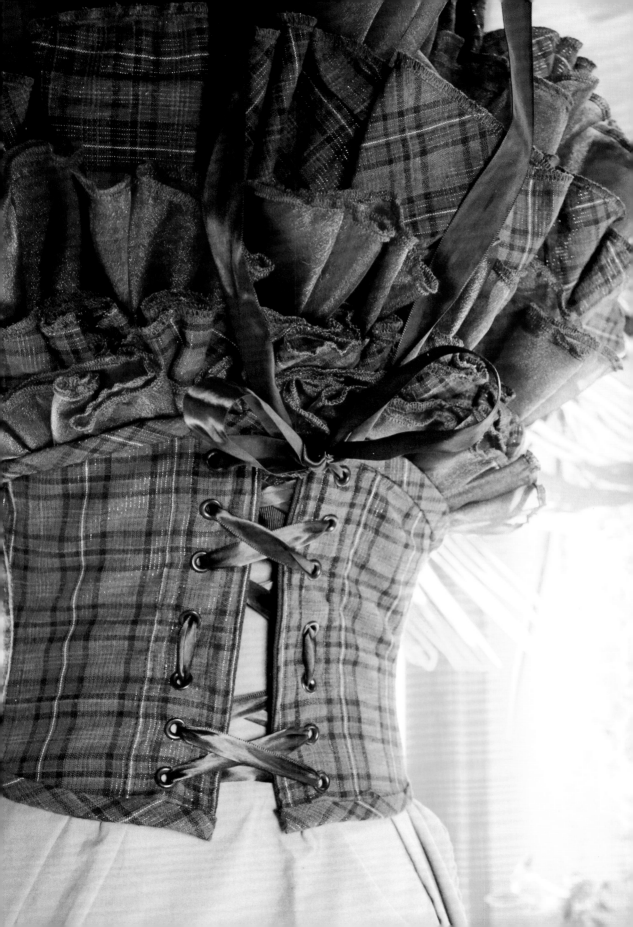

Contents

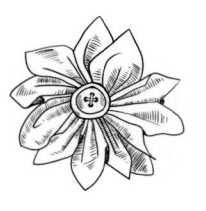
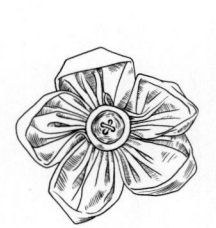

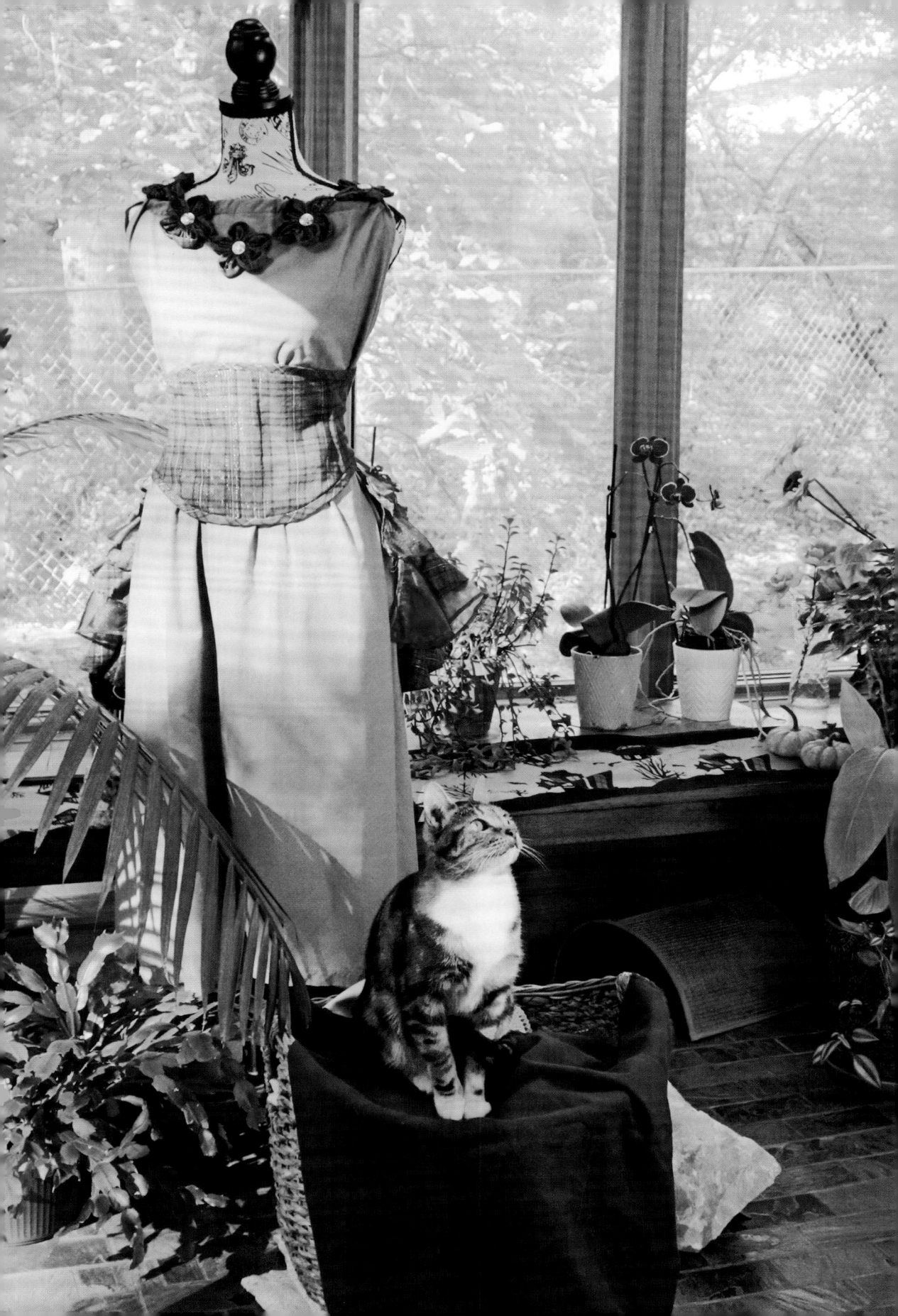

Introduction

Hello. I'm Raechel, a witch and a self-taught sewist. I've been creating and sewing garments for myself and others for twenty years. While I grew up around makers of all stripes, I never had formal training in sewing, pattern drafting, or garment construction. What I did have was access to books, YouTube, and a dislike of clothes shopping. That last bit only grew after the birth of my first child when shopping for a postpartum body left me near tears. Rather than continue to torture myself trying to fit into jeans that hadn't been made for me, I bought a pattern for a simple pair of drawstring pants. When I tried them on for the first time, I realized I would never have to buy clothes again if I didn't want to.

I love talking about that pair of pants because the experience was so liberating. I spent the next couple of years making the same pair over and over in different fabrics, learning so much along the way. Later, when I made a living sewing garments for others, I came to realize that what was true for me was true for most of us: people don't have off-the-rack bodies.

Our bodies each have unique measurements that mean most clothes need tailoring to best fit our individual shapes. But mass-market clothing can't take body diversity into account. This is why we are left with too tight or too loose fits, gaping and pulling, and other issues that leave us uncomfortable in our clothes. Even small things like garment care tags can cause discomfort.

All that experience has led me to write this book. I want to show you how to make your own clothes, those that are built to your measurements. I am going to walk you through taking measurements, drafting patterns, and making the garments. Together we'll build you a wardrobe.

This won't be any wardrobe, though. Because I'm a witch, I believe in the magic of clothes and sewing them. I wrote a whole book on sewing magic, called *Sew Witchy*—that's how much I think crafting and sewing are witchy activities. When it comes to clothes, I see their magic in multiple ways: in the way we wear them, in the effect what we wear has on us, and in the making of them.

I love long, loose clothing in natural fibers and beautiful colors. I prefer my cloak over my coat, comfy drawstring pants over jeans, and swishy skirts. I wear them for the same reason you might wear your favorite band's t-shirt, your pentagram necklace, or the political pins on your backpack. These items signal who we are and what we stand for. It is how we take up space in a society that is constantly telling anyone who doesn't fit in with the majority to make themselves smaller, less noticeable. Dressing how you want is an act of rebellion and magic all its own.

More important than how clothes present us to the outside world is the way wearing what we love makes us feel. This is especially true when it comes to magic. You don't need to wear a robe or a cape to perform magic. Your intent is the power behind your spells. However, I find that intent comes easier when what I wear is more aligned with my workings. I focus more, I feel more powerful, when I am dressed in clothing that fosters a witchy mindset.

More than that, I find wearing items I have made connects me to my creative side. That connection fuels my spellwork, as I find my visualization (another tool of magic) comes more naturally to me. I'm not saying that the garments in this book will make your spells more effective. But they may make you feel more in touch with your inner witch.

Finally, making and wearing "witchy" clothes gives me the opportunity to incorporate my magic into my wardrobe. The cloak that protects me from the cold also keeps malicious magics from clinging to me due to the spellwork I stitched into the fabric. The waist cincher (page 134) and bustle (page 140) both can be imbued with glamour magic. Sigils can literally be stitched on garments like the sigil skirt (page 44). Through your choices of fabric, thread, and notions, you can create a wardrobe that not only helps you in your spellwork but is magic in and of itself.

The style in *The Witch's Wardrobe* is a mashup of cottagecore and witchcore with a good amount of fantasy thrown into the mix. The emphasis is on long, romantic lines, layers, and lots of luscious trim. The color palette is whatever you choose. I recommend going with colors and prints that make you happy. Similarly, you shouldn't look at any of the pieces in this book through a lens of cis heteronormality. The skirts are not meant as "women's" garments any more than pants are "men's" clothing. Witches should be above such limited gender binary thinking.

You are welcome to make one or two pieces out of the book and pair them with your favorite off-the-rack piece of clothing. The single guiding principle of this book is wear what makes you feel good. (Taking into consideration weather conditions . . . frostbite will not make you feel good!) And if you are new to sewing or sewing your own clothing, you might be overwhelmed by the idea of creating a whole wardrobe. In that case, I suggest choosing one piece that you are really interested in and making it. Make multiples so that you get the hang of the techniques. Making multiples helps you adjust your pattern until it fits you perfectly.

The first part of this book introduces you to the tools and techniques you'll need to make all the garments in the book. After that, you get to dive right into the various wardrobe pieces with instructions on drafting patterns and making each piece. There are also sidebars that discuss the garment history or a magical concept. The appendix contains the templates and pattern pieces needed by some garments.

Whether you are making the breezy summer dress (page 80) for everyday wear or the pinafore (page 94) for ritual wear, I hope you find a spark of magic as you sew.

Materials, Tools + Methods

In this chapter I go over the materials, tools, and methods used in this book. For each project, you will find a section called "Terms and Concepts," which will list what methods you'll be using for that garment. I recommend reading this chapter before you start and then referring back to it as you dive into each project.

MATERIALS

All the garments in *The Witch's Wardrobe* are made with minimal notions, sticking with buttons, snaps, and grommets for closures. Waists have drawstrings or optional elastic (see "Drawstring or Elastic Waistband?" on page 13 for more information).

You can get fabric from hobby stores and online or from specialty shops like Spoonflower, but you shouldn't overlook places like thrift stores. There are even secondhand stores that specialize in craft supplies and fabric.

If you have larger measurements, items like curtains and sheets can give you more fabric to work with than the standard 44"- or 58"-wide fabric. Sheets are good for petticoats as they tend to be thinner fabric. Wool blankets make perfect material for warm, functional cloaks. Curtains make for sumptuous walking skirts.

Beyond fabric, you are going to need thread, trims, buttons, snaps, and other items. It's a good idea to pick up the notions when you are deciding on your fabric. Store everything you need for your project in one place. Each project has a section outlining what materials you will need for the garment.

Some materials, such as bias binding, can be made (see "Making Bias Binding" on page 8). Garage and estate sales, eBay, Facebook Marketplace, and thrift stores can supply you with a treasure trove of notions. Websites like Etsy can give you access to various artists who custom-make buttons.

When buying materials, make sure you get a little extra of the fabric, notions, thread, and so on. It is better to have a little left over than to find you need an extra couple of inches of fabric or another quarter of a yard of lace. Many fabrics, yarns, lace, trims, and other sewing materials are made in batches, and you can end up with something that doesn't quite match if you have to go back later for more.

Magic in Your Materials

As witches, we don't just pick any old fabric or thread and call it a day. The color, pattern, and even type of fabric influence the energies that become part of the clothing we sew. For example, corduroys in deep, earthy colors lend themselves to skirts for green witches. Black fabric of any type instantly brings to mind witchy vibes that make us feel more magically powerful. Water

witches might lean toward shades of blue and fabrics with nice drapes, such as sheer cotton gauzes and rayons, whereas glamour witches would choose velvets, shiny brocades, and metallic buttons to embellish their garments. When you are choosing fabrics, threads, and notions, take a moment to attune with them. Run your hands over the fabric. Hold the buttons up to the light. Consult color correspondences to match the material colors to your intentions with your clothes. Sewing magic, like all other types of magic, starts with intention.

How Much Fabric Do You Need?

Since most of the projects in *The Witch's Wardrobe* are made to your measurements, the answer to that question is "It depends." The other factor is the width of the fabric you are using. Most commercially available fabric comes in two widths: 44" and 58". In most cases you will be folding the fabric in half widthwise (selvage to selvage, not the cut ends) and then placing your pattern pieces on the fabric. This means how wide your pattern pieces are (and they can get pretty wide when you get to the dresses and skirts) will determine which width of fabric you can use.

Most of the time you will be drafting your pattern pieces before you start sewing, which will give you an idea of how much fabric you need. For most projects you will need enough fabric to make a front and back or multiple panels of each piece. There will also be waistbands, ties, pocket pieces, and other parts that can be made out of the fabric left over after you cut out the main pieces.

The best way to calculate how much fabric you'll need is by laying out your pattern pieces and using a yardstick to measure the length and width of each. If the longest width of your pattern piece is 22" or less, you can use fabric that is 44" wide. If the longest width of your pattern is 29" or less, you can use fabric that is 58" wide. Any wider and you will need to use single layers of fabric rather than double when cutting out your pattern. This will give you a rough estimate of how much fabric you will need. And when in doubt, get a half yard more than you think you will need, just in case.

Fabric Care

Before you embark on sewing your garments, you'll need to launder your fabric. This is especially true if you are using sheets, curtains, or other materials you got secondhand. Most thrift stores do not wash their wares before sticking them on the rack.

This isn't just a matter of cleanliness, though. New fabric can shrink when it is first washed, which can lead to warped garments. Take the time to wash and dry your fabric according to the manufacturer's instructions. Iron it as well if needed.

After you have sewn your garment, you will launder it in the same way that you did the fabric. However, some care may be needed when it comes to certain garments. If you have added trim and flourishes, like Fabric Flowers, you may want to put the garment in a laundry bag before washing it. Other garments, like the Bustle and Waist Cincher, should be dry-cleaned only. Proper care and maintenance of your garments means that your witchy wardrobe will last for years to come.

Right vs. Wrong Side of Fabric

Most fabrics will have a "right" side and a "wrong" side. The right side refers to the side that faces out and is meant to be seen. The wrong side is the side that faces inside, toward your body. These can also be thought of as the front and back sides of the fabric. With most fabrics, it is easy to tell which is the right side. If it is printed cotton, one side will be brighter and more defined. For brocades, the wrong side often looks like blocks of color as opposed to the colorful designs of the right side.

Thread

When it comes to thread, you have a dizzying array of choices. For most of the projects in *The Witch's Wardrobe*, you can use a polyester thread, which is suitable for most fabric types. Cotton thread is another choice. It is best used with cotton fabrics but should not be used for garments whose seams will be under a lot of stress (such as the waist cincher on page 134), as it isn't as strong as polyester. Silk and wool threads are usually reserved for embroidery and can be used for topstitching details on outfits. Choose thread that is close in color to your fabric so that the stitching isn't a distraction.

TOOLS

You will need a few sewing tools to make the garments in *The Witch's Wardrobe*. None of these tools is particularly expensive, and you might already have many on hand depending on your sewing experience.

- **SCISSORS:** You need two pairs: one for cutting paper and one for cutting fabric. Don't mix the two up. Paper dulls blades and makes it harder to cut through fabric, so make sure you know which is which. You might also want a pair of small detail scissors for snipping threads.

- **SEAM RIPPER:** In case of mistakes, have one on hand. This will also be used to open buttonholes and to open up seams.

- **IRON**

- **MEASURING TAPE**

- **YARDSTICK**

- **QUILTING RULER:** These transparent rulers often come in a rectangular or square shape. They are useful for finding right angles and marking 45- and 60-degree edges.

- **HAND-SEWING NEEDLES**

- **HEM GAUGE:** This is a metal tool with a sliding piece that helps you press up your hems evenly.

- **PINS**

- **SEWING MACHINE**

- **WRIST PINCUSHION:** This is one of those "nice to have" tools, as it gives you a handy place to store your pins as you work.

- **CHALK OR MARKING PENS**

- **BODKIN OR SAFETY PIN:** Use one of these for pulling laces and elastic through channels. A diaper pin is helpful as it locks the point, so you don't risk poking yourself as you work.

Make sure to choose the right needle for the fabric. Sewing machine needles are made to work with various weights and types of fabric and are marked as such. Not only does using the correct needle lead to better-looking garments and seams, but it is necessary for the correct function of your sewing machine. Consult your machine's manual to find out what brand of needle it uses. To that end, also make sure you are not using needles that have been dulled over time. Switch to new sewing machine needles every couple of garments to make sure that you get the best seams possible.

METHODS

Below are the techniques and methods you'll be using to make the garments in *The Witch's Wardrobe*.

Basting

Basting fabrics together can help avoid issues when you machine-sew the seams. Use a hand-sewing needle and a length of thread to join the fabric together with a long running stitch. Stitch ¼" from the edge. After you have sewn your seam ½" from the edge with the sewing machine, pull out the basting stitches and continue with the garment instructions.

Buttonholes

Most sewing machines will come with a buttonhole foot and feature. Read the instructions that came with your machine to learn how to use them.

Buttonholes should be long enough for the buttons you are using. Buttonholes should go through two layers of fabric. If a project has you making a buttonhole in one layer of fabric, back it first with some interfacing along the wrong side of the fabric.

Edge Stitching

Sew a scant ⅛" along a finished edge to give projects a crisp look and to close gaps that were left for turning fabrics. Use a matching thread.

Facings

Facings are pieces of fabric that are sewn inside a garment to help with structure around necklines and armholes. The fabric is sewn with right sides together, and then the facing is turned to the wrong side of the garment. It is then pressed and understitched (see page 10) so that it stays in place.

Finishing the Seams

Finishing seams is an important step in sewing and one that I am always loath to tackle. If you leave your seams unfinished, the fabric will begin to fray. Eventually, the seams will fray to the stitching, and holes will appear in your garment. Fortunately, there are several ways to finish a seam. Find one that you like from the following list and get to finishing.

PINKING

Sew the side seam. Sew the seam again, this time ⅛" inside the seam allowance. Use pinking shears to trim the seam, taking care not to cut through the two lines of stitching.

SERGING

A serger is a special type of sewing machine that stitches and finishes seams all at once. It finishes the seams by using extra thread to overlock the raw edges of the seam.

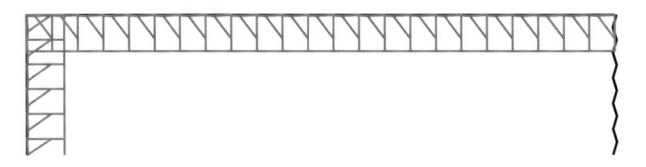

ZIGZAG

If you don't have a serger, you can mimic its finishing effect with the zigzag stitch setting on your sewing machine. After sewing the seam, set your stitch to the zigzag setting according to your machine's instructions. Then sew very close to the raw edges of the fabric.

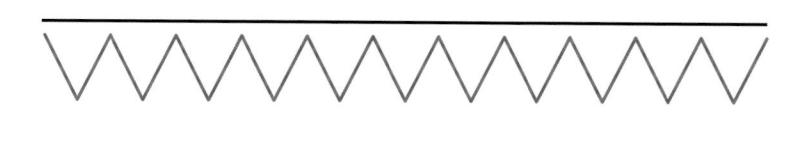

BIAS BINDING

Bias binding is a strip of fabric that has been cut on the bias (on a diagonal), which gives it great elasticity. The strip has then been folded over on both sides so there is a finished edge. Double-fold bias binding is folded yet again so that the raw edges of the fabric strip are encased in the fold and can't be seen. After sewing the seam, you can sandwich the raw edges of the fabric between the folds of the bias binding and sew it close to the folded edges.

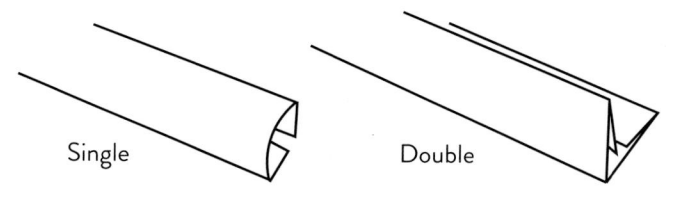

Single   Double

FRENCH SEAM

With the wrong sides together, sew a ¼" seam (A). Trim the seam (B). Turn fabric so that the right sides are together. Sew a ¼" seam so that the raw edge is encased (C).

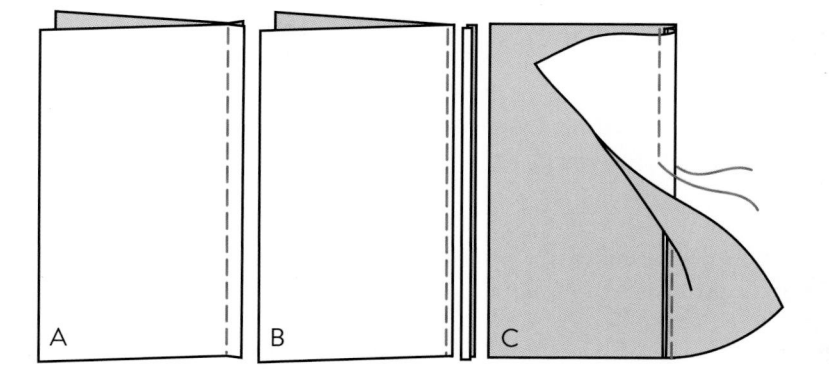

Gathering

Gathering fabric involves running a long stitch ½" from the edge of the fabric. The long stitch allows you to then pull the fabric along the stitching so that it bunches up. You can make gathering stitches either by hand or by sewing machine. To make a gathering stitch on your sewing machine, set your stitch length to its maximum length.

Gussets

A gusset is a triangular piece of fabric that is attached between a sleeve and the body of the garment. This piece gives greater movement to the arm hole and provides extra room for the bust.

Making Bias Binding

Bias binding is made from fabric that has been cut at a 45-degree angle to the selvage. The selvage is the finished edge that runs down both long sides of the fabric. This gives the binding lots of stretch, making it good for binding curves.

To make bias binding, cut 2" strips of fabric. Fold the edges in ½" down the length of the strip to the wrong side of the fabric and press. Fold the strip in half down the length of the strip, with the raw edges on the inside and press.

If you need longer lengths, take two strips of fabric and lay one on top of the other, right sides together, at a 90-degree angle. Stitch a diagonal line from outer corner to outer corner (A). Trim off the excess and open up the strip. Press the seam open (B). Continue as above.

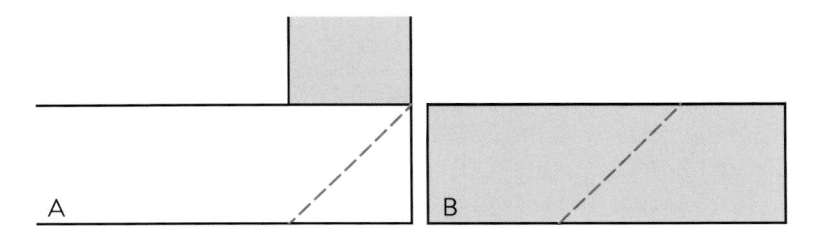

Narrow Hem

A narrow hem is made by folding the fabric ½" to the inside of the garment. The fabric is then folded in another ½". The hem is sewn on the outside of the fabric close to the first fold, throughout all layers.

Pivoting When Sewing

To pivot while stitching with a sewing machine, stop sewing while the needle is in the fabric. Lift up the presser foot and rotate the fabric. Lower the presser foot and continue sewing. To reinforce the seam, backstitch before and after you pivot.

Seams

Unless otherwise noted, all seams in this book are sewn at ½". All topstitching (stitching that is seen on the outside of the garment) is done at ⅛".

Sewing Darts

Darts are triangular seams that provide shaping for a garment. Start by marking on your fabric the point where the dart will end and drawing two diagonal lines from the edge of the fabric to the dot. Cut open the dart between the diagonal lines up to but not through the dot.

With right sides together, sew a seam along the diagonal lines to the dot. Reduce the stitch length as you approach the dot to strengthen the seam. Press the seam open.

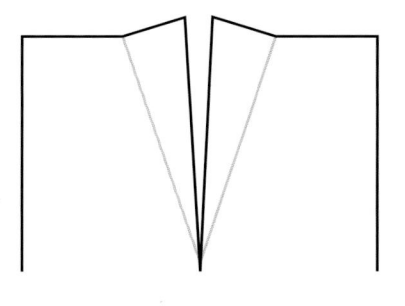 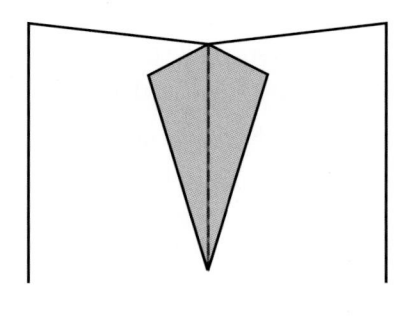

Slip Stitch

A slip stitch, also called the ladder stitch, is a way to close openings so that the stitches don't show. Start with the raw edges of the opening turned to the wrong side of the fabric. Starting from the underside of the folded fabric, bring the needle up at A. Directly across from A, push the needle into the other folded piece of fabric, slipping it between the fold at B. Run the needle ⅛" under the fabric and bring it up at C. Repeat, running the needle back and forth like the slats of a ladder until you reach the end of the gap you are sewing closed. Pull the thread tight, and the gap should close without the thread showing on the right side of the fabric. Then tie off your thread and snip the leftover.

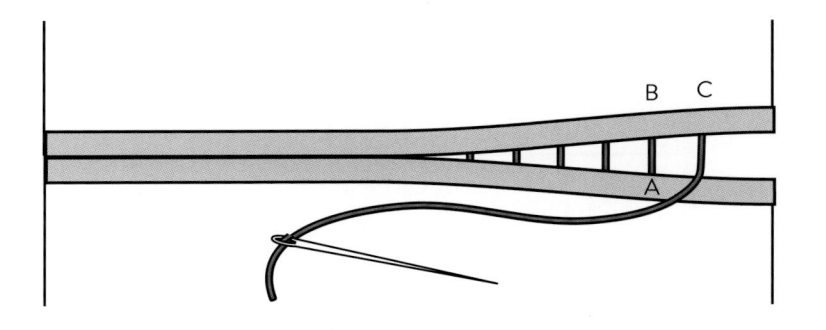

Standard Hem

To make a standard hem, do the following: Press the edge of the hem up ¼" inch. Fold the edge up again 1" and press. Sew on the outside of fabric close to the first fold.

Tailor Tacks

Tailor tacks are a way to mark fabric without chalk or quilting markers. It involves running a double-threaded needle through the fabric where you want to mark. Leave a length of about 2" on either side of the fabric, and then cut the thread. It will stay in place as you sew your garment. When you are finished, you can pull out the tailor tacks with tweezers. Use a thread color that contrasts with your fabric so that it is easy to see.

Tips for Hemming Curves

- Serge the raw edges (or zigzag the raw edges if you don't have a serger) and use the seam as a guide for folding, pressing, and hemming.
- Baste along the curves ¼" from the raw edge. Use the basting to help shape the hem as you press it in place. Remove the basting after you sew the hem.
- Use bias tape to bind the edges.
- Create a curve template from a piece of thin cardstock or a manila folder. Place the template on the wrong side of the fabric ¼" from the edge. Fold the hem up and over the template and press in place.

Understitching

Understitching is a way to keep facing from showing. Facings are pieces of fabric that are sewn to the inside of garments to help structure arm and neck holes. They also can be used behind sheer fabric in bodice sections. Sew the facing to the neck or arm opening. Press the seam out toward the facing. Then stitch very close to the seam line with the facing right-side up.

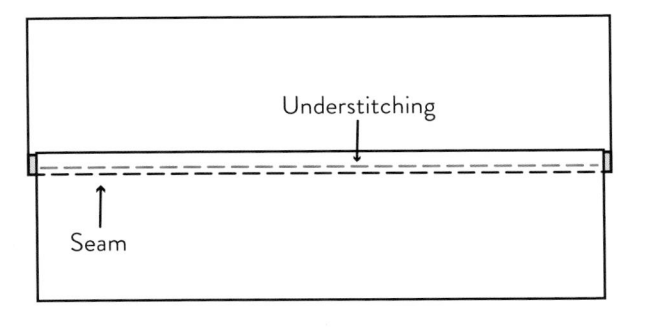

THE IMPORTANCE OF POCKETS

The garments in *The Witch's Wardrobe* all include pockets (where feasible). Pockets are essential to witchcraft, as they allow you to have your hands free and give you a place to store the cool rocks that you find when foraging. They can even be used in magic, as explored in the walking skirt on page 38. You are welcome to omit the pockets if you wish.

MEASURING TIPS

In *The Witch's Wardrobe*, you'll be charged with taking measurements. These are easier to take if you have a friend doing the measurement, but you can certainly take all the ones you need yourself. The garments in the book have very forgiving fits, and you can always use a toile (see "Your Best Friend: The Toile" on the next page) to help fine-tune the fit. All your measurements should be taken while you are in your underwear. Draw the measuring tape loosely around the part you are measuring. Don't pull it so tight that it cuts into your body. Stand straight and breathe normally as you take the measurements. Don't hold your breath, tense, flex, or suck in your body, as this can throw off the measurement.

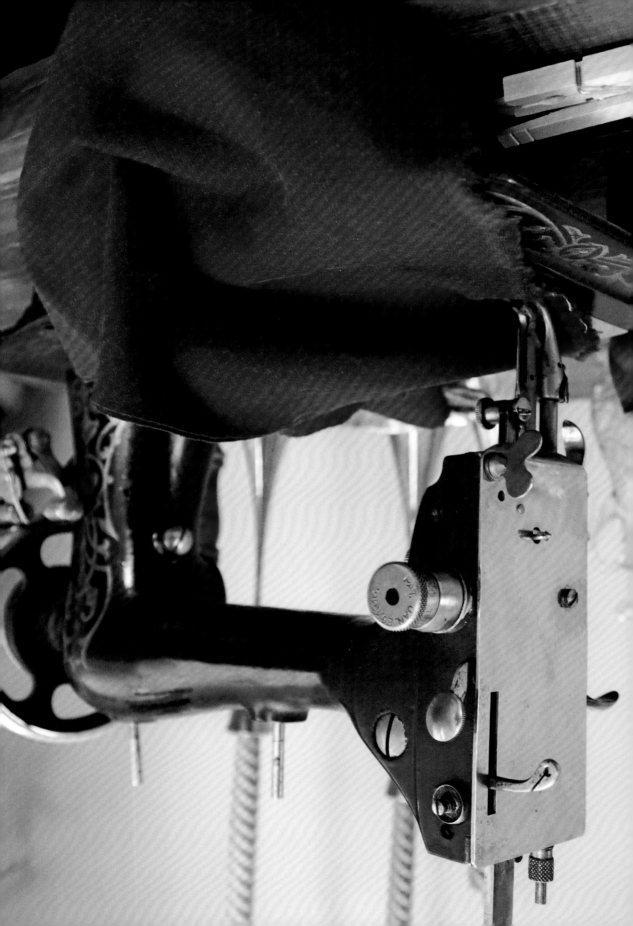

The measurements you'll be asked to take are as follows:

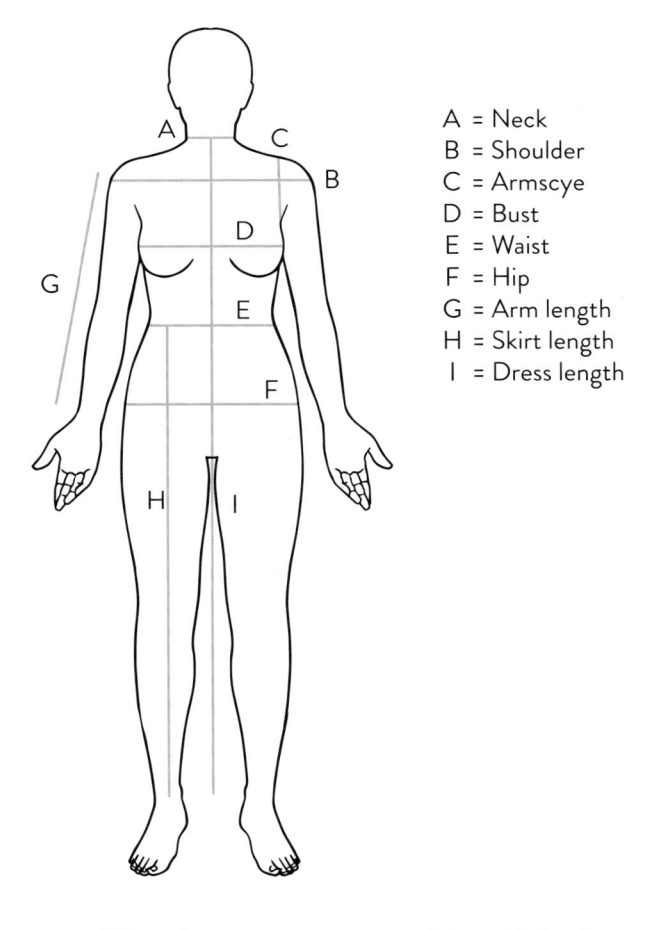

A = Neck
B = Shoulder
C = Armscye
D = Bust
E = Waist
F = Hip
G = Arm length
H = Skirt length
I = Dress length

NECK CIRCUMFERENCE: Wrap the tape measure around the middle of your neck.

SHOULDER CIRCUMFERENCE: Wrap the tape measure around your shoulders just above your biceps.

ARMSCYE: With your arm held straight out, wrap the tape measure around one of your shoulders, going over the shoulder and under your armpit. Lower your arm to your side, allowing the tape measure to adjust to the larger measurement.

BUST CIRCUMFERENCE: Wrap the tape measure around the widest part of your bust, making sure that it is kept even and straight across your back.

WAIST CIRCUMFERENCE: Wrap the tape measure around your waist. Make sure the tape measure is kept even and straight across your back.

HIP CIRCUMFERENCE: Wrap the tape measure around the widest part of your hips, including your stomach if it is rounded or hangs down. Make sure that the tape measure is kept even and straight across the back of your hips.

ARM LENGTH: With one arm hanging down at your side, measure from the top of your shoulder down to where you want the sleeves to fall (end).

SKIRT LENGTH: Measure down your front from your waist to where you want your skirt to fall (end).

DRESS LENGTH: Measure down your back from the base of your neck to where you want your dress to fall (end).

DRAFTING A PATTERN

Don't let the idea of drafting your own pattern intimidate you. The garments in *The Witch's Wardrobe* are all loosely tailored. They rely on shapes like rectangles, circles, and triangles. Most of the drafting can be done with a yardstick.

If you are new to sewing or pattern drafting, I recommend you draw your pattern onto paper first. Wrapping paper, paper bags, and newspaper can all be used for this part of the process. You can also buy specialty pattern paper from fabric stores.

Templates for projects that require tracing patterns are available at the back of the book. Large patterns are also available in PDF format at www.llewellyn.com/product.php?ean=9780738777092 at 100 percent for easy printing. Use the password "witchcrafter" to open the file.

Use your paper pattern to make a **toile** (see below) and mark any changes that need to be made on it. Then you can either alter the existing pattern or draft a new one with the alterations. The benefit is that you will end up with pattern pieces that can be used over and over again.

Ease

Ease in a garment is the difference between the finished article of clothing and the wearer's body. Ease allows one to put the garment on and have ease of movement and comfort in wearing.

Your Best Friend: The Toile

When you are making your own clothes, it is tempting to dive right in with pattern pieces and scissors, but I'm going to introduce you to the idea of adding a toile to your process. A toile is a mockup, usually made from muslin or another, cheaper material, to check the fit of a garment. Making a toile allows you to ensure not only that your garment fits but that it feels good on your body, that you like where the hem or sleeves fall, where the pockets are, and so on. You can use a pencil or pins to mark any necessary changes. Then you'll transfer those changes to your pattern. This will save you from disappointment later when you have put the garment together with your chosen fabric, only to discover that your design is too tight, loose, long, or short.

When making the toile, choose fabric like muslin or cotton. Old, worn sheets work well for this task. Also choose fabric that is close in weight to your final fabric so that you will know how it drapes.

Toiles are especially helpful if you are new to sewing or beginning a project you haven't tried before. It will give you practice with the construction, which will increase your confidence when you sew the later, final garment.

Drawstring or Elastic Waistband?

The garments in *The Witch's Wardrobe* are all made with drawstring waistbands, but if you would prefer to have an elastic waistband instead, follow these instructions:

1 Omit the buttonholes.

2 When sewing the channel at the waist of the garment, leave a gap in which to insert the elastic.

3 Measure a length of elastic that is 1" shorter than your waist measurement.

4 Using a safety pin or bodkin, thread the elastic through the channel, making sure to keep one end outside the channel.

5 Overlap the ends of the elastic and sew them together with a zigzag stitch.

6 Close the channel gap.

HOW TO MAKE A WARDROBE

There are thirty items in *The Witch's Wardrobe*, enough to fill your closet with clothes for all seasons. In order to make a cohesive wardrobe, follow these tips:

MAKE A PALETTE: Choose two or three colors for all the garments so that they coordinate. When choosing colors, have one neutral shade for base layers and undergarments like bloomers and petticoats. Then choose a couple of complementary colors for overgarments like pinafores and skirts.

PAIR ITEMS WITH EACH OTHER: The garments in *The Witch's Wardrobe* can be mixed and matched to create countless combinations. Consider:

- The panel dress (page 64) can be worn over the bloomers (page 28).
- Pair the walking skirt (page 38) with the neck warmer (page 150) and fingerless gloves (page 112).
- Wear a pinafore (page 94) over the breezy summer dress (page 80).

LOOK AT WHAT YOU ALREADY HAVE IN YOUR CLOSET: Do you have lots of graphic t-shirts? They're perfect when paired with the wrap pants (page 32). Have jeans? Wear them with the waist cincher (page 134) and bustle (page 140) for effortless whimsy.

PICK ONE GARMENT AND MAKE MULTIPLE VARIATIONS: The infinity scarf (page 146) is easy to make, and sewing a few in different fabrics allows you to change up your outfit whenever you want.

LAYER UP: Start with a chemise (page 22) in a neutral color. Add the petticoat (page 16), the walking skirt (page 38), and then a pinafore (page 94).

DON'T BE AFRAID OF ADDING A SPLASH OF COLOR: We witches love our black clothing, but an accessory of deep red, bright green, or purple can take an outfit from standard-issue witchy to green witch, storm witch, or whatever path you follow.

Petticoat History

Originally, the petticoat was constructed from two pieces of rectangular fabric. The pieces were pleated along the top and fastened to waist ties. The side seams stopped a short distance from the top to allow access to pockets, which were originally bags that were tied around the waist under the petticoats and skirts.

Around the eighteenth century, fashion revealed the petticoat in the form of the *jupe*, a skirt worn under robes *à la française* and other women's fashion that were split in the front. It was often made of lavish material, embroidered and decorated with various trims to either match or complement the robes.

With the dawning of the Regency period, simpler gowns with silhouettes meant to evoke Grecian columns came into fashion. Panniers—the structural garments that gave robes their exaggerated hip shape—were dropped. The petticoat's job now was to provide modesty, hiding the legs of women, as the gowns were made of lightweight cottons and muslin.

The bell-shaped skirt came back during the Victorian era and lasted in various forms until the 1920s. Women would wear multiple petticoats, which were often decorated with flounces and bustled at the back, to support their skirts. They also served to hide the lines and joins of steel hoop cages used for hoop skirts. And they served another function: keeping women's legs warm.

After World War I, silhouettes again contracted, and petticoats were eventually replaced with slips. With a few exceptions—the 1950s with its swing dresses and poodle skirts or Lolita fashion—petticoats have been phased out of everyday use.

Petticoat

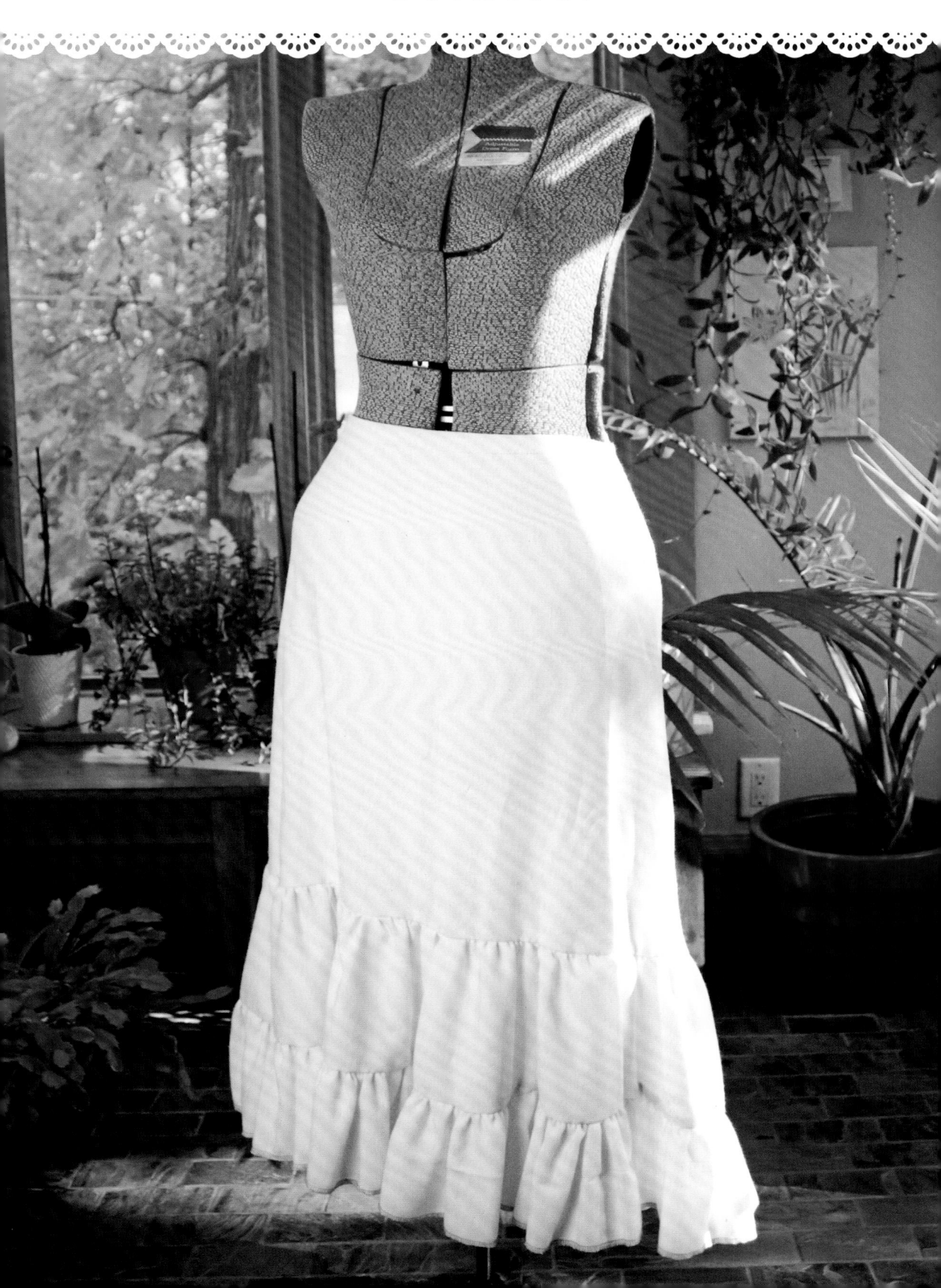

The petticoat has been a staple of various wardrobes for centuries. This easy first project for new sewists introduces various sewing techniques that will be used throughout this book. There are many reasons to create a petticoat to go with your outfits:

- It is useful for the layered look of the witchcore wardrobe.
- Petticoats help add fullness to your skirts.
- Petticoats can help keep you warm during the winter months.
- Petticoats help keep skirts from blowing up during windy days.
- There is something extremely satisfying in swishing around in a petticoat and skirt.

Magically, the petticoat can be used in spells for stability due to its function as a foundational garment. Stitch a few ivy leaves on your petticoat so you always walk in good luck and are protected from disaster. Anoint the fabric with orange blossom water to imbue it with stability. Or run it through the smoke of patchouli incense to add in vibrations of protection and good luck (especially with regard to money). When you are dressing, envision yourself donning a stable foundation of good luck, protection, and positivity when you step into your petticoat.

You can use any number of embellishments on your petticoat. You can run ribbon above the tier seams or add lace to the bottom tier. You can embroider the bottom tier so that cheeky little flowers or butterflies peak out. Really, the only limitation is your own imagination!

What Kind of Fabric to Use

Cotton is a good choice for your petticoat if you are going to use it just for warmth and fullness. Muslin is a cheap, suitable material. If you are Willendorf shaped, choose a muslin with a wider width. If you are making a petticoat that will show under your skirts, you can go with a plain muslin or cotton for the first two tiers and then a more decorative fabric for the bottom tier.

Cotton does have a tendency to cling, so if you are wearing a cotton petticoat under a cotton skirt, there could be some bunching. If this is an issue for you, pick a fabric with a little more "glide," like a lining fabric such as charmeuse or polyester. There are also anti-cling polyester linings that are specifically designed to avoid the issue.

MATERIALS
Fabric (see "How Much Fabric?" on page 18)

Matching thread (and optional coordinating thread for top stitching)

2 snap fasteners

TOOLS
Sewing machine and needle

Pins

Iron

Hem gauge

Measuring tape

Yardstick

Marking pen or chalk

Seam ripper (just in case)

TERMS & CONCEPTS
You will be drafting a pattern, gathering fabric, and hemming the bottom of the petticoat. See "Methods" on page 6 for more information.

Historically, some petticoats were made of flannel for warmth. If you are looking for something to wear to keep warm during the winter months, perhaps consider a plain, **lightweight flannel** for that.

As for thickness, choose a thinner fabric rather than a thick one. Fleece, wool felt, velvet, and the like will be too bulky. Stiff materials like canvas or denim aren't well suited for this project either.

And though the point of the petticoat is to be supportive, not seen, you shouldn't feel like you can't embellish your garment. Ribbons, lace, and embroidery have all been used before on petticoats. Make something you are going to enjoy looking at, even if you are the only one who will know it is there.

Old sheets are ideal for petticoats because they (1) are soft from many washings and (2) come in wide lengths to accommodate larger sizes. The petticoat in the photo was made from a top sheet.

How Much Fabric?

You will need a length of fabric equal to the length of your petticoat skirt piece and your two tier pieces. The width of fabric you'll need is determined by the bottom of the petticoat skirt piece. If it is under 22" wide, you'll be able to use 44"-wide fabric folded in half widthwise. If it is under 29" wide, you'll be able to use 58"-wide fabric folded in half widthwise. For any larger width you will need to cut out two of the skirt pieces on a single layer of fabric.

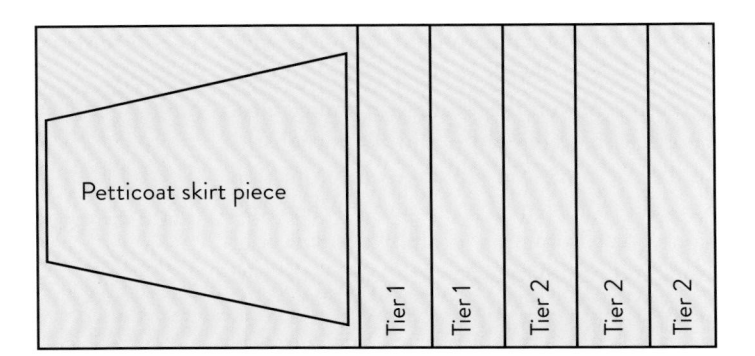

PATTERN DRAFTING

You will be drafting three pattern pieces: a petticoat skirt piece and two tier pieces.

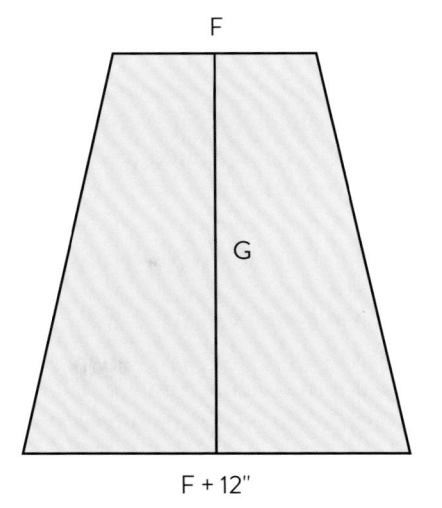

Measurements

You will need the following measurements:

- **A** = Your waist circumference
- **B** = Your hip circumference
- **C** = The length from your waist to your knees
- **D** = The length from your knees to your calves
- **E** = The length from your calves to where you want the petticoat to fall

Take your **A** measurement + 2" for the ease divided by 2, + 1" for the seam allowance. This is your **F** measurement.

Take your **C** measurement and add 1¾" for the seam allowance. This is your **G** measurement.

Take your **D** measurement and add 1¾" for the seam allowance. This is your **H** measurement.

Take your **E** measurement and add 1¾" for the seam allowance and hem. This is your **I** measurement.

Draw a vertical line equal to your **G** measurement down your paper.

Next, draw a horizontal line that is equal to your **F** measurement and that is centered perpendicular to the top of your **G** line.

Then draw a horizontal line that is equal to your **F** measurement + 12" and that is centered perpendicular to the bottom of your **G** line.

Draw two diagonal lines that connect your **F** line to the bottom line.

This creates your petticoat skirt piece.

Cut out a rectangle of fabric that measures your **H** measurement by 2 times the bottom of your petticoat skirt piece. You may have to piece the rectangle together from multiple pieces of fabric. This is the first tier of your petticoat.

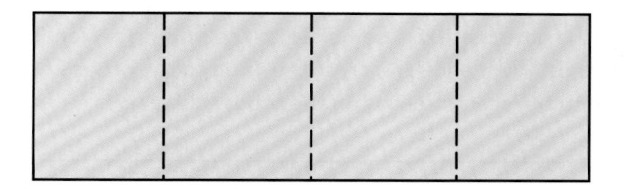

Cut out a rectangle of fabric that measures your **I** measurement by 2 times the first tier length. You may have to piece the rectangle together from multiple pieces of fabric. This is the second tier of your petticoat.

CONSTRUCTION

1 On the wrong side of the petticoat skirt, mark each side 7" down from the top edge. This is for the opening of the side seams so the petticoat can be pulled over your hips.

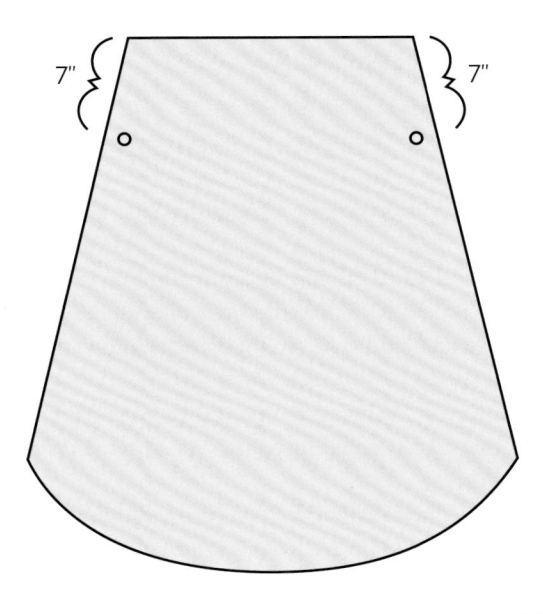

2 With right sides together, sew the sides of the petticoat skirt with a ½" seam using a basting stitch from the top of the petticoat skirt to the mark. At the mark, switch to a shorter stitch and continue to the bottom. Repeat on the other side.

3 Press the seams open.

4 On the outside of the petticoat skirt, sew close to the side seam from the top edge to where the basting stitch ends. Pivot and sew across the seam to the other side. Pivot again and sew up to the top close to the seam. Repeat on the other side seam.

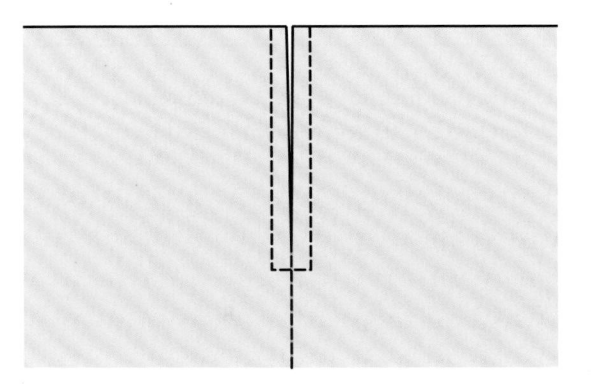

5 Make the first tier by sewing the short ends of the first tier fabric together, creating a circle. Press the seams open.

6 Sew a gathering stitch ½" from one long edge of the tier.

7 Mark two points at the bottom of the petticoat skirt at the center front and center back.

8 Mark four points equal distance apart on the long side of the first tier with the basting.

9 Match the points and the side seams of the petticoat skirt with the points on the tier with right sides facing.

10 Gather up the tier between the points so that the tier is the same length as the skirt. Pin in place and distribute the gathers evenly.

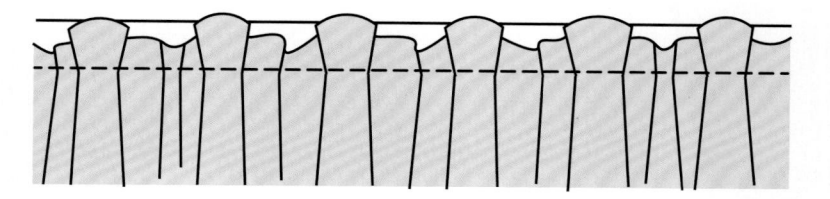

11 Sew a ½" seam attaching the tier to the petticoat skirt. Press the seam up toward the top of the petticoat.

12 Repeat steps 5–6 with the second tier.

13 Repeat steps 7–11 to attach the second tier to the first.

14 Open the basting at the waist side seams with a seam ripper.

15 Fold the top of the petticoat under ¼". Press. Fold under again 1". Press. Sew close to the first fold.

16 Attach snaps to the side openings of the waist.

17 Hem the second tier.

Chemise

The chemise is constructed from rectangles and triangles. Gussets provide ease of movement in the sleeves, and drawstrings at the neck allow for a neckline that can be adjusted to accommodate outerwear fashions. This makes for a garment that is easy to construct.

The chemise is one of the most versatile patterns in *The Witch's Wardrobe*. It can be made up to serve as a nightgown, a blouse, or even a dress depending on the fabric you use. The pattern makes economical use of your fabric and can be adjusted to fit all sizes. Combine the chemise with the petticoat on page 16, and you'll have all the undergarments you need as a foundation for the rest of the clothing in the book.

This garment can be embellished with lace, ribbon, and trims. The way the sleeves are constructed gives you a ruffled edge that could be embroidered before it is put together. This will hide the backside of the embroidery in the cuff.

What Kind of Fabric to Use

As the chemise is meant to be an inner layer, you want to use a lightweight breathable material like **linen** or **cotton**. If you plan to make this as a blouse or dress, you can use **synthetics** and **poly-blends**. A lightweight fabric is suggested, as it drapes better.

For this garment choose 44"-wide fabric. This will give you a finished bust measurement of 86", which should fit most figures. If you need more room, then go up to 58"-wide fabric.

How Much Fabric?

You will need fabric that measures 44" wide, or 58" if you usually fit a size 4XL or larger. Of that, you'll need a length that measures twice your **A** measurement + your **B** measurement.

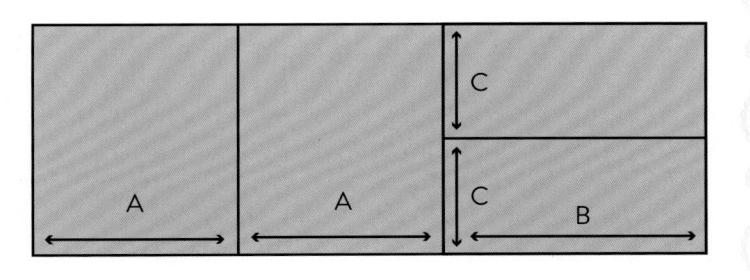

MATERIALS

Fabric (see "How Much Fabric?" below)

Matching thread

1 package of ⅛" elastic

54" of rattail or similar-size cording in a color matching the fabric (if you will be using a drawstring at the neckline)

TOOLS

Sewing machine and needle

Pins

Iron

Measuring tape

Scissors or a rotary cutter

Quilting ruler that shows 45-degree angles

Hem gauge

Small safety pin

Seam ripper (just in case)

TERMS & CONCEPTS

You will be creating **narrow hems**, using **gussets**, and **finishing seams**. See "Methods" on page 6 for more information.

PATTERN DRAFTING

Measurements

You will need the following measurements:

- The length from the bottom of your neck (where your neck meets your back) down your back to where you want the chemise to fall. Historically, it stopped at mid-calf.
- The length from the top of your shoulder (where your shoulder meets your arm) to your wrist.
- Your shoulder circumference (around your shoulder, under your armpit, and back up to the top of your shoulder). Loop the tape measure around your shoulder. Make sure your arm is down at your side, as that gives a more accurate measurement than if your arm is stretched out.

Take your body length measurement and add 2" for the neckline and hem. This is your **A** measurement.

Take your arm length measurement and add 8" to account for seam allowances and neckline adjustments. This is your **B** measurement.

Take your shoulder circumference measurement and add 2" for seam allowances and ease. This is your **C** measurement.

For the body, cut two rectangles measuring 44" by your **A** measurement.

For the sleeves, cut two rectangles measuring your **B** measurement by your **C** measurement.

CONSTRUCTION

1 Fold one body piece in half widthwise. Using the quilting ruler, mark a line 9" in length across the top corners at a 45-degree angle. Cut the corners off. Fold the other body piece and sleeve pieces in half widthwise and repeat the marking and cutting of corners at the top of each. When you are done, you should be able to align the tops of the sleeves and body to form a rectangle, with the diagonal sides matching. Keep the cut corner triangles for the gussets.

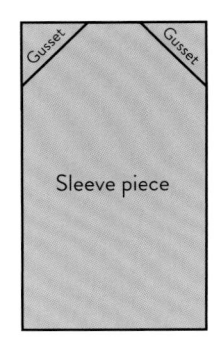

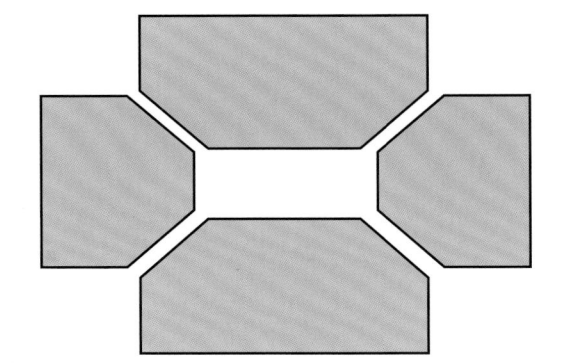

2 Make the drawstring channels along the top of each body and sleeve piece by sewing a hem. To do so, fold the top of each piece to the wrong side ½". Press. Fold in another ½" and press again. Sew close to the first fold.

3 You will make gussets to help with ease of movement. Do this by aligning one corner triangle piece to one sleeve piece with straight edges together and right sides facing. The diagonal edge of the gusset should face away from the hemmed edge of the sleeve. Sew a ½" seam. Repeat for the other three gussets and sleeve sides.

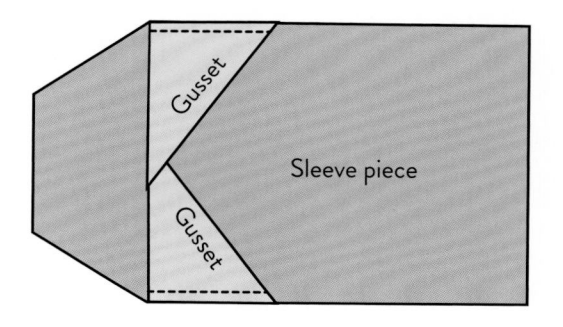

4 Once you have sewn the gusset pieces to both sides of each sleeve, it is time to attach them to the sides of the body. Align the unsewn straight edge of the gusset to the straight edge of the body, right sides facing. The diagonal edge should face away from the hemmed edge of the body piece. Sew a ½" seam. Repeat for the other three gussets and body sides.

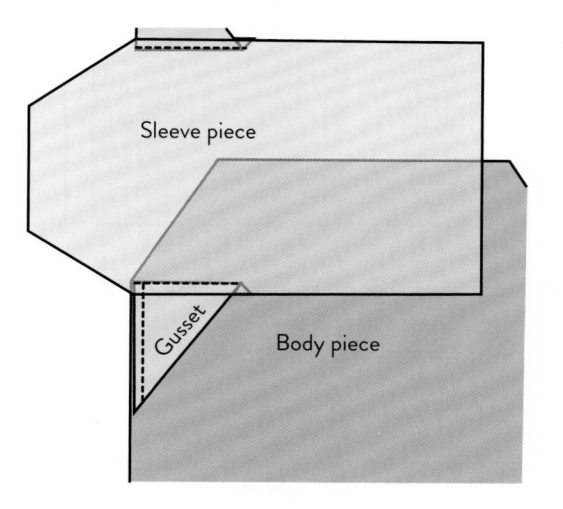

5 Now sew the sleeves to the body pieces by sewing the diagonal sides together. Start just after the neckline channels so they stay open. Stop where the other two seams meet. Press the gusset seams toward the gusset. Here are two views of this step:

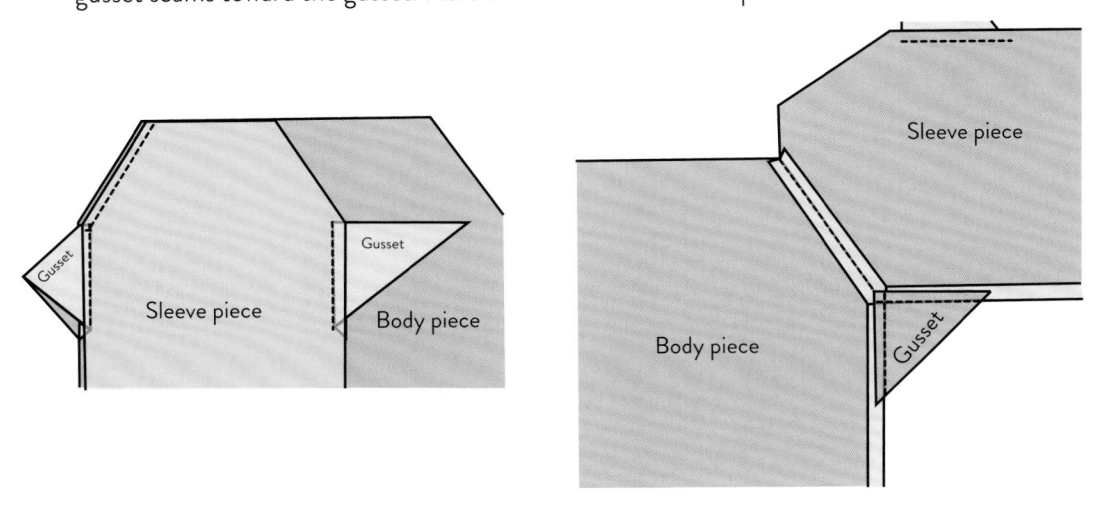

6 Finish the sleeves in the following manner: Press the hem of each sleeve up ½" and then another ½". Press the hemmed sleeve up 4" and press. Sew close to the first fold and then sew another seam ¼" from that seam to make an elastic channel.

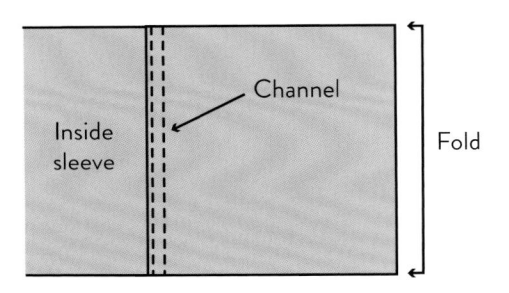

7 Cut a piece of ⅛" elastic long enough to fit around your clenched fist. Using the safety pin, thread the elastic through the sleeve channel. Sew the end of the elastic at each opening of the channel. This will cause the sleeve to gather.

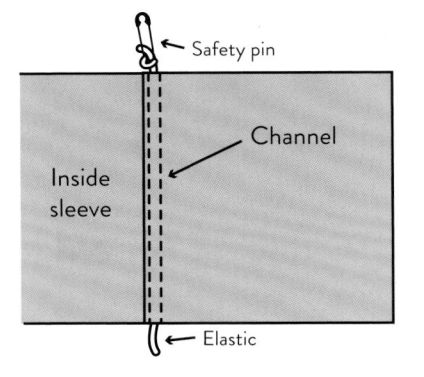

8 It's time now to sew the sides. First fold the chemise so that the raw edges are aligned with the right sides together. Starting at the sleeve end, sew a ½" seam along the sleeve, down the gusset, and down to the bottom of the chemise. When you reach the gusset seams, make sure you have them face toward the gusset to help secure them and to cut down on any itchy seams.

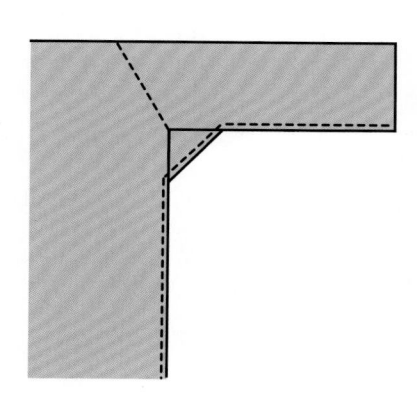

9 Give the bottom of the chemise a narrow hem.

10 Using a safety pin, run the cording through the neckline channel. You can either cut the cording into four pieces and tie bows at each opening, or you can run the cording through all the channels and draw it closed at one opening.

Chemise History

The chemise (or smock, camisole, shift, etc.) was the innermost layer for a good portion of fashion history. Usually made of linen or cotton, it served as undergarment and sleepwear. Depending on era and economic status of the wearer, the chemise could be simple and meant to be hidden under layers of clothing, or it could be elaborate with lace and embroidery, meant to show. The main purpose of the chemise was to protect clothing from the oils and sweat produced by the body. Most people would own at least two chemises, with eighteenth-century marital guides recommending at least two dozen for a wedding trousseau.

Bloomers

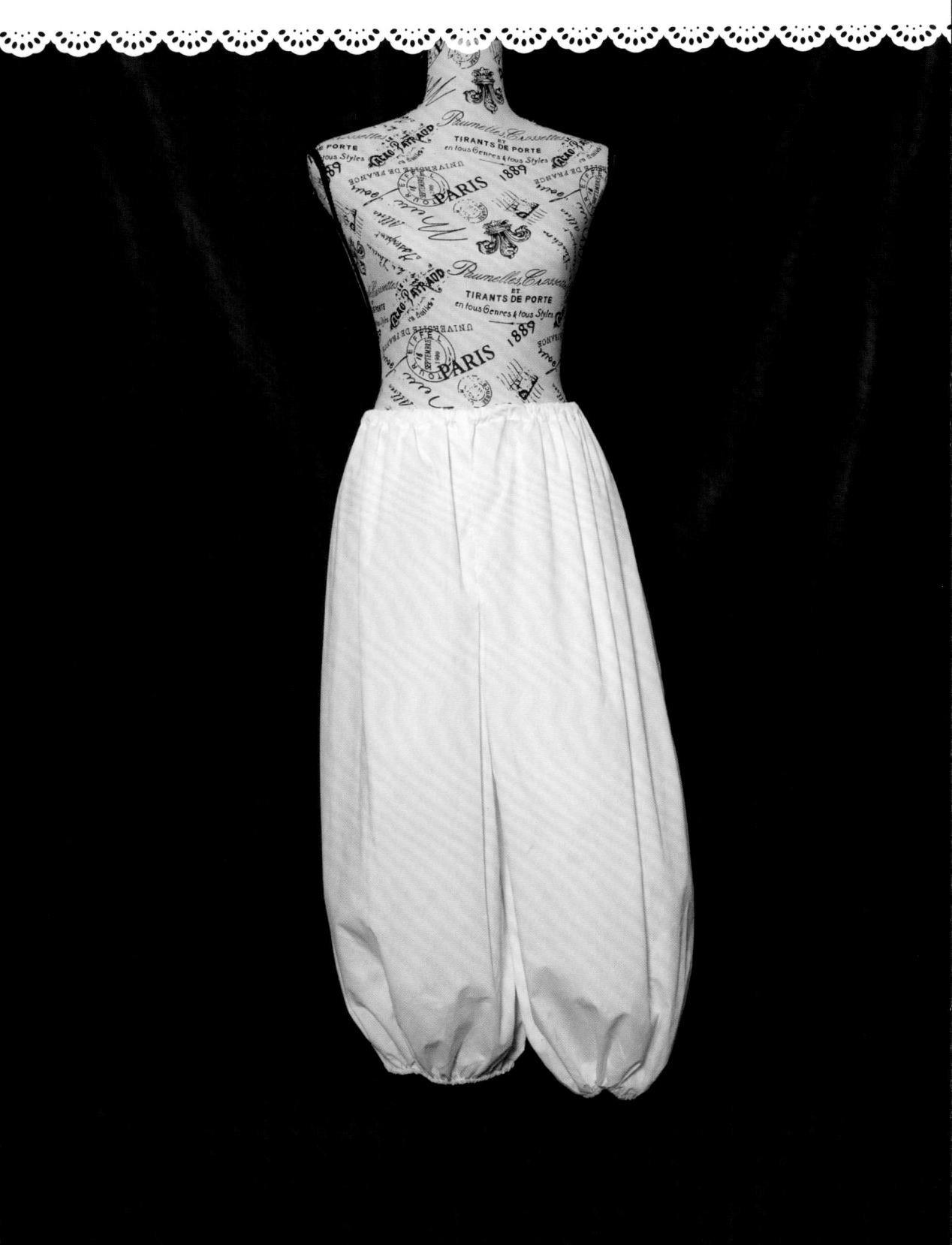

Bloomers served as underwear for a good couple of centuries. Wars, which commandeered fabrics like cotton and wool, led to smaller undergarments. Today, bloomers can provide warmth under skirts and dresses and can even be worn on their own with a blouse or pinafore.

Like the petticoat, bloomers have magical correspondences to stability, as well as fertility, due to their closeness to reproductive organs. If you are working spells for fruitfulness, embroider symbols that represent your goals on the bloomers. If you want to tap into your sexuality, add lace and ribbons to the bloomers to bring romantic and sensual energies into your life.

What Kind of Fabric to Use

Cotton is the best choice for your bloomers. Choose a lightweight **muslin** for undergarments or a heavier weight like **quilting cotton** for bloomers that will be seen.

PATTERN DRAFTING

There is no pattern needed for the bloomers. You can draw the crotch cutout directly on the fabric.

Measurements

You will need the following measurements:

- **A** = your hip measurement
- **B** = waist to just below your knees or to your calves

CONSTRUCTION

1 Cut two pieces of fabric with your **A** measurement by your **B** measurement. If you are using the entire width of your fabric, you need only cut it the length of your **B** measurement.

2 Fold the two pieces of fabric in half widthwise and lay one on top of the other, folds even.

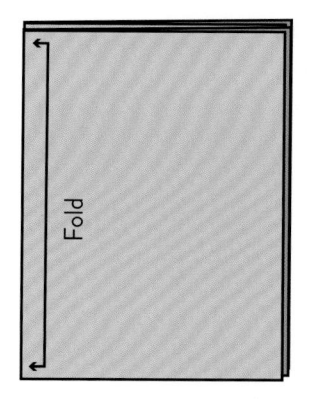

Fold

MATERIALS

44"-wide fabric in a length that is double your **B** measurement from below

Matching thread

1 piece of ¾"-wide elastic cut to your waist circumference – 2"

2 pieces of ¼"-wide elastic cut to your calf or knee circumference

TOOLS

Sewing machine and needle

Pins

Iron

Measuring tape

Yardstick

Scissors or a rotary cutter

Seam ripper (just in case)

TERMS & CONCEPTS

You will be **basting**, creating **bias binding**, making a **standard hem**, and **finishing the seams**. See "Methods" on page 6 for more information.

3 Determine how deep you want the crotch of the pants to be. The standard depth is 10–12". If you have a larger rear end or stomach, you will want to make the crotch deeper so that it will be comfortable and reach your waist. Start with a shorter crotch if you are uncertain, as you can deepen it if you need. Draw a rectangle on the fabric that measures your desired crotch depth from the top edge and 4" from the fold. Draw a curve where the lines join to make a half U shape. Cut along the lines.

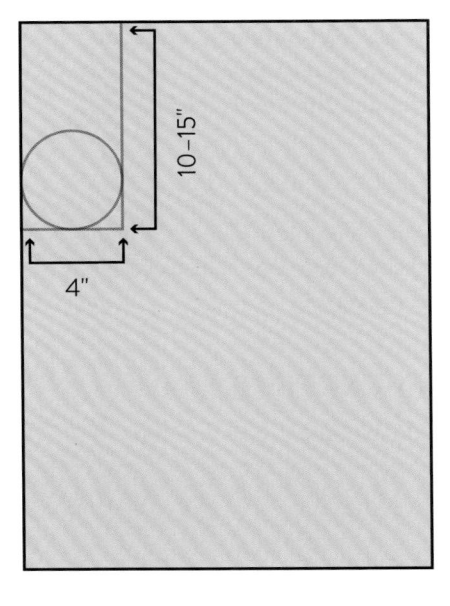

4 Open up the fabric. With wrong sides together, sew a ¼" seam along the crotch. Trim the seam. Turn the fabric so that the right sides are together. Press the curved seam. Sew a ¼" seam along the curved lines. This creates a strong seam that keeps the edges from unraveling.

5 Sew the side seams. Press the seams open.

6 Turn the waist edge of the bloomers under ¼". Press. Turn again 1". Press. Sew near the first fold, leaving a gap to thread the ¾" elastic.

7 Thread the elastic through the channel. Sew the ends of the elastic together.

8 Sew the gap closed.

9 Turn the leg edges under ½". Press. Turn again ½". Press. Sew near the first fold, leaving a gap to thread the ¼" elastic.

10 Thread the elastic through the leg channel. Sew the ends of the elastic together.

11 Sew the gaps closed.

Notion Magic

With bloomers as well as other garments, you can add magic through the use of lace, ribbons, and other embellishments, also known as notions. These items fall under the realm of the element of spirit, which is associated with creativity and is where one's individual power is found. More than that, however, each notion taps into other energies on its own.

- **Lace** is associated with beauty, sexuality, and sensuality. If you are adding lace to your bloomers or other garments, choose one that feels good on your skin. No need for stiff, itchy lace in your life.

- **Ribbons** correspond with binding but not in the constrictive sense—in joining things together. Take time to choose colored ribbons that are aligned with your purposes, and you can bind those color energies into your garment.

- **Flowers**, such as the fabric ones on page 164, bring in energies of growth, happiness, and abundance. Decorating your clothing with flower embellishments can give you a boost of joy when you wear them.

- Notions like **rhinestones** and **gems** are associated with energies of luxury and prosperity. Add them to a bag, belt, or neckline to tap into those correspondences whenever you carry or wear those items.

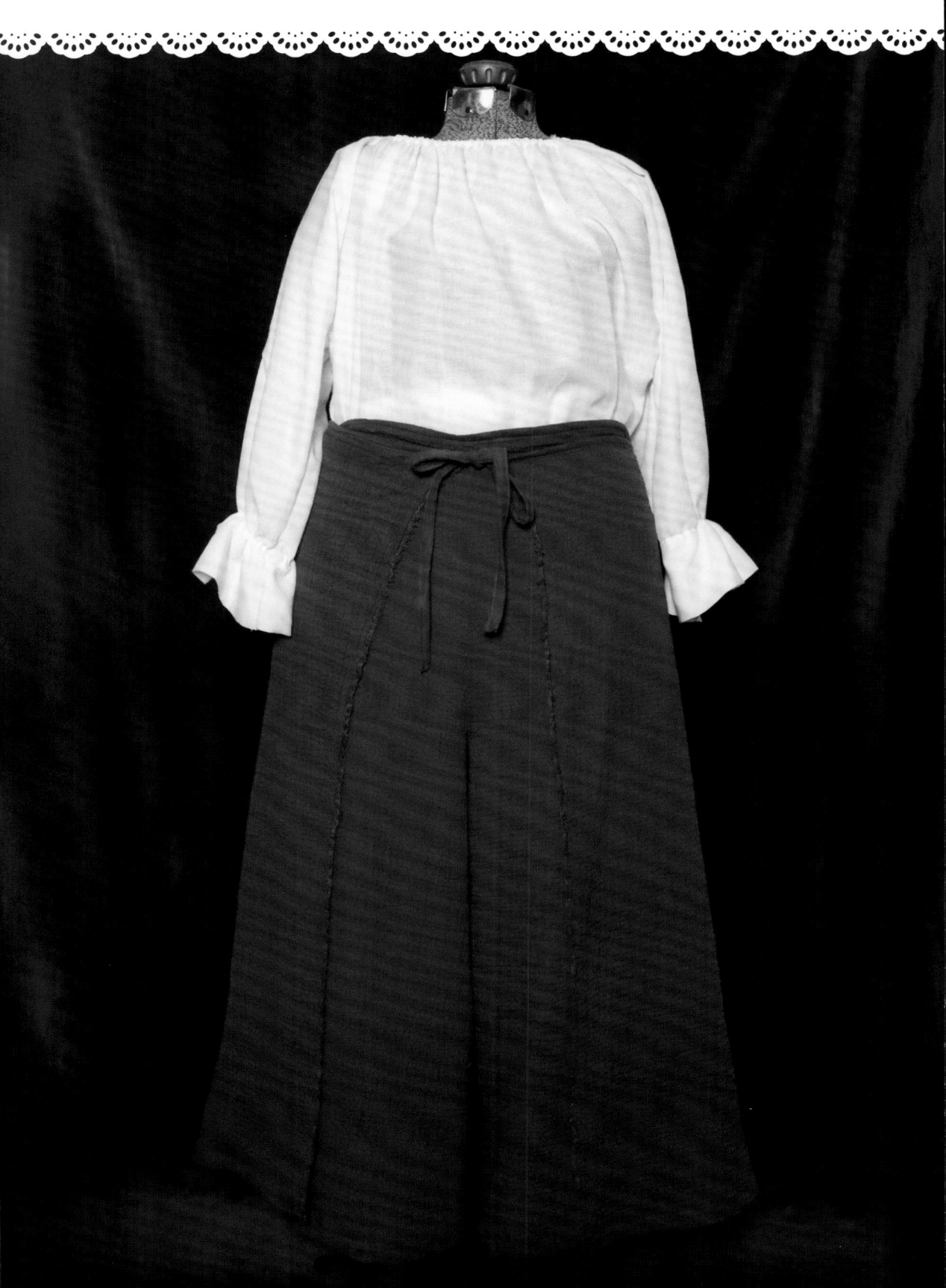

Pants may not seem to fit into the witchy wardrobe, which often emphasizes dresses and skirts. However, there are situations when having a pair of pants is beneficial. They can be worn under tunics and skirts as an extra layer of warmth and protection, or worn with a tank top to beat the heat when the sun is out. They also make for great around-the-house loungewear.

The pattern for the wrap pants is similar to the bloomers on page 28. The exception is that instead of sewing the sides and making an elastic waist, you'll be leaving the sides open and finishing the waist of the pants with ties that will wrap around your body.

To wear the pants, you will first tie the front around your waist using the waist ties, tying them in the back. Then pull the pants through your legs to the back and tie the pants around your waist to the front with the waist ties.

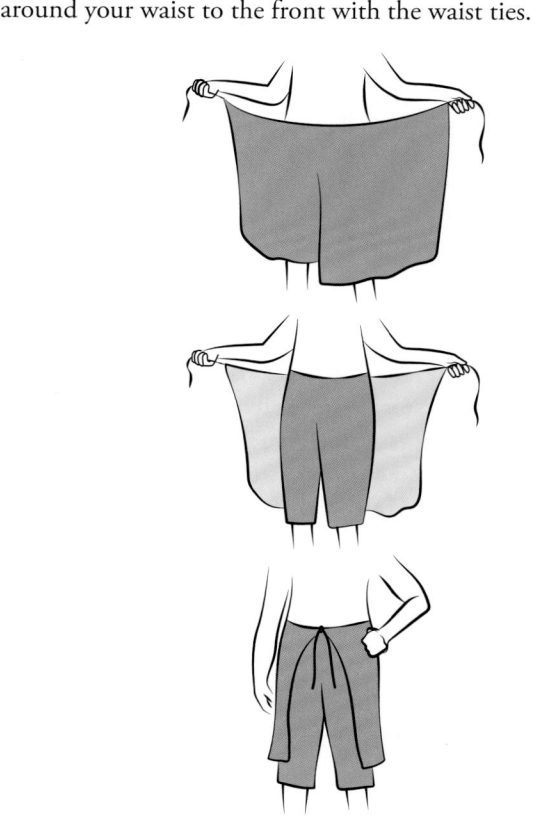

What Kind of Fabric to Use

Lightweight, drapey fabrics are best suited for this project. **Cotton** and **linen** provide cooling, breathable pants for hot weather. **Knits** give the pants extra stretch for activities like hiking and yoga. **Polyester** and **other blends** bring sophisticated polish to the pants for when you need to sweep into a royal palace to deliver a prophecy.

MATERIALS

Fabric measuring double the desired length of the pants plus the seam allowance. So, for example, pants measuring 24" long require at least 50" of fabric ([24" + 1"] × 2). Use 44" or 58" fabric.

Matching thread

2 packages of double-fold bias binding or self-made bias binding

TOOLS

Sewing machine and needle

Pins

Iron

Measuring tape

Yardstick

Scissors or a rotary cutter

Seam ripper (just in case)

TERMS & CONCEPTS

You will be basting, creating bias binding, making a standard hem, and finishing the seams. See "Methods" on page 6 for more information.

PATTERN DRAFTING

There is no pattern needed for the wrap pants. You can draw the crotch cutout directly on the fabric.

Measurements

You will need the following measurements:

- **A** = your hip measurement

- **B** = waist to where you want the pants to fall

CONSTRUCTION

1 Cut two pieces of fabric with your **A** measurement by **B** measurement. If you are using the entire width of your fabric, you need only cut it the length of your **B** measurement.

2 Fold the two pieces of fabric in half widthwise and lay one on top of the other, folds even.

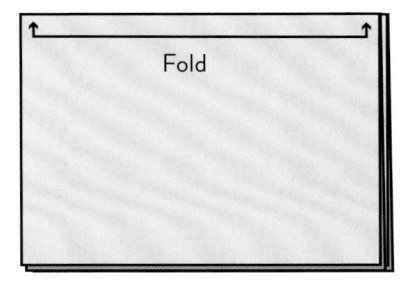

3 Determine how deep you want the crotch of the pants to be. The standard depth is 10–12". If you have a larger rear end or stomach, you will want to make the crotch deeper so that it will be comfortable and reach your waist. Start with a shorter crotch if you are uncertain, as you can deepen it if you need. On the fold of the fabric, draw a rectangle that measures your desired crotch depth from the top edge and 4" from the fold. Draw a curve where the lines join to make a half U shape. Cut along the lines.

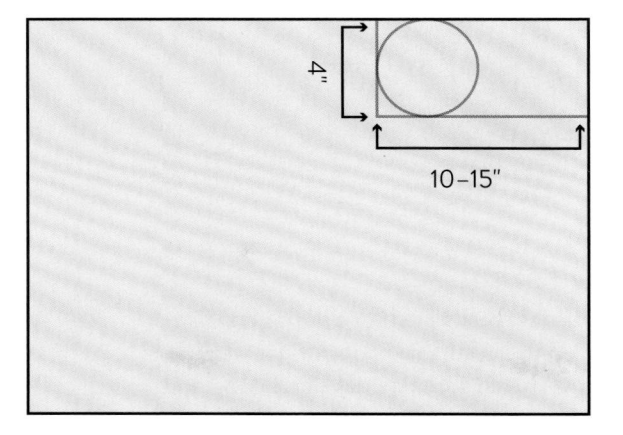

4 Open up the fabric. With wrong sides together, sew a ¼" seam along the crotch. Trim the seam. Turn the fabric so that the right sides are together. Press the curved seam. Sew a ¼" seam along curved lines. This creates a strong seam that keeps the edges from unraveling.

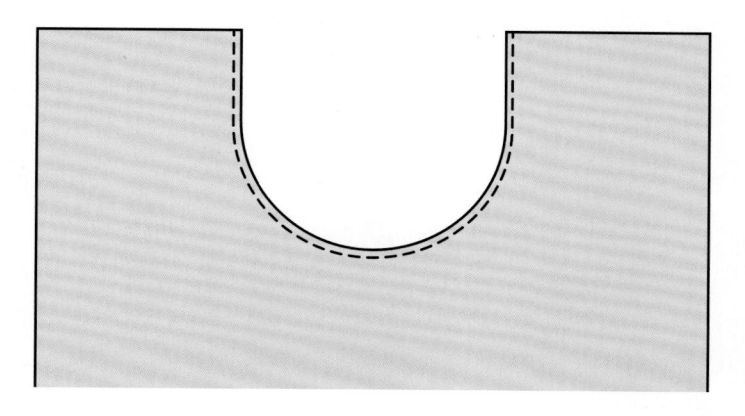

5 Hem the bottom of the pants using a standard hem. If you are not using the selvages of fabric for the sides of the pants, hem the sides as well.

6 Cut the bias binding or your self-made bias binding the width of the top edge of the pants + 24".

7 Find the center of the bias binding and match it to the center seam created by the crotch on each top edge. Pin the bias binding to the right side of the waist, raw edges even.

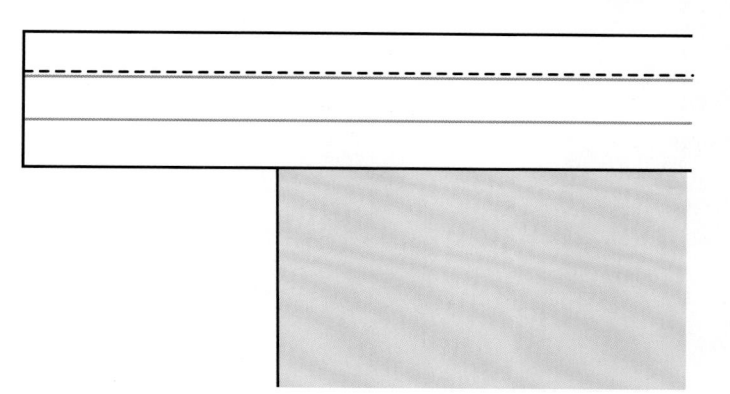

8 Sew next to the first fold of the bias binding. Fold the bias binding to the inside. Sew along the bottom edge of the bias binding through all layers.

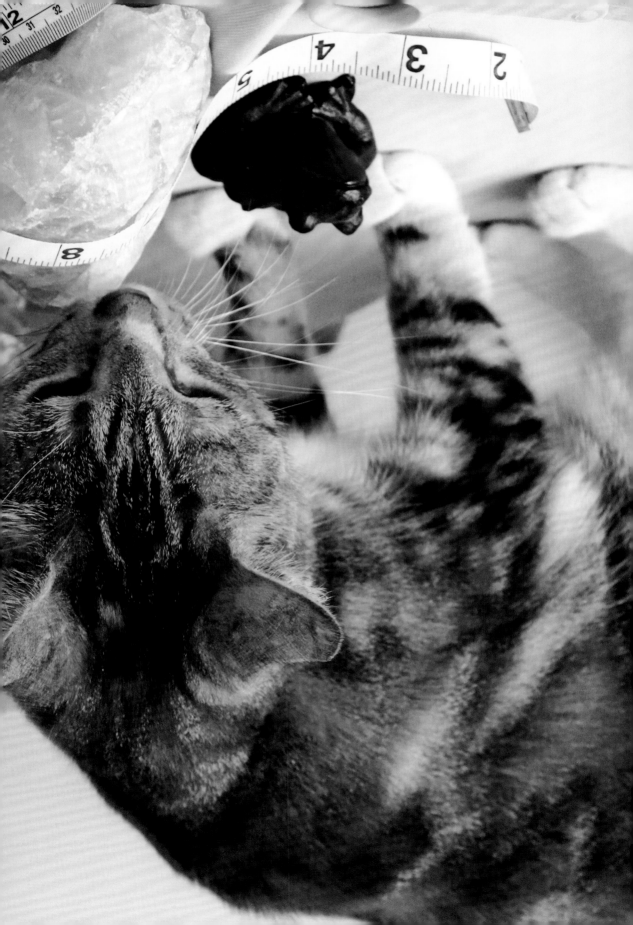

Crystal Magic

While many witches use crystals in their practice, you don't have to spend big bucks at the store for stones to use in magic. There is a plethora of magical rocks all around if you just look.

When walking out in nature, or even just across the parking lot, you can keep an eye on the ground for rocks that are shaped like animals, striped rocks, rocks with holes in them (also known as "hag stones"), and others. Quartz is one of the most common and easily identifiable crystals out there and can be found just chilling with other stones.

Rocks from special places can be used to help you connect with that space even when you aren't there. River rocks or stones gathered from the beach can be used to tap into water energy. Lava rocks, often used in landscaping, carry fire energy. Flat stones can serve as an altar or hearthstone for your home.

Make sure to forage rocks responsibly. Give thanks to the environment you take them from. Happy rockhounding!

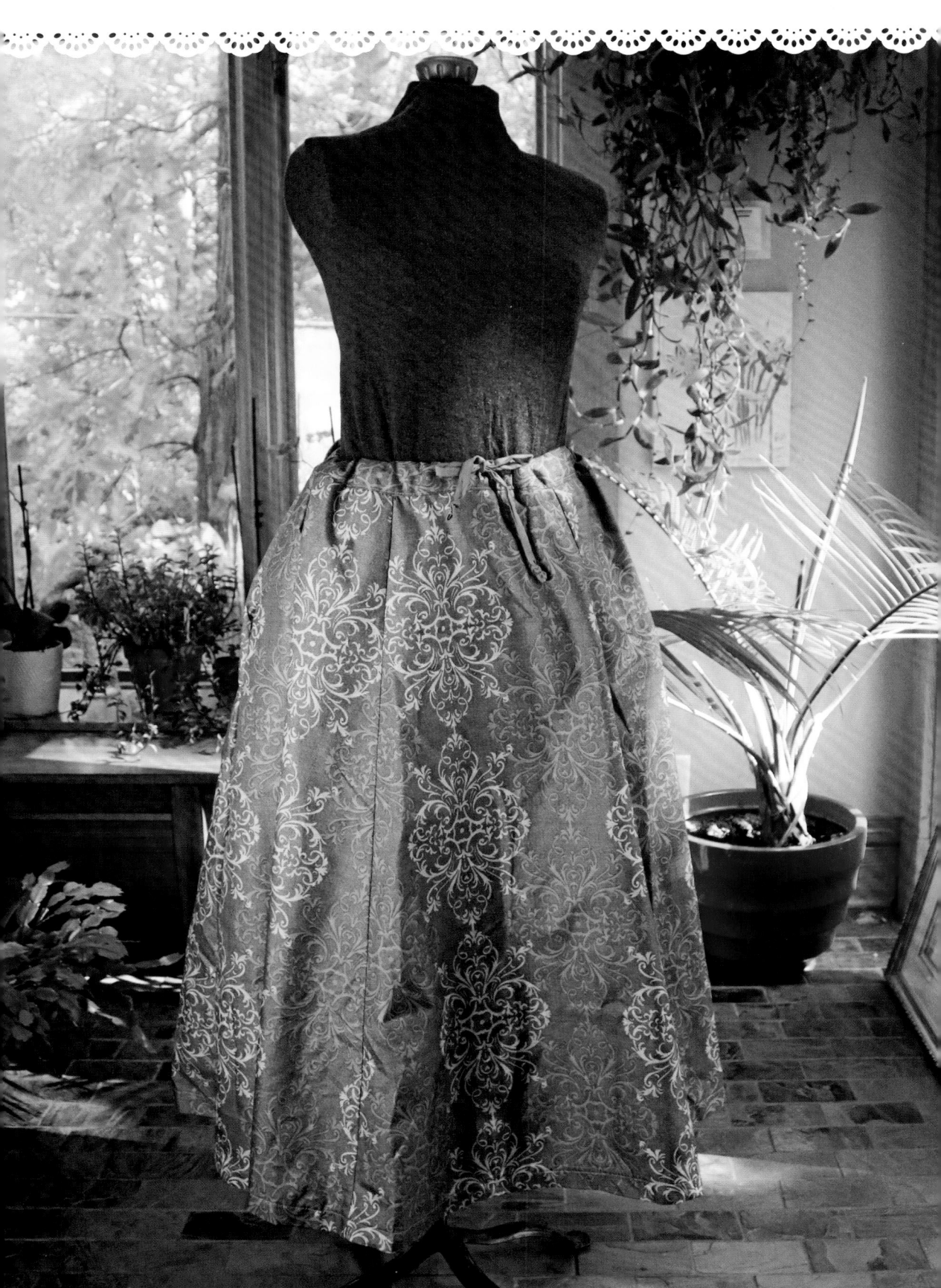

Sweeping, swirling skirts are some of the most recognizable garments when it comes to the hedgewitch style. They're romantic. They're striking. And they can take anything from a t-shirt to a frilly top from ordinary to over-the-top witchy.

The concept of the walking skirt originated in Edwardian fashion, when women wanted an outfit that was more suited for their increasingly active lifestyle. These skirts were slightly shorter, keeping hems out of the way. They included flat front panels that were often decorated with ribbon and braiding. The back was pleated and gathered to fit over a bustle.

The skirt presented in this chapter is my interpretation of the historical walking skirt, rather than a faithful reproduction. It is a skirt that is meant for everyday wear and is cut to be flattering and comfortable for every body shape. In keeping with my philosophy that pockets should be universal, functional, and deep, pockets are included in the pattern.

What Kind of Fabric to Use

The walking skirt is suitable for a wide range of fabrics. **Cottons** and **linens** are great choices if you want something you can roam the forest in. You can fancy it up by using **poly-blends**, **silks**, **crepes**, or **satins**, creating a skirt for a night out. Heavier-weight fabric like **denim** will provide you with a more structured, but still very wearable garment. I wouldn't suggest fabrics like fleece, as they will be too bulky.

If you decide on a heavier fabric, consider using **muslin** or a lighter-weight fabric for your pockets to reduce bulk around the waist and hips.

How Much Fabric?

Once you have drafted your pattern, you can figure out how much fabric you need. To do so, look at the bottom width of your skirt panel. If it is less than 22", you can use fabric that is 44" wide. If it is less than 29", you can use fabric that is 58" wide. In both cases, you will want a length of fabric that is 3 times as long as your **B** measurement. You will then fold the fabric in half widthwise (selvage to selvage) and lay your pattern piece on the fabric to cut out six panels. If the bottom of your skirt panel is wider than 29", you will need a length of fabric that is 6 times as long as your **B** measurement. You will then cut out six panels from the fabric, laying your pattern piece on single layers of the fabric. The pocket and waistband pieces can be cut out of the leftover fabric.

MATERIALS

Fabric (see below)

Matching thread

Pocket pattern piece on page 174

Fusible interfacing

TOOLS

Sewing machine and needle

Pins

Iron

Measuring tape

Yardstick

Scissors or a rotary cutter

Hem gauge

Seam ripper

TERMS & CONCEPTS

You will be **drafting a pattern**, making a **standard hem**, adding **pockets**, making **buttonholes**, and **finishing the seams**. See "Methods" on page 6 for more information.

PATTERN DRAFTING

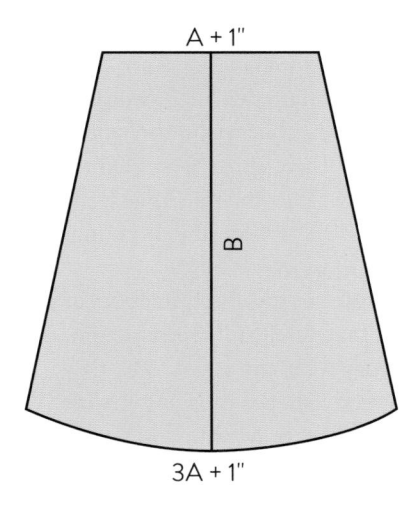

Measurements

You will need the following measurements:

- Your hip circumference
- Desired length of skirt

Take your hip measurement and add 4" for your ease to it. Then divide the result by 6, as there will be six panels to the skirt. This is your **A** measurement.

Next, take your desired length of the skirt and add 1¾" for the hems. This is your **B** measurement.

Now on to drawing your pattern. Start by drawing a vertical line the length of your **B** measurement down the middle of your paper.

Next, draw a horizontal line the length of your **A** measurement + 1" for the seam allowance centered on the top of your **B** line.

At the bottom of your **B** line, draw another horizontal line that measures 3 times your **A** measurement + 1" for the seam allowance.

Finally, draw two diagonal lines to connect the top and bottom horizontal lines. Give the bottom hem a gentle curve.

Cut out your pattern piece.

CONSTRUCTION

1 Cut out your pieces as follows:

- 6 skirt panel pieces
- 4 pocket pieces (see page 174)
- 1 waistband piece measuring 4" by your **A** measurement + 1" for seam allowance

2 Add the pockets first by positioning one pocket piece 1" down from the top edge of a skirt panel, right sides together. Sew a ⅜" seam attaching the pocket to the panel. Press the pocket out. Repeat with the other three pocket pieces and three other skirt panels. Make sure that the pockets are attached on the right side for two panels and the left side for the other two panels.

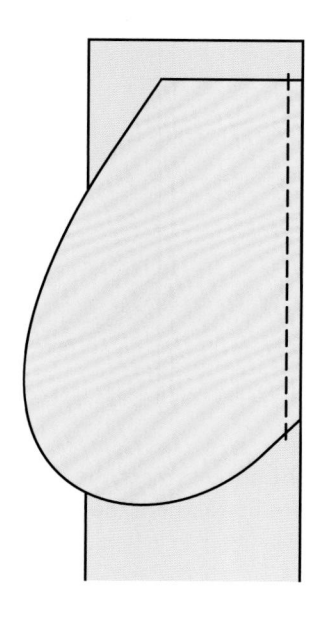

3 Now create a front and back of the skirt by sewing one pocketed panel to either side of an unpocketed panel, right sides together, using a ½" seam. Repeat with the remaining two pocketed panels and unpocketed panel.

4 Pin the front of the skirt to the back, right sides together. Sew ½" from the raw edge of the skirt panel down ½" past the top edge of the pocket, pivot 90 degrees, and continue across the pocket.

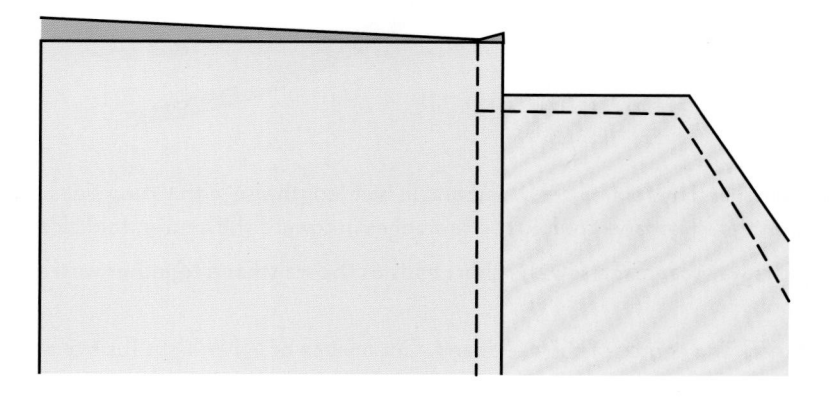

5 Sew a ½" seam around the pocket. Sew into the skirt panels ½". Pivot sharply and continue down to the hem.

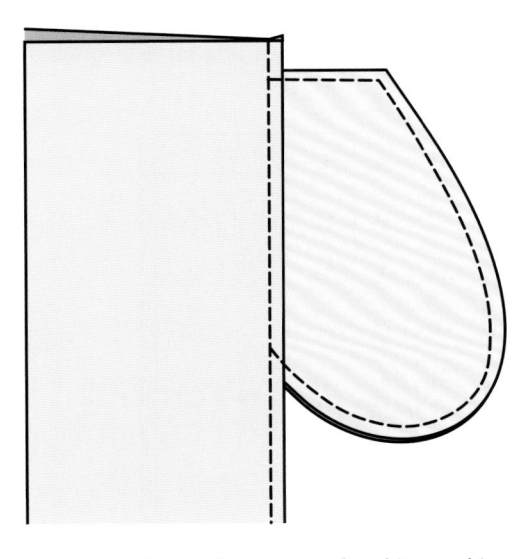

6 Clip the seam allowance where the pockets meet the skirt, making sure not to cut through the stitching. Finish the side seams up to where the seam is clipped.

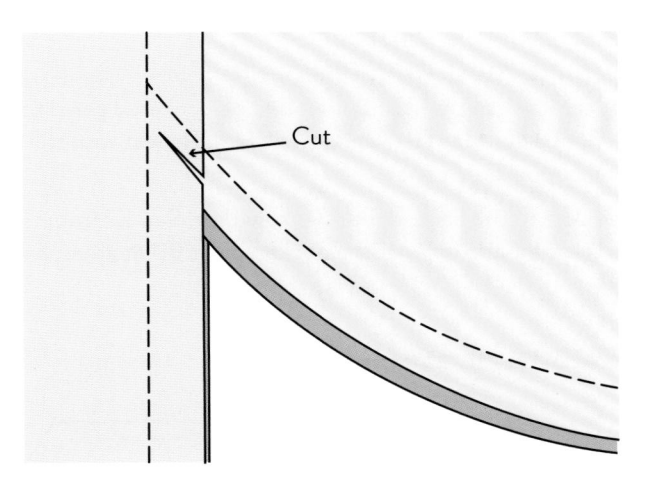

7 Add the waistband by folding the waistband in half lengthwise with wrong sides together and press. Open the waistband up, fold the raw edges in toward the center, fold closed, and press.

8 Open up the waistband and sew the short ends of the waistband together with a ½" seam to create a loop.

9 Find and mark the center of the waistband. Cut a piece of lightweight fusible interfacing 1" by 2". Using manufacturer's directions, adhere the interfacing to the wrong side of the fabric 1¼" down from the top edge centered over the center front marking.

10 On the right side of the fabric, mark two lines on either side of the center front measuring 1" long. Sew buttonholes on these marks.

11 Open up the buttonholes with a seam ripper.

12 Pin the waistband to the skirt with right sides facing and the buttonholes matching the center front of the skirt. Sew with a ½" seam.

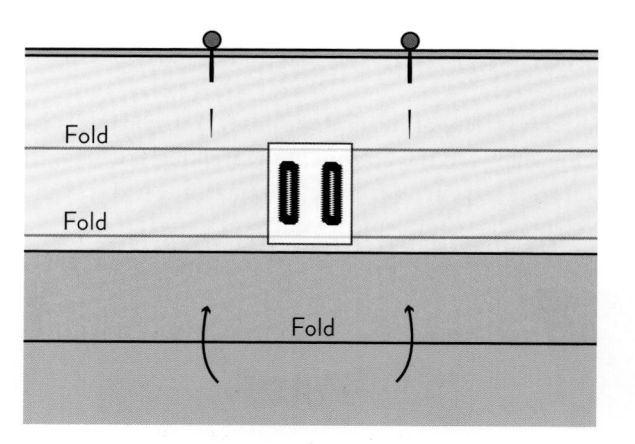

13 Fold the waistband over to the wrong side of the skirt, encasing the raw edges, and sew in place.

14 Make the drawstring by cutting a piece of fabric measuring 2" long by your hip measurement × 2 wide. Fold the fabric in half lengthwise with the right sides of the fabric facing. Sew ¼" from the long edge. Turn the fabric tube right-side out.

15 Thread the drawstring through the channel, entering in one buttonhole and coming out the other. Knot the ends of the drawstring. You can add beads or charms to the ends of the drawstring.

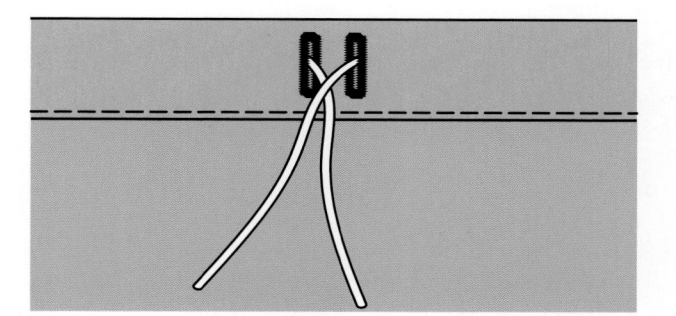

16 Hem the skirt using a standard hem.

VARIATIONS

Ruffled Skirt

To create a ruffle for the skirt, you will need to shorten your skirt pattern by the length you want your ruffle to be. Cut a rectangle that measures how long you want your ruffle to be by twice the width of the bottom circumference of your skirt.

Sew the skirt as per the earlier instructions, leaving out step 16. Sew the short edges of the ruffle together. Add a hem to the bottom of the ruffle. Gather the top edge of the ruffle and pin it to the bottom of the skirt with right sides together. Adjust the gathers so that they are evenly distributed and so that the ruffle is the same width as the bottom of the skirt. Sew a ½" seam around the gathered edge.

Sigil Skirt

A sigil is a symbol used for a variety of magical purposes. You can add sigils to any of your clothing, but it looks especially witchy on the bottom of the walking skirt. Transfer the sigil for self-love from page 173 to the bottom of your skirt once you have finished it. Embroider the design with straight stitches and in colors that complement your skirt's fabric.

Pocket Magic

Historically, pockets were separate garments that were worn under outerwear. Imagine purses but tied around your waist. Women's clothing has been particularly lacking in the pocket department for many years. Part of the reason for this is that changing silhouettes, starting in the early eighteenth century with the empire dresses of the Regency era, stopped supporting substantial pockets. Later, flapper dresses, miniskirts, and tight silhouettes didn't have room for storage. And once women got used to not having pockets and instead carrying around purses, the fashion industry found no reason to add them back in.

Fortunately, pockets in women's fashion have been experiencing a comeback, at least in some places, which is a reason to rejoice. Not only do pockets provide a place to put our magical tools, but they offer the opportunity for some unique sewing magic.

Pockets are portals and secret keepers. No one but the wearer knows what is in them. This gives you a place to work low-key magic, especially if you aren't open about your practice. Embroider prosperity sigils into your pockets to give you access to money magic. Use color theory to make pockets from a different color fabric than your garment (see "Color Magic" on page 124 for more information). Use quilting markers to write your intentions on the pockets. The marks from the pens disappear when exposed to heat or water, so they'll wash away when you launder your garment. Pockets are especially useful for protection spells, for which you can sew a charm like a hamsa hand or nazar inside the pocket.

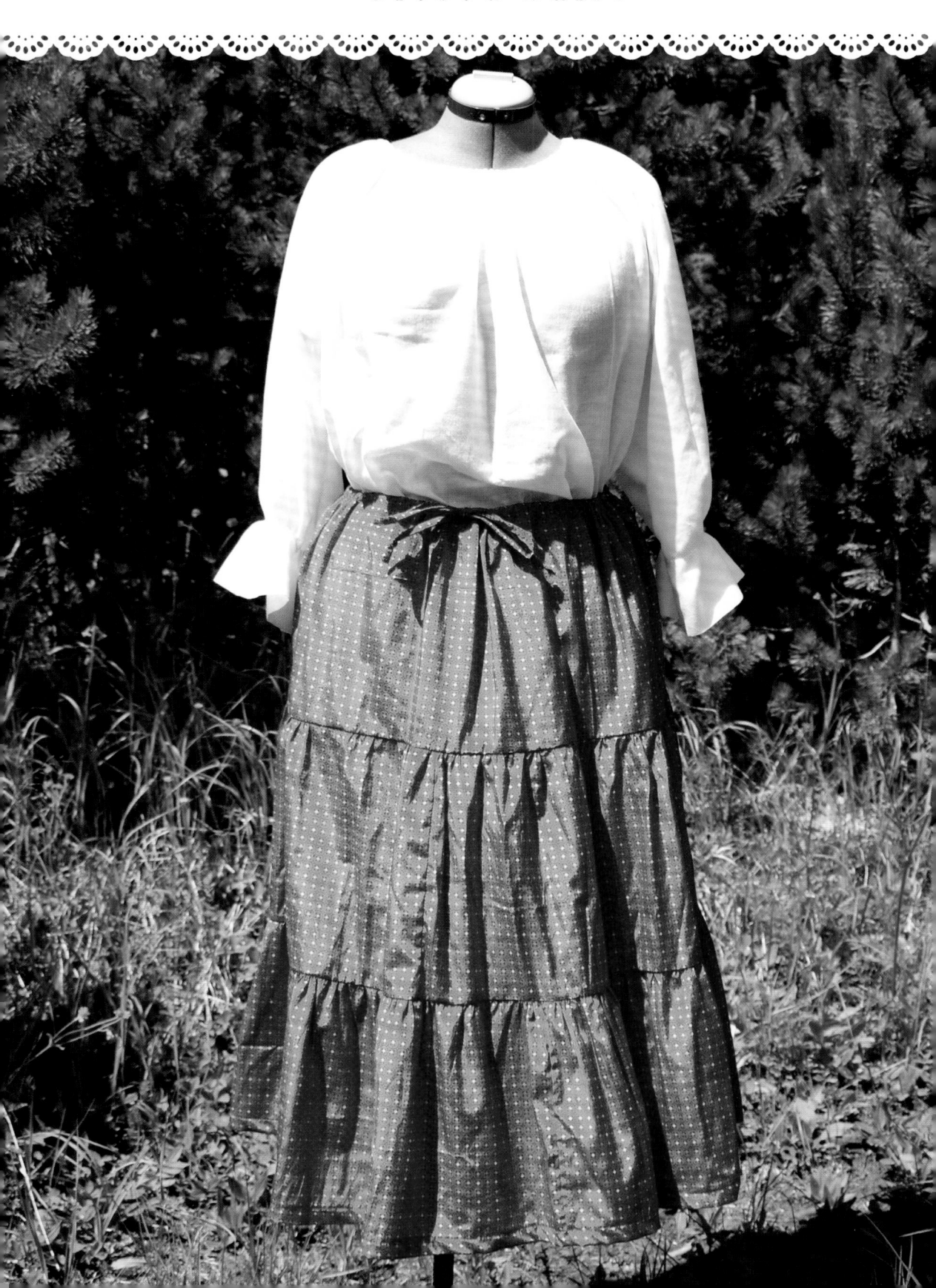

The tiered skirt is a staple of many wardrobes, and for good reason. The gathered tiers are very romantic looking, especially when you are frolicking in a mountain meadow.

More than just a skirt to dance under the moonlit sky in, the tiered skirt has its own magic. Three, a number of increase and action, features prominently in the construction. There are three tiers, each one a circle that reduces in size as it moves up from the ground to your waist, bringing energy from the earth up to your torso.

The skirt accommodates a variety of fabrics, so you can make a couple of different options for your closet.

What Kind of Fabric to Use

This skirt is suitable for **most fabrics**, although thick or stiff fabrics (like fleece or denim) might prove difficult to use. For very fine materials or fabrics that easily unravel, you will want to finish the edges with a serger or zigzag stitch before you gather the tiers. This will make the gathering process easier.

How Much Fabric?

You will need a length of fabric at least equal to your **B** measurement + 5". If your third tier measures longer than 132" wide, you'll need extra length of fabric to make all the tiers if you are using 44"-wide fabric.

PATTERN DRAFTING

The basic design is making three or more circles of increasing diameter from rectangles of fabric. The first circle or tier measures 1.5 times your waist measurement. Each subsequent tier is larger than the last.

Measurements

You will need the following measurements:

- **A** = Your waist measurement

- **B** = Length from your waist to where you want your skirt to fall

Your first tier will be ⅓ your **B** measurement + 1¾" in length by 1.5 × your **A** measurement in width.

Your second tier will be ⅓ your **B** measurement + 1" in length by 1.5 × your first tier measurement in width.

MATERIALS

Fabric (see below)

Thread

Fusible interfacing

Beads or charms (optional)

TOOLS

Sewing machine and needle

Pins

Iron

Measuring tape

Yardstick

Scissors or rotary cutter

Hem gauge

Seam ripper

TERMS & CONCEPTS

You will be making a **standard hem, gathering**, and creating **buttonholes**. See "Methods" on page 6 for more information.

Your third tier will be ⅓ your **B** measurement + 1¾" in length by 1.5 × your second tier measurement in width.

You may run into an issue that the length you need for the tier is more than the width of the fabric you have. In that case, you will need to cut your tiers in more than one piece and sew them together to get your needed length.

CONSTRUCTION

1 Start by cutting out all the fabric for the tiers.

2 Next, assemble all the tiers. Do so by sewing the short ends of the first tier fabric together to create a circle. Press the seams open. Repeat with the second tier and third tier fabrics so that you end up with three circles.

3 Sew a gathering stitch ½" from one long edge of the second tier.

4 Mark two points at the bottom of the first tier at the center front and center back. If you only have one side seam on your first tier, mark the point opposite from it on the bottom of the tier.

5 Mark four points equal distance apart on the long side of the second tier with the basting.

6 Match the points and the side seams of the first tier with the points on the second tier, with right sides facing.

7 Gather up the second tier between the points so that the second tier is the same length as the first tier. Pin in place and distribute the gathers evenly.

8 Sew a ½" seam attaching the second tier to the first tier. Press the seam up toward the top of the skirt.

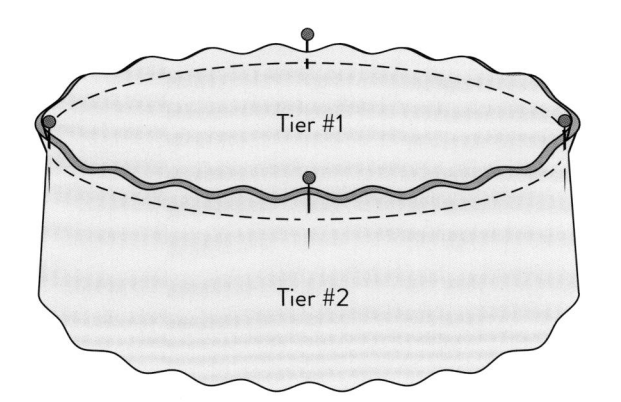

9 Repeat steps 2–8 with the third tier, attaching it to the second tier.

10 Give the third tier a standard hem.

11 Find the center front of the first tier by folding one length of fabric in half. Mark the center front with a pin, chalk, or tailor tacks.

12 Cut a piece of lightweight fusible interfacing 1" by 2". Using manufacturer's directions, adhere the interfacing to the wrong side of the fabric, placing the interfacing 1 ¼" down from the top edge centered over the center front marking.

13 On the right side of the fabric, mark two lines on either side of the center front measuring 1" long. Sew buttonholes on these marks.

14 Open up the buttonholes with a seam ripper.

15 Turn the top edge of the first tier under ¼". Press. Turn again 1". Press. Sew near the first fold, making sure not to catch the buttonholes.

16 Cut a piece of fabric 2" in length and measuring 2 × your waist circumference in width. Fold the fabric in half lengthwise with the right sides of the fabric facing. Sew ¼" from the long edge. Turn the fabric tube right-side out.

17 Thread the drawstring through the channel, entering in one buttonhole and coming out the other. You can add beads or charms to the ends of the drawstring. Knot the ends of the drawstring.

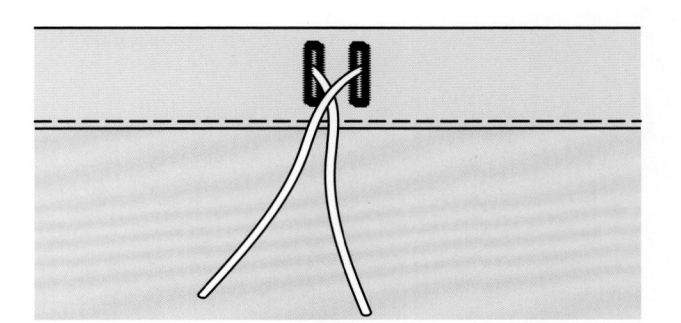

Knot Magic

When you are working on your tiered skirt, you can bring in a bit of sewing magic through knots. Tying a knot once you have finished a seam is a powerful bit of magic. It signifies to the universe that you are done, a physical manifestation of the phrase "So mote it be."

When I am sewing, I like to tie my knots in three, saying, "**For Maiden, Mother, and Crone**" as I do so. In this way, I am tying in the youthful energy of the Maiden, the nurturing nature of the Mother, and the wisdom of the Crone in all the clothes I sew for myself. This also taps into the power of three, which is a number of rising action. You don't have to tie your knots three times (which some people might find excessive), but you can call on whatever deities or helper spirits you work with when you finish sewing. Use the action as a way to say, "**My work here is done and I release my intent into the universe.**"

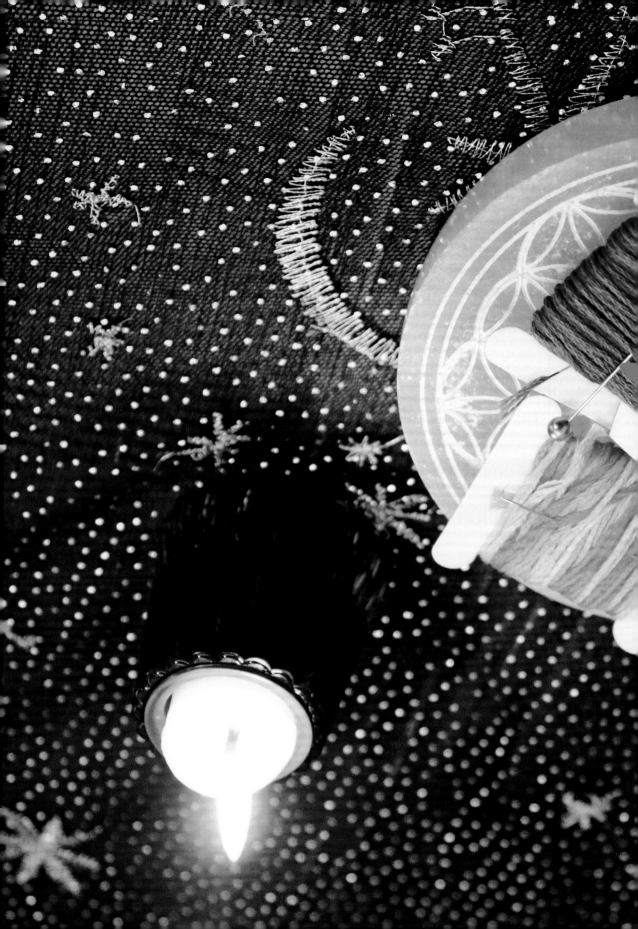

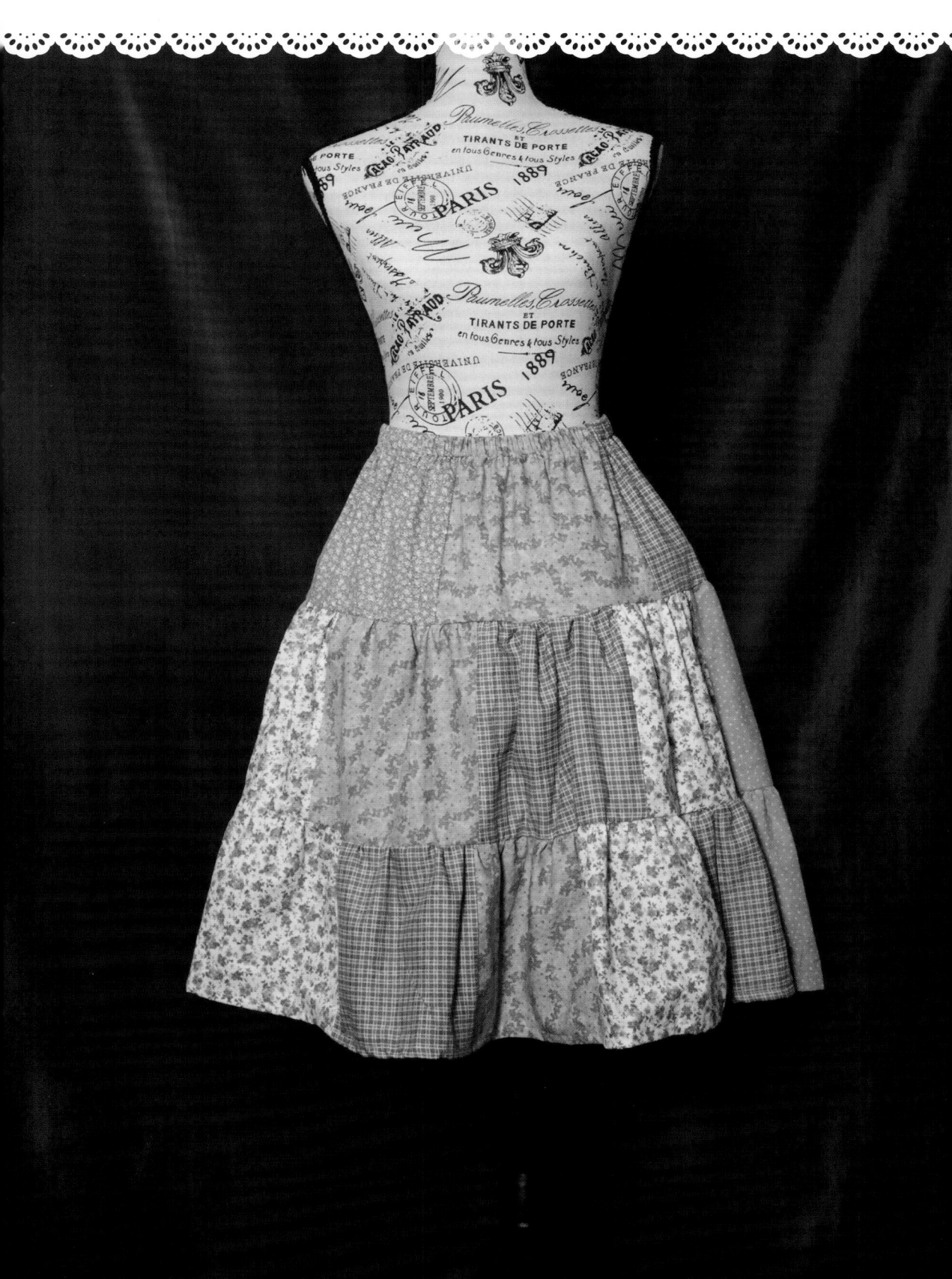

The patchwork skirt is another staple of many different types of wardrobes. From cottagecore to witchcore, its appeal is universal. This chapter will walk you through creating a patchwork skirt that fits your measurements. You can work with scraps you have on hand or get fabric solely for this garment. The skirt is put together in much the same way as the tiered skirt. You will be cutting out patchwork pieces for each tier, sewing them together, and then sewing the tiers to each other.

This skirt offers you the opportunity to play around with color and patterns to create a garment with a magical vocabulary and correspondences sewn in. Choose various shades of red for a skirt to evoke passion and energy. Sew it with botanical patterns to connect to plant magic. Your options are unlimited when it comes to matching the various pieces of fabric to your intentions.

What Kind of Fabric to Use

The patchwork skirt works with any light- or medium-weight fabric. Printed **cottons** are ideal, but you could also use **silks**, **jacquards**, and even **brocades**. The skirt is not suitable for heavyweight or thick materials. Don't be afraid to mix and match different fabrics as well. A patchwork skirt with differing textiles provides additional visual interest beyond just pattern and color.

How Much Fabric?

The amount of fabric used by this skirt is determined by the number of different textiles you use. On average, plan on the equivalent of 3 yards of fabric.

PATTERN DRAFTING

Measurements

You will need the following measurements:

- **A** = Your hip measurement
- **B** = Length from your waist to where you want your skirt to fall

Your first tier will be ⅓ your **B** measurement + 1¾" in length by 1.5 × your **A** measurement in width.

Your second tier will be ⅓ your **B** measurement + 1" in length by 1.5 × your tier one measurement in width.

Your third tier will be ⅓ your **B** measurement + 1¾" in length by 1.5 × your tier two measurement in width.

MATERIALS

Fabric (see below)

Thread

Fusible interfacing

Beads or charms (optional)

TOOLS

Sewing machine and needle

Pins

Iron

Hem gauge

Measuring tape

Yardstick

Marking pen or chalk

Seam ripper

TERMS & CONCEPTS

You will be making a **standard hem**, **gathering**, and creating **buttonholes**. See "Methods" on page 6 for more information.

Now take your first tier width and divide it by its length. For example, if your first tier width is 44" and the length is 9¾", divide 44 by 9.75, which will give you a result of 4.51. Round this result up to the nearest whole number, in this case 5. You will need to cut 5 almost-squares measuring 9¾" × 10¾" (adding 1" to the width of the square for the seam allowance), which you will then sew together to make a tier that is slightly over the 44" width you started with.

Repeat the same mathematics with the second tier and the third. This will give you the number of squares you'll need for each one.

CONSTRUCTION

1 Start by sewing the squares for each tier together using a ½" seam, making three tiers. Press the seams open.

2 Sew the short ends of the first tier together, creating a circle. Press the seams open. Repeat with the second tier and third tier.

3 Sew a gathering stitch ½" from one long edge of the second tier.

4 Mark two points at the bottom of the first tier at the center front and center back.

5 Mark four points an equal distance apart on the long side of the second tier with the basting.

6 Match the points and the side seams of the first tier with the points on the second tier, with right sides facing.

7 Gather up the second tier between the points so that the second tier is the same length as the first tier. Pin in place and distribute the gathers evenly.

8 Sew a ½" seam attaching the second tier to the first tier. Press the seam up toward the top of the skirt.

9 Repeat steps 2–8 with the third tier, attaching it to the second tier.

10 Give the third tier a standard hem.

11 Find the center front of the first tier by folding one length of fabric in half. Mark the center front with a pin, chalk, or tailor tacks.

12 Cut a piece of lightweight fusible interfacing 1" by 2". Using the manufacturer's directions, adhere the interfacing to the wrong side of the fabric, placing the interfacing 1¼" down from the top edge, centered over the center front marking.

13 On the right side of the fabric, mark two lines on either side of the center front measuring 1" long. Sew buttonholes on these marks.

14 Open up the buttonholes with a seam ripper.

15 Turn the top edge of the first tier under ¼". Press. Turn again 1". Press. Sew near the first fold, making sure not to catch the buttonholes.

16 Cut a piece of fabric 2" in length and measuring 2 × your waist circumference in width. Fold the fabric in half lengthwise with the right sides of the fabric facing. Sew ¼" from the long edge. Turn the fabric tube right-side out.

17 Thread the drawstring through the channel, entering in one buttonhole and coming out the other. You can add beads or charms to the ends of the drawstring. Knot the ends of the drawstring.

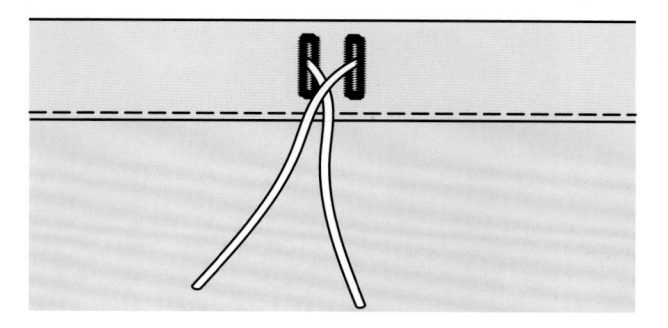

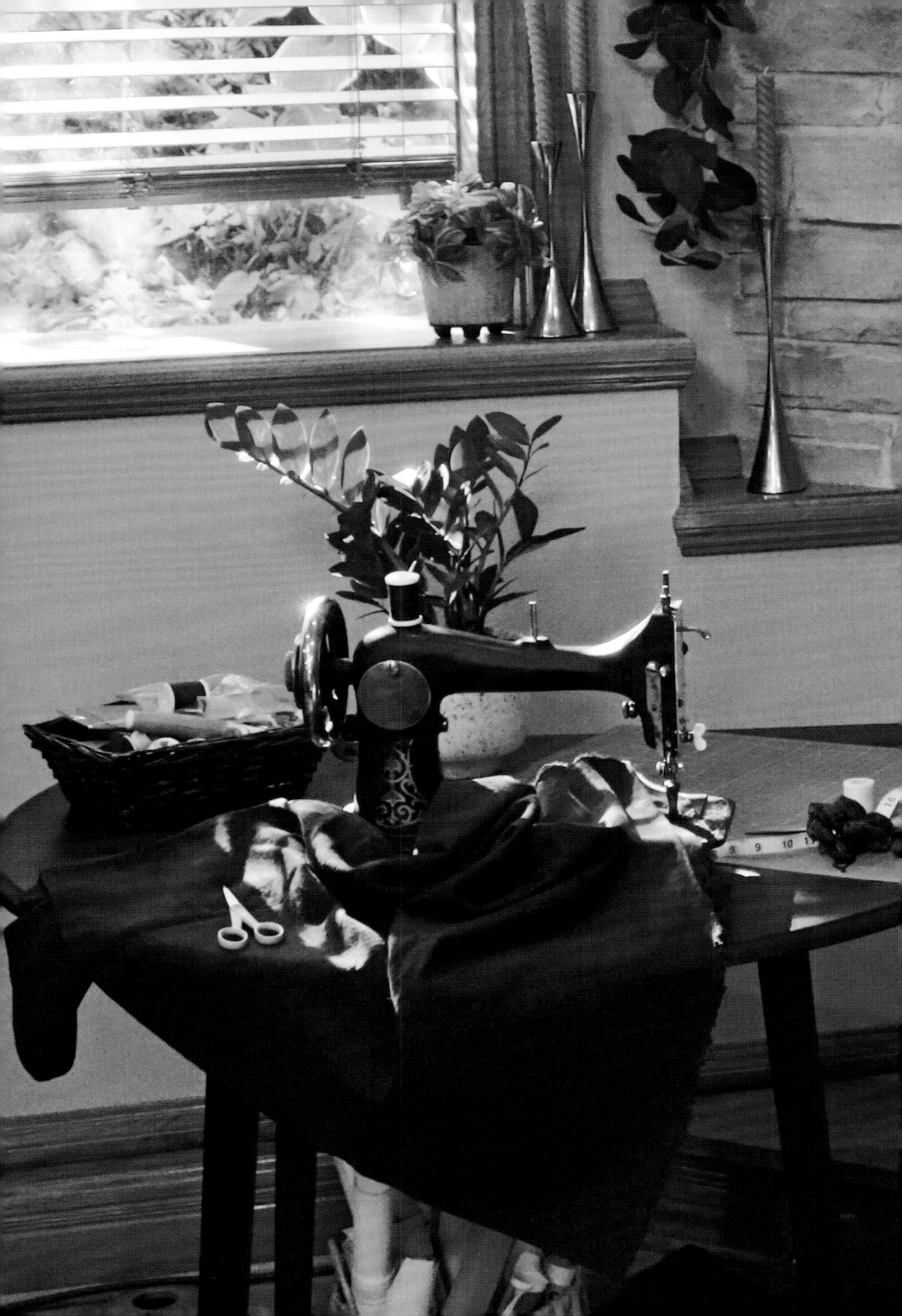

Clothing Sachet Magic

When storing your skirts, dresses, and other witchy garments, you can help boost their magic properties by creating a spell bag as a sachet and storing it with your clothes. Creating a clothing sachet with herbs, crystals, and symbols aligned with your intentions can work on both the mundane and magical levels. Many herbs that are associated with protection were also used in sachets to keep insects from infesting clothing.

Fill a sachet with **cedar chips** not only to prevent fleas from taking up residence in your drawers but to also purify your clothing. Add **black tourmaline** to the sachet to amplify the purification energies and for cleansing your clothing from any negative influences.

Other herbs for clothing sachets include **cloves**, **bay leaves**, **lavender**, and **rosemary**. They all protect against insects as well as provide protective and cleansing energies. **Amethyst** and **selenite** are good crystals to use for the same purposes.

Why add magical protection to your clothing? Simply because clothing is our second skin when we go out into the world. Our clothing picks up the dust, hair, odors, and energies that are swirling around on the outside. Normally, doing the laundry can both clean and cleanse them (see "Laundry Magic" on page 86 for more information). However, if you have clothes that don't get washed after every wear or that are dry-clean only, you want to make sure that negative or malicious energy isn't clinging to them.

Ruffled Wrap Skirt

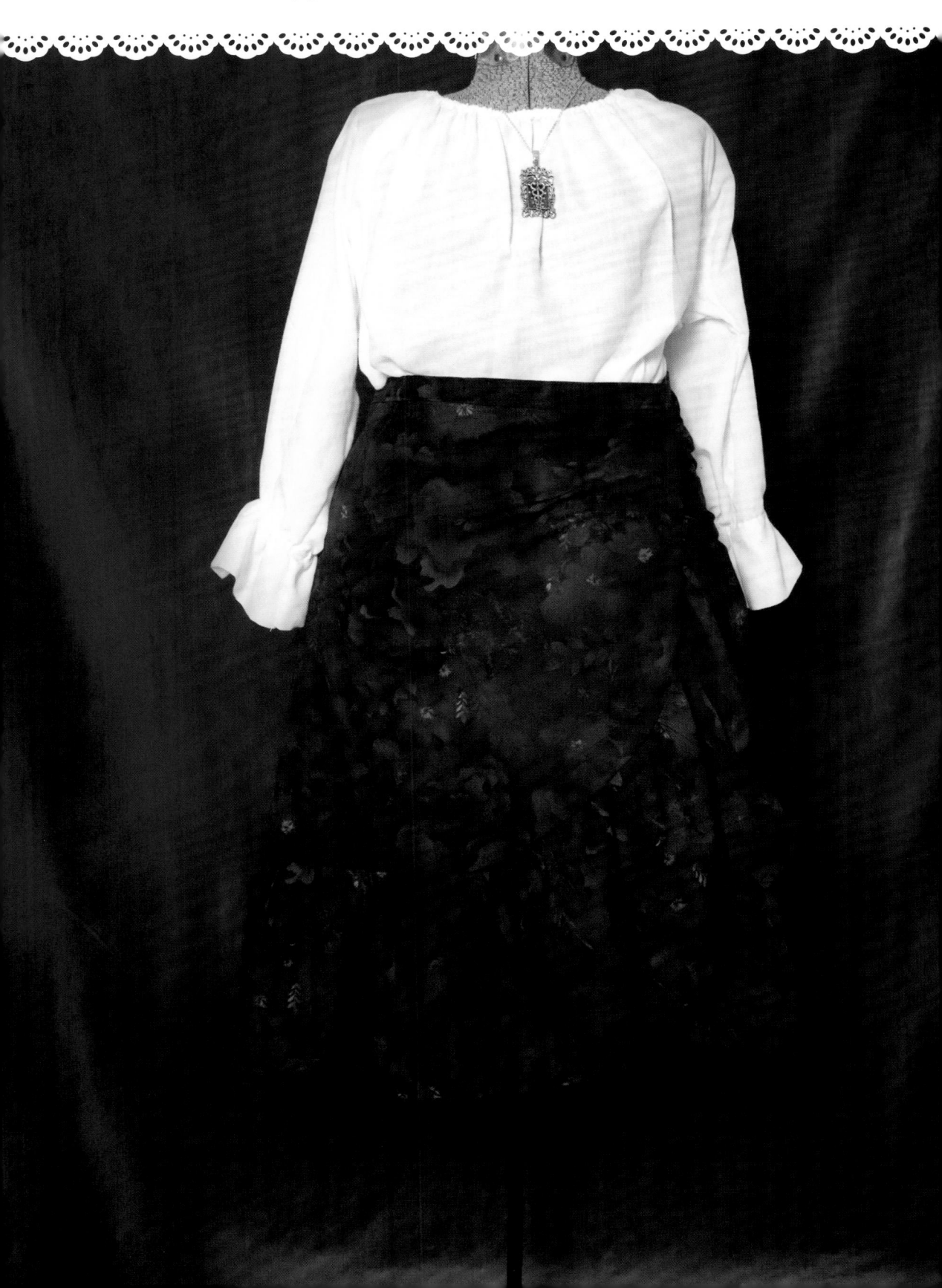

The wrap skirt is one of the simplest skirts to make. At its core, the wrap skirt is a piece of cloth wrapped around the waist. The skirt in this project has a curved bottom and a ruffle layer to make for a visually interesting garment. Use the same fabric for the ruffle as the skirt or use a complementary fabric for a touch of whimsy. The waistband has a buttonhole to give a more secure fit.

What Kind of Fabric to Use

Fabric that has a nice drape is suitable for this skirt. Either a **woven** or **knit** fabric can be used.

How Much Fabric?

You will need fabric measuring your waist circumference × 1.5 in width and your **B** measurement in length. For example, if you have a waist measurement of 30", you can use 44"-wide fabric. If your waist is larger, use 58"-wide fabric. You will also need extra fabric for your ruffle and waist tie.

PATTERN DRAFTING

You'll be drafting a simple curved shape for your skirt. Starting with a rectangle and then curving the bottom corners is the fastest and easiest way to create the shape. You'll draft a pattern that can be placed on the fold of the fabric.

Measurements

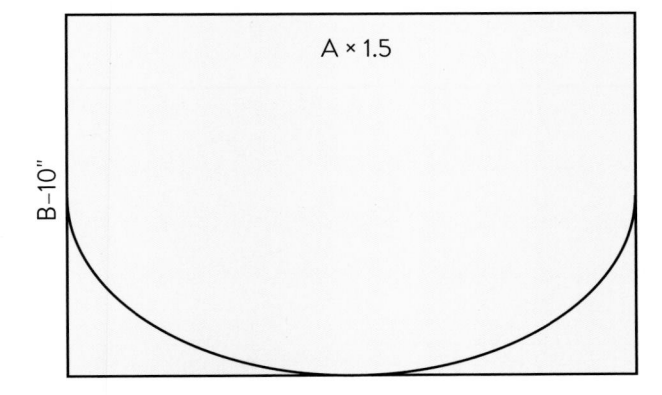

You'll need the following measurements:

- **A** = Your waist circumference
- **B** = The length from your waist to where you want the skirt to end

MATERIALS

Fabric (see below)

Matching thread

TOOLS

Sewing machine and needle

Pins

Iron

Hem gauge

Measuring tape

Yardstick

Marking pen or chalk

Seam ripper

TERMS & CONCEPTS

You will be **drafting a pattern**, **gathering**, making a **narrow hem**, and sewing a **buttonhole**. See "Methods" on page 6 for more information.

If you have a large (over 10") difference between your waist and hip circumference, you might consider using your hip measurement in place of your waist for the **A** measurement above. This will ensure that the wrap skirt will cover the largest part of your lower body and you won't have to worry about gaping.

Start by drafting a rectangle measuring ([**A** × 1.5] ÷ 2) – 10" wide by **B** – 10" long.

Round the lower right-hand corner starting at halfway from the top of the rectangle.

You will also be cutting out a ruffle. Measure the curved sides of the skirt to know how much ruffle you will need. Multiply that number by 1.5. This is your **C** measurement.

Cut a ruffle that measures 10" by your **C** measurement. You may need to cut several smaller pieces and sew them together to make a ruffle that matches your width measurement.

CONSTRUCTION

1 Start by folding your fabric in half with the right sides together. Place your pattern piece with the long straight edge against the fold. Cut out your skirt piece.

2 Give one long edge of the ruffle a narrow hem.

3 Run a gathering stitch on the unhemmed side of the ruffle. With the right sides together, pin the ruffle to the skirt at the tops of each side and at the center of the skirt. Pull up the gathering thread until the ruffle is the same length as the curved edge of the skirt. Distribute the gathers evenly. Sew the ruffle to the skirt using a ½" seam.

4 Press the ruffle seam up toward the skirt.

5 Measure the top of your skirt from one side to the other. Cut out a rectangle of fabric measuring 4" in length by 2 × the top of your skirt in width. You may need to cut smaller pieces and sew them together to make a waist tie that meets the length you need.

6 Fold the waist tie in half lengthwise. Press. This marks the center of the length of the waist tie. Open the tie out and fold the edges into the center. Fold the tie closed and press. The tie will have the following folds:

Fold
Fold
Fold

7 With the right sides facing, center the waist tie on the upper part of the skirt, raw edges matching. Sew a ½" seam across the top of the skirt, attaching the waist tie to the skirt.

8 Fold the waist tie over, enclosing the seam, with folded edges together. Baste or pin along the top of the skirt, through all fabric.

9 Finish the waist tie end by opening up one short end. Fold the fabric in ½". Refold the waist tie. Pin to keep the end closed. Repeat with the other end.

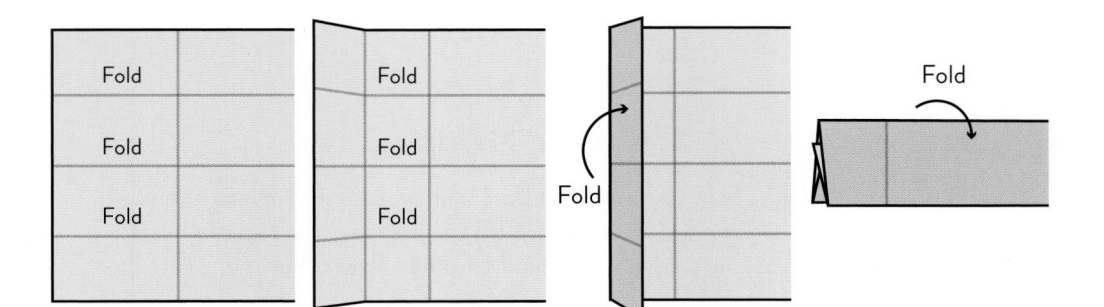

10 Sew a seam around all of the waist tie ⅛" from the edges, making sure to go through all thicknesses when you get to the skirt top.

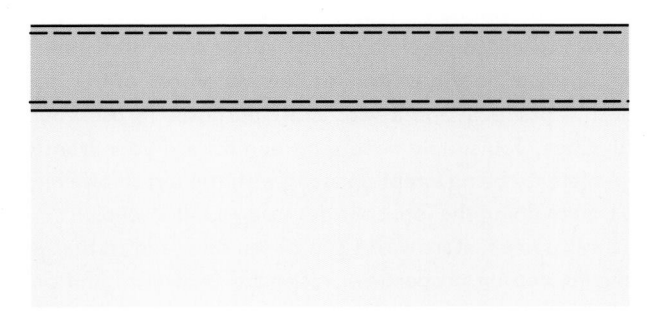

11 Try on the skirt. Make a mark where the left top of the skirt meets the right side of the skirt. Sew a 1" buttonhole at that mark to allow the left half of the waist tie to pass through to the front of the skirt.

Sweeping Magic

There is something about the swish of a skirt that evokes fanciful images and emotions. From dancing to frolicking through the meadow, the feel of a skirt swirling around your legs takes your mind to other places. For me, one of those places is sweeping. The movement of the skirt always brings to mind the back-and-forth rhythm of the broom. And to a witch, the movement of a broom evokes magic.

It's not surprising that the broom is associated with witches. Up until recently, most witches worked in the home and most witchcraft involved domestic tools. A broom didn't just clear away the dust on the floor; it was used to cleanse a space, to repel negativity, and to even bring rain.

Sweeping, however, is the way that I use my broom in my magic, due to it serving both a practical and a witchcraft purpose. To use your broom to cleanse your space, you simply need to sweep toward your front door, envisioning any negativity being swept up along with the dirt. However, if you feel like that isn't quite doing the job, consider using a salt sweep.

To make a **salt sweep**, start with 1 cup of sea salt. Add to that juniper berries (for their exorcizing properties), rosemary (exorcism and purification), chamomile (purification), thistle (exorcism and hex-breaking), or any combination of those herbs. You can also add a few drops of moon water or rosemary or lavender essential oils to the mix for their protective and purifying properties. Finally, add a couple of tablespoons of baking soda (for its absorbent properties).

Sprinkle the salt sweep on hardwood floors, making sure to get under furniture and into corners. Visualize the negativity being broken up and then absorbed by the baking soda. Now sweep it all up, sweeping toward the front door. Carry the dustpan out the front door to take the remaining bad energy out of your home.

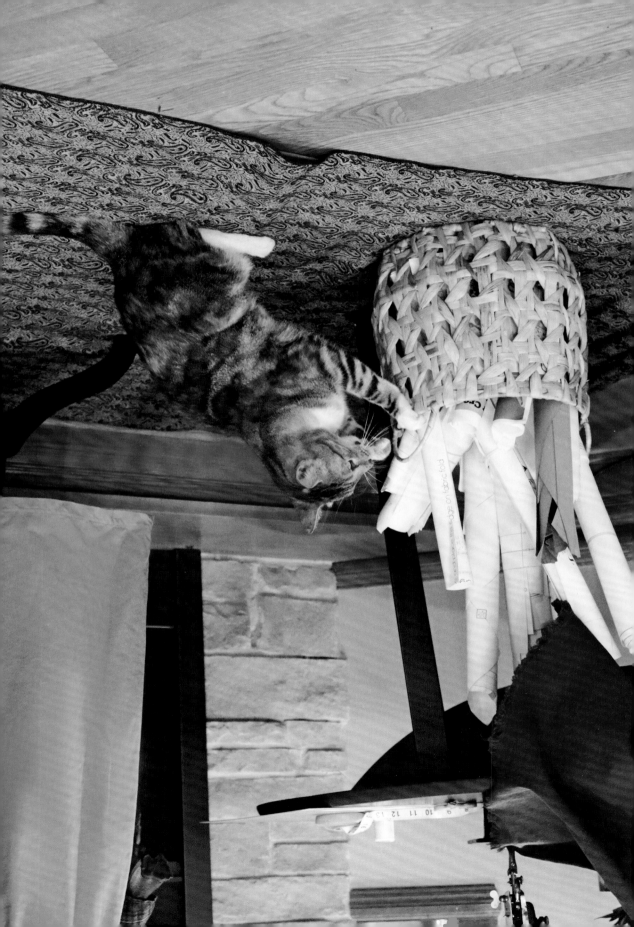

Panel Dress

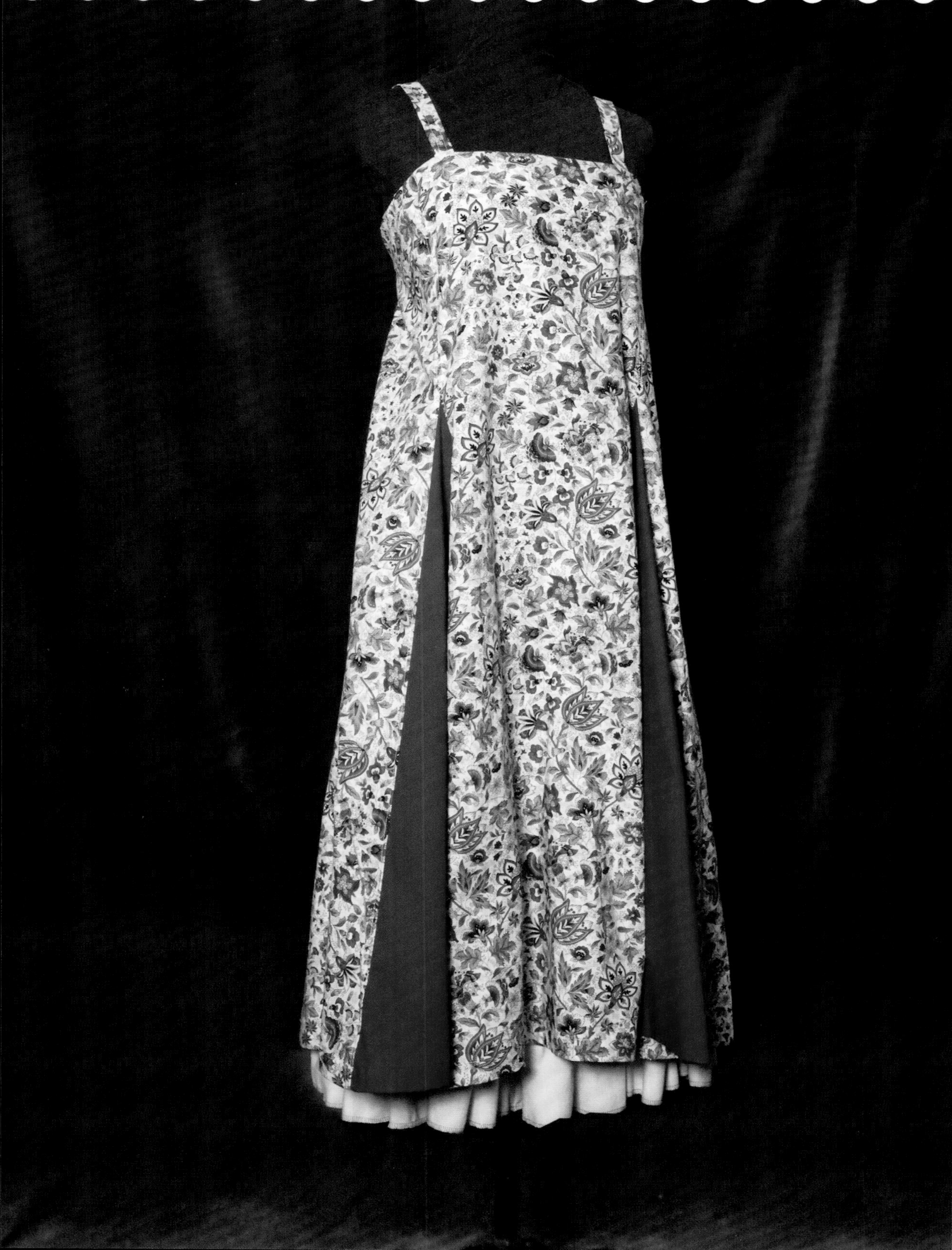

This dress is based on the Norse apron dresses. The gores and A-line bottom section of the body panels gives it a very full skirt for maximum swishiness. The instructions in this chapter include customization options of a waist tie, back or side lacing, and pockets. You can further embellish the dress with trim or even use multiple fabrics in one dress for visual interest.

What Kind of Fabric to Use

You can use pretty much any fabric for this dress. Choose a lightweight **cotton** or **linen** for the summer. Pick a heavier fabric like **suede** or **wool** for colder weather. You can use a variety of **blends** and **synthetics**.

How Much Fabric?

Once you have drafted your pattern pieces, you can figure out how much fabric you will need. If the bottom of your body panel is less than 22", you can use fabric that is 44" wide. Otherwise, you'll be using fabric that is 58" in width. You'll need a length of fabric that is twice as long as your body pattern piece. The gores, straps, facing, and pockets (if adding) can be cut out of the leftover fabric.

PATTERN DRAFTING

I do recommend you draft your pattern rather than drawing the measurements directly on the fabric. This is simply because you'll be cutting out four pieces of the body panels and the gores. I use wrapping paper to draft patterns because it is wide and cheap (especially if you buy it the day after Christmas).

Measurements

You will need the following measurements:

- Your bust circumference
- The length from the top of your bust to your waist
- The length from the top of your bust to where you want the dress to end

Decide how much ease you want in the dress. An ease of 2" will allow you to pull the dress on, and it is best for a dress that you will be wearing alone. If you are making a pinafore style of dress that will be worn over other clothing, you'll want an ease of around 4". If you are going to be adding side or back lacing to the dress, you can have more ease as you will be able to adjust the fit with the lacing.

MATERIALS

Fabric (see below)

Thread

Trim such as rickrack, ribbon, or piping (optional)

⅝" grosgrain ribbon in a coordinating color for lacing loops (optional)

¼" braided cord or organza ribbon in a coordination color for lacing (optional)

½"-wide elastic (optional)

Lightweight fusible interfacing (optional)

TOOLS

Sewing machine and needle

Measuring tape

Ruler

Scissors or a rotary cutter

Paper for pattern making

Pins

Seam ripper (just in case)

TERMS & CONCEPTS

You will be **drafting a pattern**, figuring out **ease**, **basting**, **understitching**, **topstitching**, creating **bias binding**, making a **standard hem**, and **finishing the seams**. See "Methods" on page 6 for more information.

With those measurements, calculate the following:

- A = ([Bust measurement + ease] ÷ 4) + 1" seam allowance
- B = Bust to waist + ½" seam allowance
- C = Length − B + 1½" hem
- D = 2 × A

Body Panel

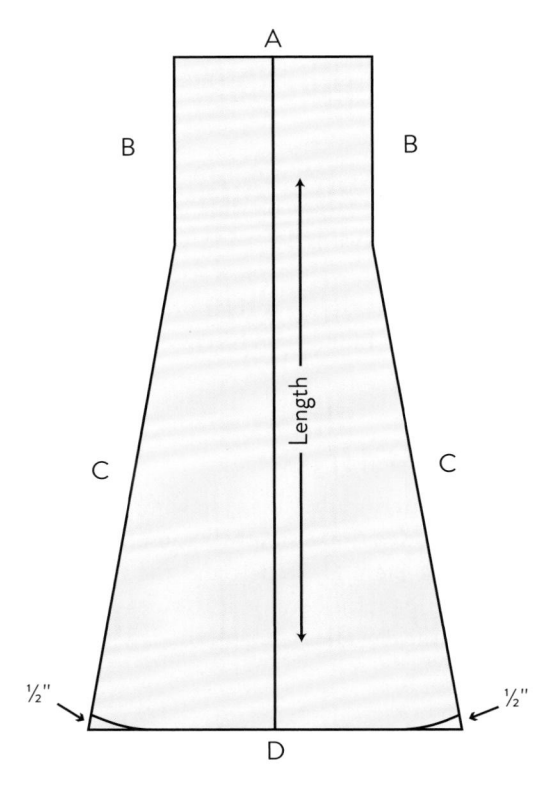

1 Using a yardstick or ruler, draw a line your desired length + 2" for the top seam allowance and the hem down the middle of your paper.

2 Draw a line the length of your **A** measurement centered at the top of the length line.

3 Draw a line the length of your **D** measurement centered at the bottom of the length line.

4 At each end of the **A** line, draw down a line measuring your **B** length parallel to the length line.

5 Connect the end of your **B** line to the **D** line on both sides.

6 Curve the bottom hem of the body panel by marking a spot ½" up on each side and drawing a curve connecting this spot with the **D** line.

Gore

1 Draw a horizontal line the length of your **D** measurement.

2 Find the center of this line and measure up the length of your **C** measurement. Make a mark.

3 Draw a line from the mark to each end of your **D** line. These lines should measure your **C** length and will not meet up with the end of your **D** line. Draw a curve from your **D** line to the ends of each vertical line, connecting them to make a triangle piece with a curved bottom.

4 Curve the bottom hem of the gore by marking a spot ½" up on each side and draw a curve connecting this spot with the **D** line.

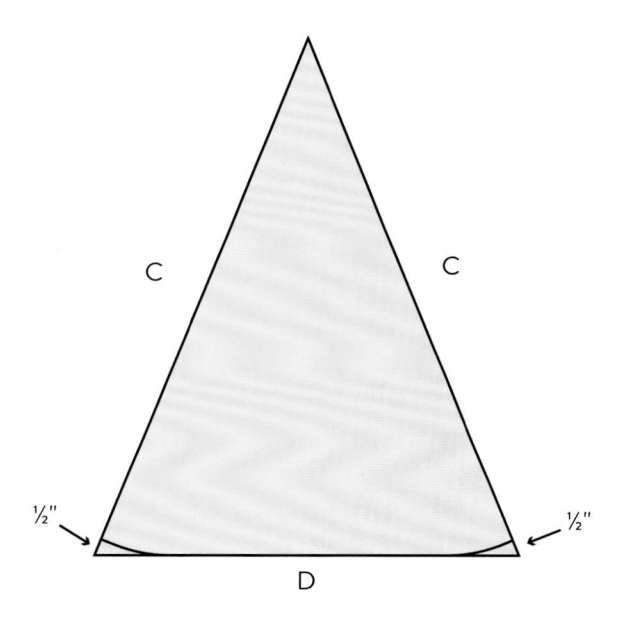

Cut out both pattern pieces. Cut four pieces of the body panel and four of the gore from your fabric. Designate one panel as the back panel, two as the side panels, and one as the front panel.

CONSTRUCTION

Back Panel Options

If you are going to include a waist tie or back lacing, do the following:

FOR A WAIST TIE

1 From your fabric cut two rectangles 2½" wide by 25" long. Fold the fabric in half lengthwise, with right sides facing. Sew along one short edge and the long edge with a ½" seam. Turn the waist tie right-side out and press. Repeat with the other waist tie piece.

2 Pin the ties to the right side of the back panel, 2–3" above the waist, matching raw edges. Baste. Tie the waist ties together or pin them to the back panel to keep them out of the way for the remainder of the construction.

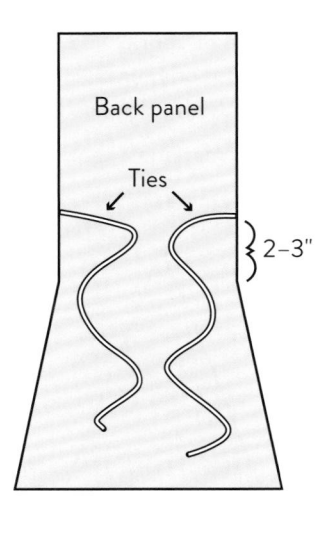

FOR BACK LACING

1 Cut the grosgrain ribbon into 2" lengths. You will want to space the loops no more than ½" apart. I recommend setting them every inch. Cut enough pieces of ribbon to fit the length of your **B** measurement, leaving 1" at the top and 1½"–2" above the waist.

2 Mark the ribbon placement. Fold ribbons in half and pin them along each side of the right side of the back panel, raw edges matching. Baste.

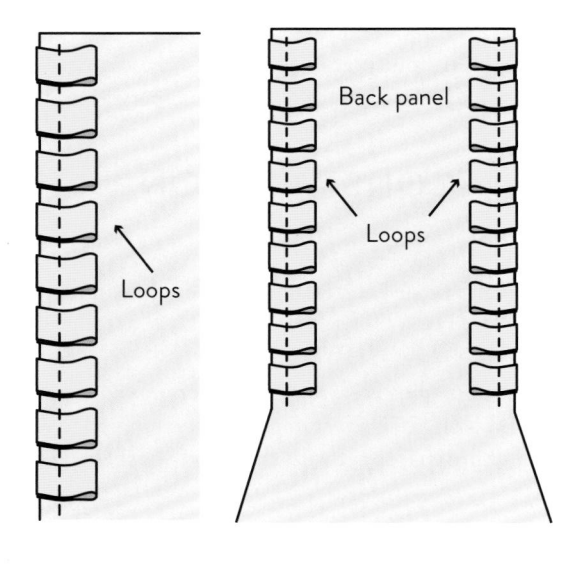

Side Panel Options

If you are going to include side lacing or pockets, do the following:

FOR SIDE LACING

Follow the above instructions for back lacing, but make the ribbons on both side panels.

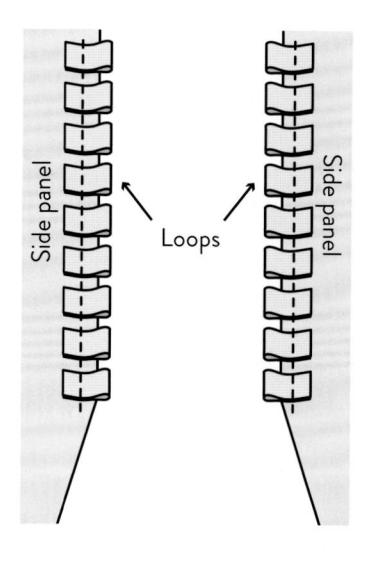

FOR POCKETS

1 On paper draw a square 8" × 8" in size. Round the bottom corners to give you a curved shape.

2 Cut out two pieces of fabric from your paper pattern.

3 Give the top of each pocket a narrow hem. You can add embellishments such as embroidery, piping, etc.

4 Sew a basting stitch around the other three sides of the pocket ½" from the edge. Fold the fabric to the inside along the stitching and press. Remove the basting.

5 Determine where you want the pockets to be on the side panels by measuring from your bust to where the top of your hand falls along your side. Mark that distance down the side panels from the top. Place the top edge of the pocket at this mark, centered horizontally on the panel.

6 Stitch a scant ⅛" from the edge of the pocket around the curved sides. Backstitch at the beginning and end of the stitching to anchor and reinforce the pocket corners.

Assembling the Dress

1 Pin one gore to the front panel (one that has no lacing loops, waist ties, or pockets), matching hems. Mark a dot at the point of the gore where it meets the waist. This will show you where to stop stitching. Stitch a ½" seam from the hem to the waist. Backstitch at the point to reinforce the seam.

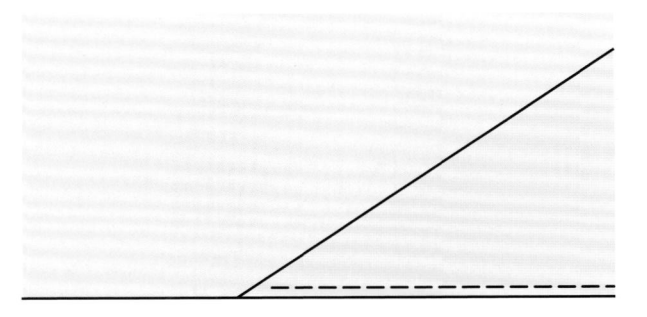

2 Repeat step 1 with a second gore on the other side of the front panel.

3 Pin one side panel to the one of the front panel gores. Sew from the bottom hems up to the gore point. Backstitch at the point. Pin the top of the side panel to the front panel above the gore. Starting right above the gore stitching, sew a ½" seam up to the top of the panels. Again, backstitch at the start of the seam to reinforce that point. If you have side lacing loops on the panel, make sure the folded ends do not get caught in the stitching.

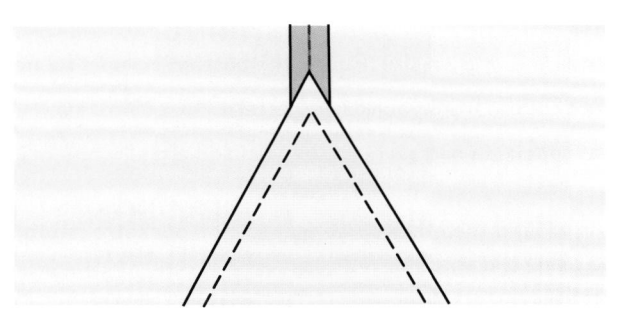

4 Repeat step 3 on the other side with the remaining side panel.

5 Attach the remaining gores to the back panel as in steps 1 and 2.

6 Attach the back panel to the side panels as in steps 3 and 4.

7 Finish the seams and press them.

8 If you have included any lacing loops, top stitch close (⅛") to the seam on either side of the loops to reinforce them.

Fitting the Straps

1 Cut two rectangles from your fabric that measure 2½" wide by 20" long. Fold each rectangle in half lengthwise, right sides together. Sew a ½" seam along the long side of each strap. Turn the straps right-side out and press.

2 Try on the dress. Check how it fits at the top. Note any gaping and mark if you need to shorten the top at the sides. If there is gaping, you can fix it either by adding darts, pinning the excess and sewing a new seam, or using elastic (see page 72 for instructions on how to insert the elastic).

3 Position the straps in the front where you want them. Mark the position on the dress or use safety pins to secure them in place, matching the raw edges. Pull the straps over your shoulders and mark where you want them to attach to the back. Mark the placement on the dress or pin them in place. Mark the excess of the straps.

4 Remove the dress.

5 With right sides together, position the straps and baste them into place. Trim off the excess.

Shaping the Side Underarm & Facing

1 If you found the top needed shaping when you tried on the dress, shape it now. Pin the two side panels together at the top and draw out the shaping according to your marks. Cut out the fabric. Save the cut-away piece for step 4.

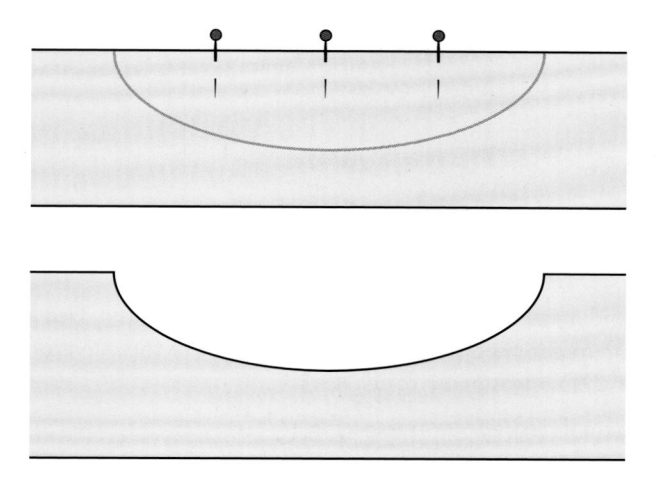

2 If you marked darts or new seams, stitch these now.

3 Measure the width of each body panel along the top to create the facing pieces. Cut out rectangles from your fabric that measure each width + 1" for the seam allowance by 4" long. If you are working with a thin or slippery fabric, you can add a lightweight fusible interfacing to the wrong side of the facing to give it a bit of stiffening.

4 Using the cut-away fabric from step 1 as a template, shape the side panel facings to match.

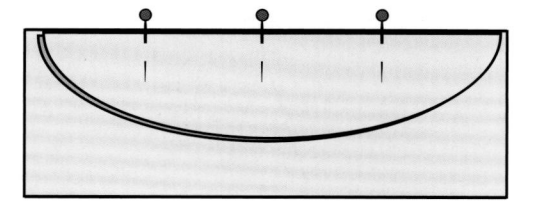

5 Sew the short sides of the facing pieces together, right sides together, with a ½" seam. Press the seams. Finish the bottom of the facing with a narrow hem.

6 Pin the facing to the dress top, right sides together, so that the straps are sandwiched between the fabric and facing. Sew a ½" seam. Clip the curves and trim the seam.

7 Press the seam toward the facing and understitch the facing.

8 To insert elastic to deal with any gaping at the top, do the following: Cut a length of ½" wide elastic 2" shorter than the finished top panel width. Attach one end of the elastic to the inside of the facing at the side seam. Attach the other end of the elastic to the facing at the opposite side seam. If you want added security, stretch the elastic out to the full length of the panel and stitch in the middle. This will give the top a slight gathered look as it pulls the fabric close to your body.

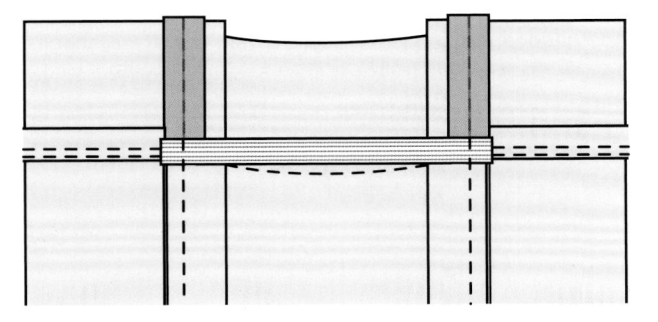

9 Turn the facing to the inside of the dress and press.

Hemming and Finishing

1 Try on the dress and make note of the length. Shorten it if desired. Use a standard hem. On the inside, the hem might need tucking at the seams due to the curvature of the gores and panels. This is okay. No one is going to see it.

2 Add trim to the hem if desired.

3 The join at the point of the gore is particularly vulnerable to tears. Reinforce the seams with a bar tack by sewing a zigzag stitch with a short stitch length over the point, backstitching to secure the threads.

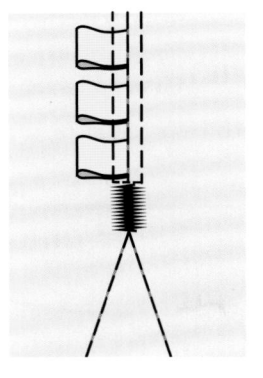

4 If you are adding lacing, run cording or ribbon through the lacing loops.

Mending Magic

There will come a time when your clothing needs to be repaired. Maybe it's a simple matter of reattaching a button. Or you may find that a seam has torn or a rip opened up in the gore in your panel dress. Rather than throwing the garment out or relegating it to the rag pile, consider mending it instead.

There has been a movement over the last few years to visibly mend clothing. This has been documented in books like *Visible Mending* by Arounna Khounnoraj and *Creative Mending* by Hikaru Noguchi. It is based on a Japanese form of mending called *sashiko*, which is a tradition of stitching that is meant to be seen. What this practice provides, though, is an opportunity to work more magic into your wardrobe.

Use embroidery thread in colors like white for renewal, blue for healing, or green for prosperity to darn rips. Go the patchwork route and cover unsightly tears and stains with appliques. You can add a fabric heart for loving energies, a sun to bring in its protective properties, or any other symbol that encapsulates your intentions.

As you sew, feel gratitude for the use you have already gotten out of the clothing item. Pour that gratitude back into the fabric with each stitch. When you are finished, sit with your mending for a moment. Much like magic, sewing is an art. It is the ability to make something out of almost nothing. And the magic doesn't have to end just because the fabric has become a little worn.

Fairy Dress

Are you a fairy witch? Fairy witches work with the Fae beings in their magical rituals. This dress combines a flowing, romantic layer over a solid color layer to give a unique look. Use a sheer or very lightweight cotton like dotted Swiss or lawn for the overlayer.

What Kind of Fabric to Use

This dress is made of a base and overlayer. The overlayer should be a lightweight, drapey fabric. Embroidered organza, tulle, and even very lightweight cotton are ideal for the overlayer. The base layer can be cotton, linen, or any other medium-weight fabric that will provide structure and stability for the overlayer.

The straps are made from the base layer fabric.

How Much Fabric?

For both the base layer and overlayer, you will need a length of fabric that is double your pattern piece. If the hem of the pattern piece is 22" or less, you will be able to use fabric that is 44" wide. For larger widths, use fabric that is 58" wide.

PATTERN DRAFTING

Measurements

You will need the following measurements:

- **A** = The distance from shoulder to shoulder across your chest

- **B** = Shoulder circumference

- **C** = Your bust circumference

- **D** = Bust to waist

- **E** = Your waist circumference

- **F** = Bust to hip

- **G** = Your hip circumference

- **H** = Bust to where you want the dress to end

To make the pattern (see next page), do the following:

Start by drawing a horizontal line measuring ½ your **A** measurement + 1" for the seam allowance.

Draw a vertical line from the left end of the **A** line measuring your **H** measurement + 1¾".

MATERIALS

Fabric for the base and overlayers (see "How Much Fabric?" below)

Matching thread

TOOLS

Sewing machine and needle

Pins

Iron

Measuring tape

Yardstick

Scissors or a rotary cutter

Hem gauge

Small safety pin

Seam ripper (just in case)

TERMS & CONCEPTS

You will be creating hems and adding straps. See "Methods" on page 6 for more information.

Draw a horizontal line from the bottom of the **H** line out to the right measuring your **G** measurement + 4" for the ease divided by 4 and then add 1" for the seam allowance. This is your hemline.

Measure down from the **A** line ½ your **B** measurement and then out from the **H** line your **C** measurement + 4" for the ease divided by 4, and then add 1" for the seam allowance. Make a dot here and label it **C**.

Draw a line from the right end of the **A** line down to the **C** dot.

Measure down from the **A** line your **D** measurement and then out from the **H** line your **E** measurement + 4" for the ease divided by 4, and then add 1" for the seam allowance. Make a dot there and label it **D**.

Draw a line from the **C** dot to the **D** dot.

Measure down from the **A** line your **F** measurement and then out from the **H** line your **G** measurement + 4" for the ease divided by 4, and then add 1" for the seam allowance. Make a dot there and label it **G**.

Draw a line from the **D** dot to your **G** dot.

Draw a diagonal line from your **G** dot down to the right end of your hemline, connecting the two. Then draw a slight curve inside the angle there.

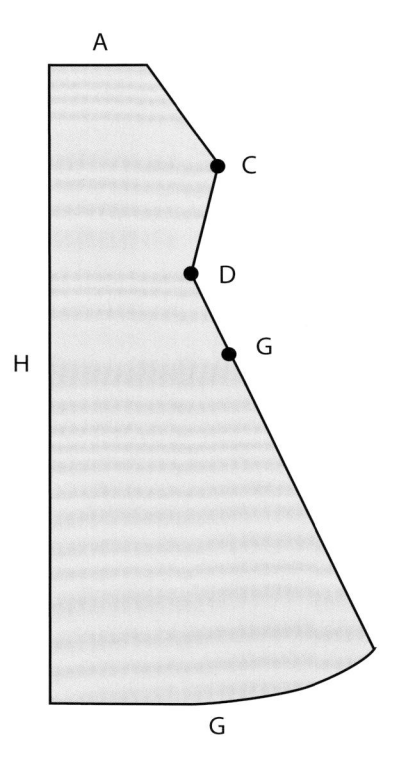

CONSTRUCTION

When cutting your pattern, the front and back of the base layer will be cut on the fold. The back of the overlayer will be cut on the fold, while the front of the overlayer will be cut on the selvages to make two pieces. The overlayer will not be sewn together at the front.

Making the Straps

1 Cut two pieces of the base fabric measuring 14" long by 2" wide.

2 Fold one strap in half widthwise with right sides together so that it now measures 14" long by 1" wide. Sew a ½" seam down the long side of the strap.

3 Trim the seam and turn the strap right-side out. Repeat with the other strap piece.

Making the Dress

1 Finish the center front edges of the overlayer with a narrow hem.

2 With right sides together, sew the front and back of the base layer together on the sides using a ½" seam. Repeat on the overlayer.

3 Hem the bottom of both the base layer and the overlayer.

4 Tack the straps to the front of the base layer on the wrong side ½" from the sides.

5 With the right side of the overlayer facing the wrong side of the base layer, match the side seams, center back, and top edges of the two layers. Because the front panels of the over-layer are not as wide as the front of the base layer, the center front edges of the overlayer will not match up to the center front of the base layer. Pin.

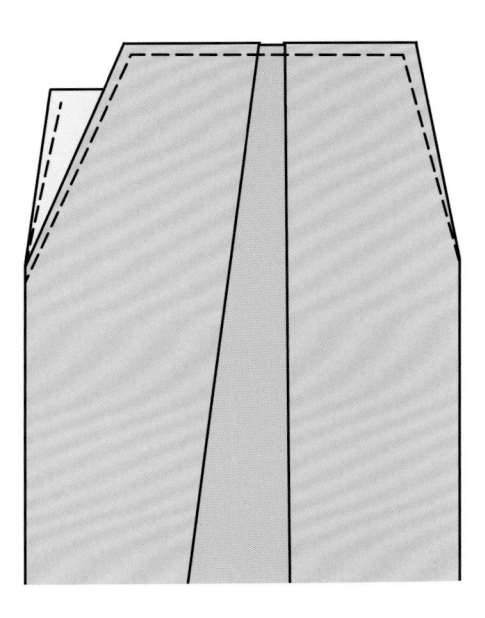

6 Sew a ½" seam all the way around the top of the gown. When stitching, leave a ½" gap at the back ½" from each side for the straps.

7 Trim the corners and seam.

8 Turn the dress right-side out with the overlayer on top of the base layer. Press the seam.

9 Try on the dress. Pin the straps in place at the back of the dress and adjust until you are pleased with their placement. Mark the straps and remove the dress.

10 Using a safety pin as a bodkin, thread the straps through the gaps in the back. Turn the dress inside out and sew the gaps closed, securing the straps. Trim off the excess.

Folk Names for
Common Herbs

Many common herbs and plants have standardized names now, along with scientific names, which makes identification easier. However, in the past those same plants might have had a variety of folk names. Depending on the area where you are, chicory might be known as witloof, blue sailors, or coffee-weed. As a hedgewitch, I love this kind of information because I can then get fanciful with labeling my herbs. Chamomile gets labeled "Blood of Hestia" and the dried dandelion leaf is "Priest's Crown," both terms that come from the Greek magical papyri.

What is interesting to me is that oftentimes the folk names of plants that might sound weird at first make sense once you think about them. For example, the holly leaf was once referred to as bat's wing. The shape of the holly leaf makes clear why people would refer to it as such. And the folk name often marks out those plants that have magickal uses. Take for example the following plants and their folk names:

FOXGLOVE: witch bells

MUGWORT: witch herb

DODDER: witch's hair

DATURA: witch's thimble

ROWAN: witchbane

All five have a long and storied history of folklore and magic. Each can be used in various ways in spellwork, to enhance a witch's psychic powers and in protection and in divination.

So when you are going through your spice rack, consider adding labels with folk names. Cinnamon can be labeled as sweet wood. Garlic powder becomes stinking rose. You can also add folk names to the herbs and plants you keep in your cabinet for witchy purposes. Just make sure to add the common and scientific names as well so there isn't any confusion later on.

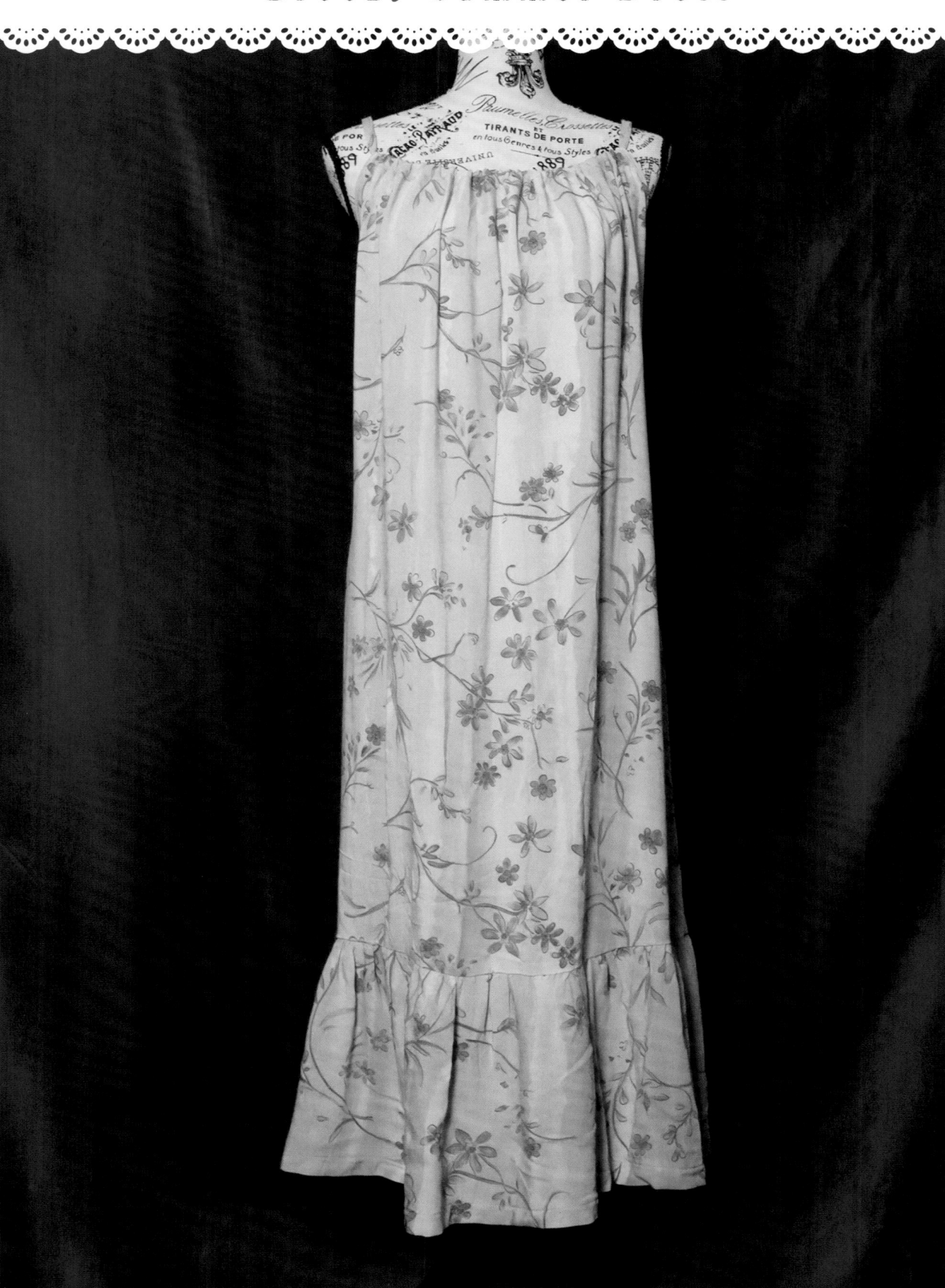

Sometimes what you need is a comfortable house dress with pockets. Make this dress out of linen that will get softer the more you wear and wash it. Or choose a slinky synthetic fabric to make a fancy going-out dress. You could always be like me and make one out of a jersey sheet you picked up for $2.50 from the thrift store.

The waist tie gives it a slightly fitted look, and the pockets are large enough to hold crystals, tarot cards, cell phones, and so on, leaving your hands free for witchery. This pattern allows for a ruffle at the bottom if you desire.

You can also shorten the length of your pattern to make this as a shirt, giving you even more wardrobe options.

What Kind of Fabric to Use

This dress is suitable for nearly all types of fabrics, although I wouldn't recommend any really stiff ones like denim or duck cloth. Use a nice **linen** or **cotton** for a lightweight everyday summer dress. Or use a **slinky synthetic** fabric for something a little more sophisticated.

How Much Fabric?

You will need a length of fabric that is twice as long as your pattern. If the hem of your pattern piece is 22" or less, you will be able to use fabric that is 44" wide. For larger widths, use 58" wide fabric. Pocket and tie pieces can be cut from leftover fabric. You will need extra fabric to add a ruffle if desired.

PATTERN DRAFTING

Measurements

You will need the following measurements:

- **A** = The distance from shoulder to shoulder across your chest
- **B** = Your bust circumference
- **C** = Your hip circumference
- **D** = Bust to waist
- **E** = Bust to hips
- **F** = Your shoulder circumference
- **G** = Bust to desired length

To make your pattern (see next page), start with the top edge and mark a line that is ½ of your **A** measurement + 2" (for the ease) + ½" (for the seam allowance).

MATERIALS

Fabric (see below)

Matching thread

TOOLS

Sewing machine and needle

Pins

Iron

Measuring tape

Scissors or a rotary cutter

Quilting ruler

Yardstick

Hem gauge

Small safety pin

Pocket pattern piece from page 174

Paper for making the pattern

Seam ripper

TERMS & CONCEPTS

You will be **drafting a pattern**, adding **pockets**, **gathering** fabric (if you are including a ruffle on the dress), and **hemming**. See "Methods" on page 6 for more information.

Perpendicular to that line on the left side, draw a line down the paper that is your **G** measurement + 1¾".

From the bottom of your **G** line, measure out ½ of your **B** measurement + 10". Measure down ¼ your **E** measurement from the top of the **A** line and then measure out ¼ of your **C** measurement + 2" (for the ease) + ½" (for the seam allowance) and make a dot. Label this dot **E**.

From the right end of your **A** line, draw a diagonal line down your **G** measurement + 1¾". Make sure the diagonal line runs through your **E** dot. This line will not meet up with the hemline. Draw a slightly curved line to connect the **G** line hem with the end of the **B** line side seam.

Marking Your Pattern

There are three points you will want to mark on your pattern. The first is where the side seams will begin. Make the mark ½" in from the edge of the pattern down the side seam ½ the length of your **F** measurement. This is your **H** mark.

The second is where your waist ties will be. You want to mark the **D** measurement on the side of your pattern. Make the mark ½" in from the edge of the pattern. When you add your ties to the dress, you will place them at these marks with the raw edges matching. This is your **I** mark.

The third mark is where your pockets will go. Measure down about 1" from the waist tie mark and make a mark for where the top of the pocket will start. When you add your pockets to the dress, you will align the top of the pocket to this mark. This is your **J** mark.

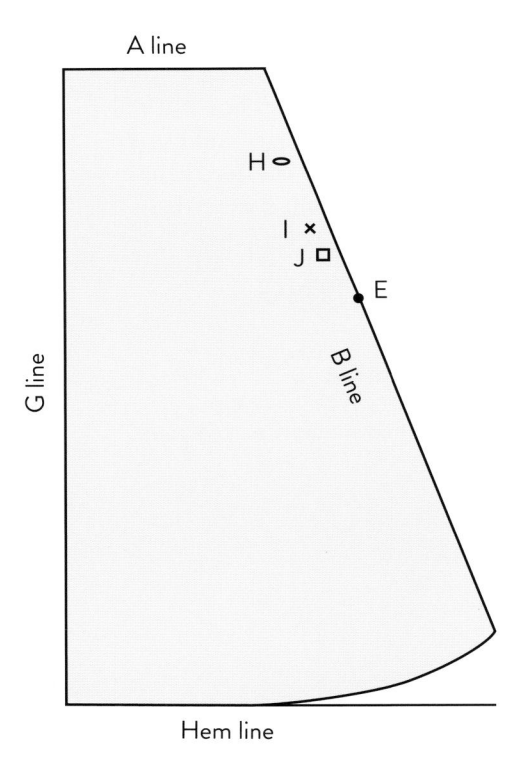

Adding a Ruffle

A ruffle is a sweet addition to this dress, requiring only a little more advance planning. You will draft your pattern as above; however, when drawing your **G** line, you will need to make it shorter

by the length of your ruffle. For example, if you want your dress to be 36" long and want to have a 6" ruffle, draw your **G** line 30½" inches long. The ruffle piece you will add will be 7¾" long and 2 times your hem width. The math will look like this:

- **G** line = **G** measurement − ruffle length + ½"
- Ruffle length = Desired ruffle length + 1¾" for hem and seam allowance
- Ruffle width = Hem width × 2

CONSTRUCTION

Making Your Ties

You will need a set of ties for the waist and a tie for the top of the dress. These can be made from leftover material after you have cut out the other pattern pieces from your fabric.

Waist ties should be cut 2" long by 25" wide. You can make the ties longer if you desire or need them to be longer. To make the waist ties, fold the fabric in half lengthwise with the right side together. Sew a ¼" seam along one short side and the long side of the fabric. Turn right-side out. Press.

The top tie should be cut 2" long by 44" wide. Fold the fabric in half lengthwise with the right side together. Sew a ¼" seam along the long side of the fabric. Turn right-side out. Press.

Making the Dress

1 Tack the ties to the right side of the front dress piece at the **I** markings with the raw edges even.

2 Position one pocket piece at the **J** marking, right sides together. Sew a ⅜" seam attaching the pocket to the panel. Press the pocket out. Repeat with the other three pocket pieces and three other dress body pieces.

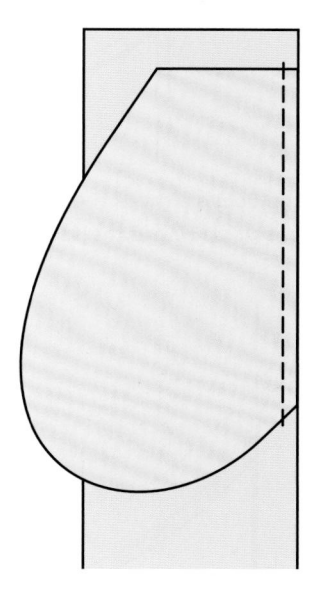

3 Sew the side seams together starting at the top with a basting stitch. When you reach the **H** side seam mark, switch to a shorter stitch length. Make sure to backstitch at the start of the shorter stitches to anchor the seam.

4 When you reach the pocket, sew down ½" past the top edge of the pocket, pivot 90 degrees, and continue across the pocket.

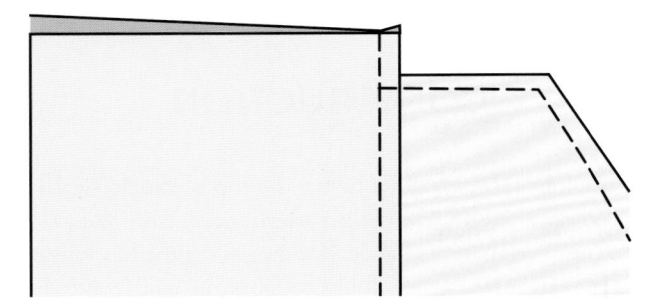

5 Sew a ½" seam around the pocket. Sew into the dress ½". Pivot sharply and continue down to the hem.

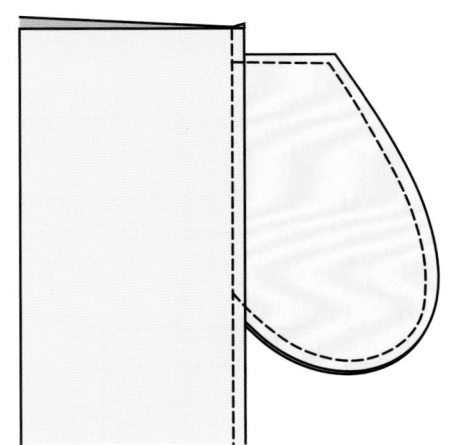

6 Clip the seam allowance where the pockets meet the dress, making sure not to cut through the stitching. Finish the side seams up to where the seam is clipped.

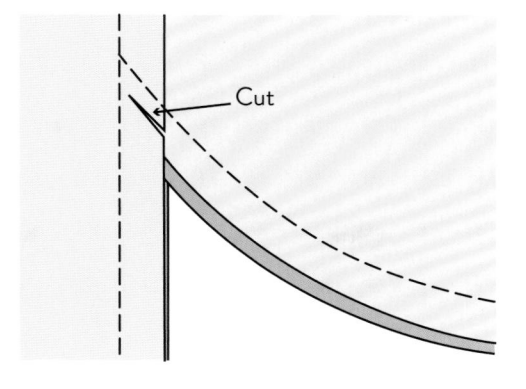

7 Press the armhole edges under ¼" and then again ¼" above the side seam marking. Topstitch close to the first fold. Open up the seam with a seam ripper to the marking, taking out the basting stitches.

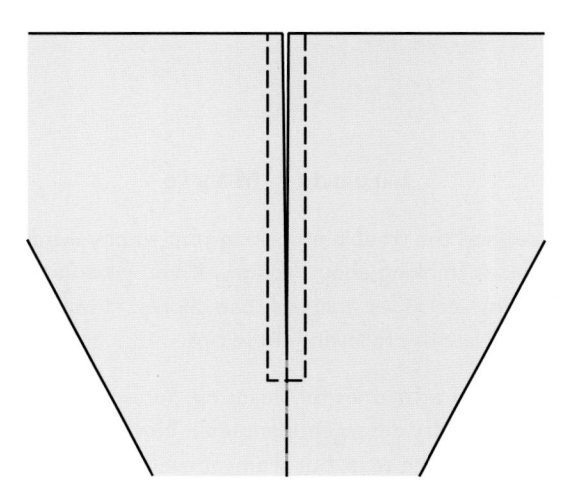

8 Make a top tie channel by pressing the top edges under ¼" and then again 1". Topstitch close to the first fold.

9 If adding a ruffle: Sew the short edges of the ruffle together. Add a hem to the bottom of the ruffle. Gather the top edge of the ruffle and pin it to the bottom of the dress with right sides together. Adjust the gathers so that they are evenly distributed and so that the ruffle is the same length as the bottom of the dress. Sew a ½" seam around the gathered edge.

10 If not adding a ruffle: Hem the bottom of the dress.

11 Using a safety pin, thread the tie through the top tie channel. Try on the dress. Adjust the top tie to desired length. Mark this on the tie.

12 Sew the ends of the tie together. Rotate the tie until the sewn edge is hidden inside the channel.

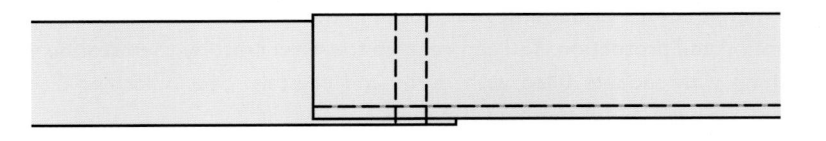

Laundry Magic

After going through all the trouble of making your witchy wardrobe, you want it to last. This means thinking about laundry. If you groan at that thought, I sympathize. Nothing seems less magical than chores. However, you can work witchcraft into your laundry following these tips:

- Use **sigils**. You can write ones for cleansing, purification, and protection on your laundry detergent container. Not only will the sigil work its magic on the soap, but seeing it every time you do a load of laundry will remind you to wash with intention. You can also add the sigils to the bottom of your hamper to do the same work on your clothes while they wait to be washed.

- Add drops of **essential oils** like rosemary, lavender, and lemon to wool dryer balls to imbue clothes with their magical properties. Don't have dryer balls? You can do the same with old dryer sheets.

- Add **vinegar** to the rinse cycle not only to soften fabric but to make use of its purification properties. You can also add sun water to your washer for the same magical effect.

- Speaking of the sun, if you can, try to **hang your clothes** on a line or even hang them on a drying rack where sunlight will fall on them. This will add the protective and purifying magic of the sun to your clothes.

When it comes to washing your clothing, the name of the game is magical cleansing and protection. You can keep up the witchcraft by then storing your clothing with sachets filled with herbs and crystals. See "Clothing Sachet Magic" on page 57 for more information.

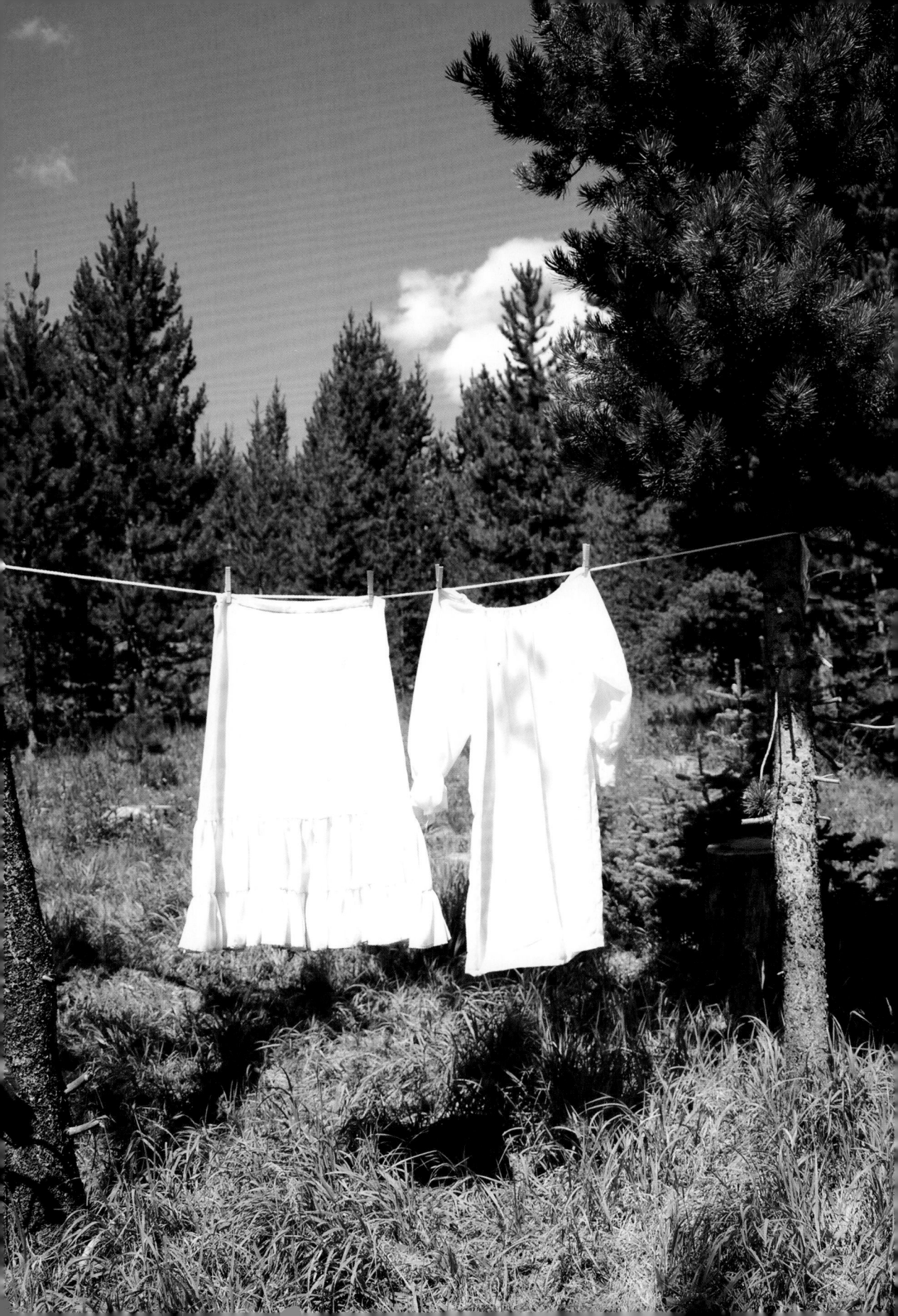

Loose House Jacket

This jacket is constructed much like a very simplified kimono. It consists of three panels (one body and two sleeves). It is meant to be a loose layering garment for chilly mornings. It includes features such as optional pockets and gathered sleeves and vented sides for ease of movement. It is unlined.

What Kind of Fabric to Use

This jacket is made using **flannel** fabric. You could also use **cotton** or **linen** if you want a more lightweight garment. For a warmer jacket, choose **wool**. Stiff, heavyweight fabric is not recommended for this project.

How Much Fabric?

You will need a length of fabric measuring twice your **C** length and as wide as ½ your **A** measurement + your **B** measurement. An extra ¼ yard of fabric is needed for the pockets.

PATTERN DRAFTING

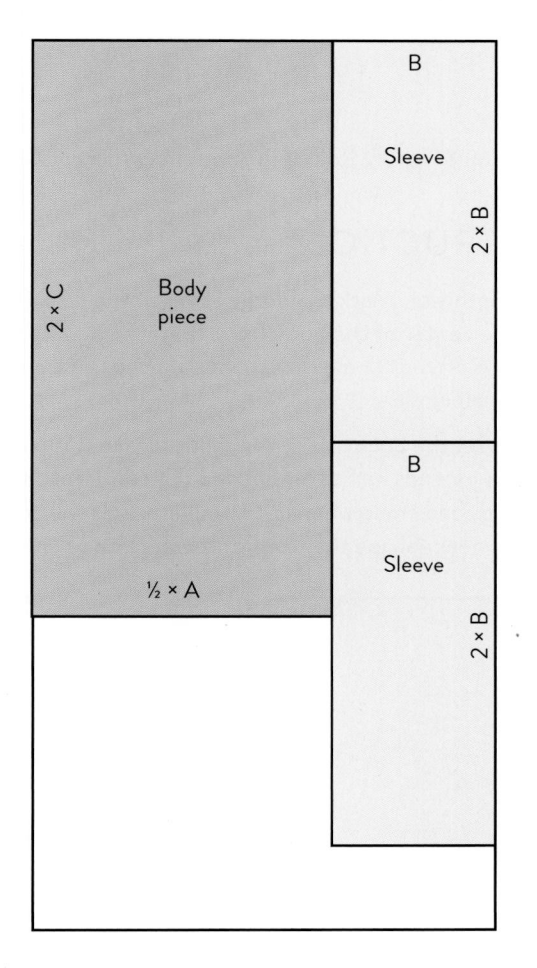

MATERIALS

Fabric (see below)

Thread

1–2 packages of single-fold bias tape (optional)

TOOLS

Sewing machine and needle

Measuring tape

Ruler

Scissors or a rotary cutter

Pins

Compass or half-circle quilting ruler (optional)

Seam ripper

TERMS & CONCEPTS

You will be **drafting a pattern**, adding **pockets**, **finishing seams**, **hemming**, and **edge stitching**. See "Methods" on page 6 for more information.

Measurements

You will need the following measurements:

- **A** = Your bust circumference + 1" for the seam allowance + 4" for the ease
- **B** = The top of your shoulder to your elbow + ½" for the seam allowance + ½" for the hem
- **C** = The length you want of your jacket + 1¼" for the hem
- **D** = Your neck circumference divided by 3.14 (π). Then divide your result by 2.

NOTES

1 The ease is necessary, as this is a loose-fitting jacket. Use the bust measurement even if it isn't your largest width measurement so that it will fit at the shoulders.

2 When calculating your **D** measurement, round down to the nearest ½". If the neck ends up being a bit smaller than you would like, you can always cut it larger, but you can't make it smaller after your initial cut.

This jacket is constructed from rectangles and only involves three pieces. You can draw your pattern directly onto the fabric, if you wish, or make a paper pattern.

Cut out a rectangle measuring 2 × **C** long by ½ of **A** wide.

Cut out two rectangles measuring 2 × **B** long by **B** wide.

Cut out the pocket pieces, if using.

For the Pockets

For two side pockets, draw a square that measures 8" by 8". Round the bottom corners of the pocket.

CONSTRUCTION

1 Start by folding the body piece in half lengthwise. Mark the outer edges of the fold. These will be your shoulder marks. Draw a line at the center of the body front from the hem to the fold. On the fold, draw a half circle with a radius of your **D** measurement. You can use a compass or a half-circle quilting ruler to draw the half circle.

2 Open out your fabric and finish the circle on the back half of the fabric. Make this part of the circle smaller than the front half so that it extends half as far beyond the center of the fabric as the front half. You will end up with a lopsided circle when it is complete. This will ensure the jacket rests snug against the back of your neck. Shape the front of the neck to your liking.

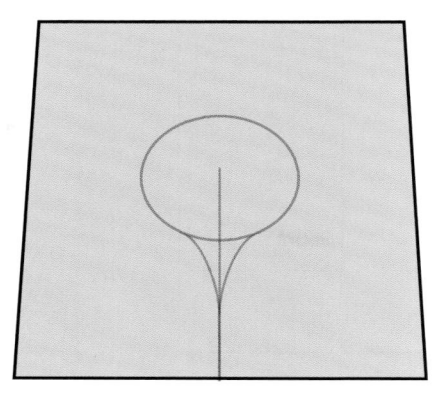

3 Cut along the line and around the neck opening. Finish the opening either with bias binding or by sewing a narrow hem.

4 If you are adding pockets, try on the body, draping it over your neck and making sure the shoulder marks align with your shoulders. Note where you want the pockets to be and mark the placement.

5 Give the top of each pocket a narrow hem. Fold the other, unfinished edges of each pocket ½" to the wrong side and press. Pin the pockets to the body piece.

6 Stitch a scant ⅛" from the edge of the pocket around the curved sides. Backstitch at the beginning and end of the stitching to anchor and reinforce the pocket corners.

7 Finish one long edge of each sleeve piece with a narrow hem.

8 Fold your sleeve pieces in half crosswise. Mark the center fold on the unfinished long edge. On the same unfinished long edge, mark ½" from each short edge. With right sides facing, match the sleeve and shoulder marks and pin. Sew the sleeves to the body between the two marks (as per red line in the illustration), leaving ½" of the seam unsewn on either end. Backstitch at the start and stop of the seam.

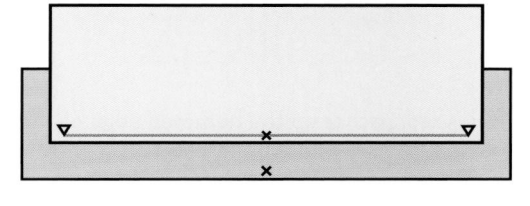

9 Fold the jacket in half crosswise, matching up the sleeves and sides. Sew the sleeves closed, stopping at the seam that attaches the sleeve to the body.

10 On the side seams, mark a point 8" below the sleeve seam. Sew the side seams together from the end of the seam that attaches the sleeves to the body down to the marking. Then switch your stitch length to a longer, basting stitch and continue the seam down the rest of the body. This will leave a small gap in the armpit of the jacket, giving more ease of movement.

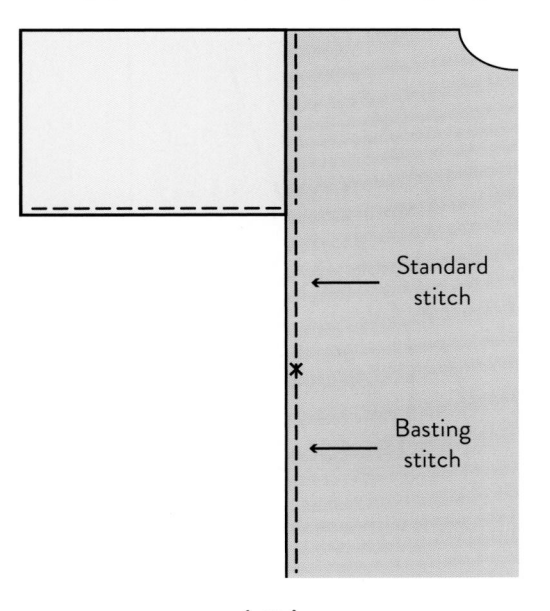

Standard stitch

Basting stitch

11 Press the side seams open.

12 Hem the bottom of the jacket with a standard hem. When you reach the side seams, sew upward, ¼" away from the seam to your marking. Sew across the seam and back down ¼" to the hem.

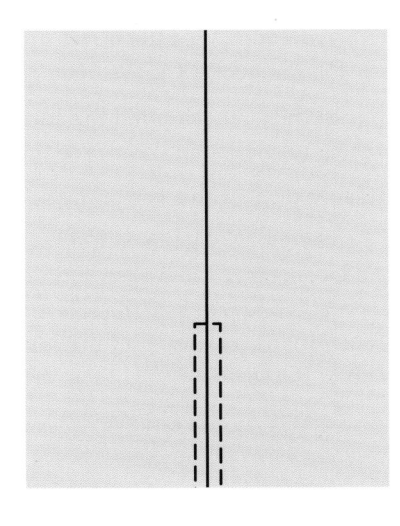

13 Try on the jacket and, if desired, gather up the hemmed edge of the sleeve until it is above the crease in your elbow. Use safety pins to secure the gathered edge in place.

14 Cut two pieces of fabric each measuring 5" by 2½". With the right sides together, fold the strips in half lengthwise. Sew a ¼" seam along the three unfinished edges, leaving a 2" gap in the middle of the long side for turning. Turn the strips right-side out and press. Edge stitch around all sides.

15 Position one loop at the center of the sleeve, with one end on the outside and one on the inside of the sleeve. Hand baste the loop to the sleeve. Once the loop is secure, remove the safety pin and stitch the loop in place. Remove the basting stitches. Repeat on the other side.

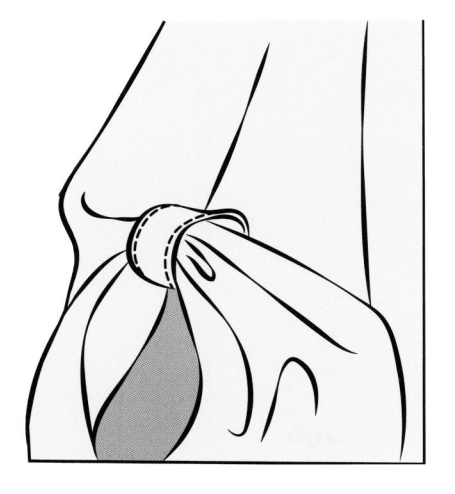

16 Open up the basted side seams with a seam ripper.

Magical Sprays

Burning herbs like sage and rosemary or incense like frankincense and myrrh is a traditional method for cleansing items. However, you may live in a place where burning anything is out of the question. You might have roommates or family members who are allergic or sensitive to smoke. Burning anything stronger than a candle could set off your smoke detectors. In that case, consider using magical sprays to cleanse your clothing.

To make a magical spray, all you need is 2 ounces of distilled water, 2 teaspoons of witch hazel or high-proof vodka, and an essential oil aligned with your purpose. Add the water and witch hazel together in a 4-ounce spray bottle. Then add 20 drops of the essential oil to the bottle. Give the bottle a shake to mix the ingredients. Also shake it before every use. Then spray your clothing before you go out, when you come home, or whenever you feel the need for an energetic cleanser.

Essential oils for cleansing include lemongrass, rosemary, lemon, cedarwood, sage, and patchouli. Once you've cleansed your clothing, you can spray a layer of protection with another spray. Essential oils for protection include rosemary, peppermint, tea tree, eucalyptus, lemon, and chamomile.

You don't have to use a lot of the spray, either. A few spritzes from a couple of inches away will cleanse the clothing without making it damp.

Pinafore

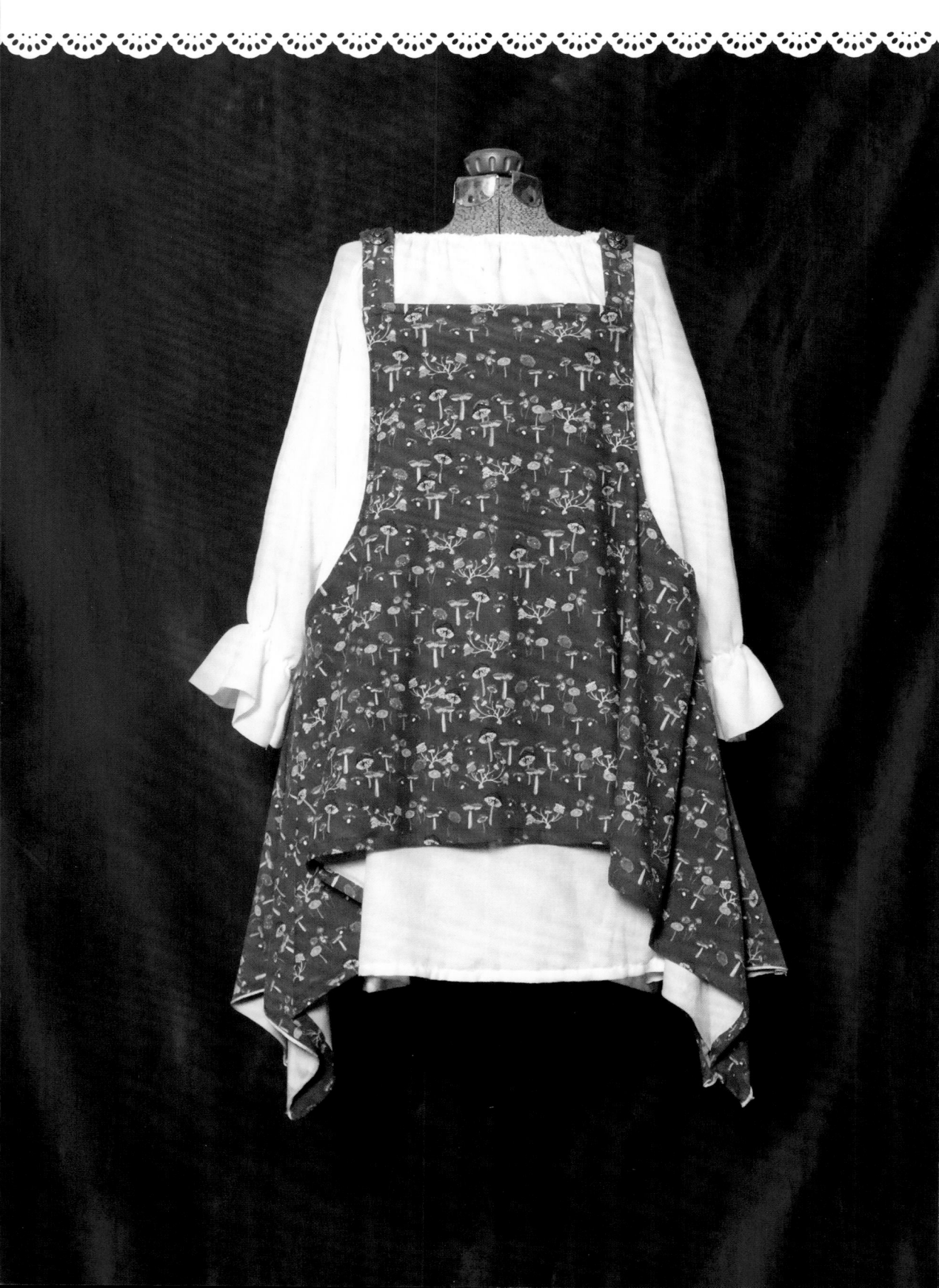

A pinafore is a sleeveless apron dress that is usually worn over other clothing to protect it when working. Pinafores have become more than a protective garment, however. Many pinafores are worn loose over an underdress or other clothing. They may include pockets, fancy trims, and other embellishments.

The pinafore here has sides that hang lower than the front and back. How long they extend is up to your desires. A front pocket can be added. Otherwise, the side openings are large enough to allow you to access pockets in your clothing underneath. The straps have button closures that you will adjust to fit your measurements.

What Kind of Fabric to Use

You can use just about any fabric you fancy for your pinafore. If you are making it to be a protective layer for when you are out foraging or working kitchen witchery, you'll want to stick with durable fabrics like **cotton** and **linen**. Materials like **duck cloth**, **denim**, and **corduroy** are all good choices for pinafores that will be used in gardening and cottage witch chores. If the pinafore you're making will be a showy outer layer, you can use **brocade**, **silk**, **synthetic materials**, or even **knits** that will give you a lovely drape. The wrong side of the fabric will be visible, so keep that in mind when choosing a fabric.

How Much Fabric?

You will need a rectangular piece of fabric that measures 2 × your **E** measurement in length by your **A** measurement plus 2 × your **D** measurement in width.

PATTERN DRAFTING

Measurements

You will need the following measurements:

- **A** = The measurement from shoulder to shoulder divided by 2 + 1" for the seam allowance
- **B** = Your hip measurement divided by 4
- **C** = The length from midbust to your waist
- **D** = The length from your waist to where you want the sides of the pinafore to fall + 1¼"
- **E** = The length from midbust to where you want the front of the pinafore to reach + 2¾"

MATERIALS

Fabric (see below)

Matching thread

2 buttons

Small scraps of a contrasting fabric if making the optional triple moon applique along the bottom of the pinafore

TOOLS

Sewing machine and needle

Pins

Iron

Measuring tape

Scissors or a rotary cutter

Hem gauge

Seam ripper (just in case)

TERMS & CONCEPTS

You will be creating **buttonholes** and sewing a **standard hem**. See "Methods" on page 6 for more information.

The pinafore doesn't require a pattern piece, but you are free to make one, especially if you plan on sewing several. Otherwise, you can use sewing chalk to mark out the cutting lines onto the wrong side of your fabric.

If your fabric has a non-directional print, meaning that the pattern does not go in one direction only, you can start by folding your rectangle of fabric in half lengthwise and then again in half widthwise. Fold with the right sides together so that the wrong sides face out.

If your fabric has a one-direction print, you will need to first cut your fabric in half lengthwise and turn the fabric so that both sides have the print facing up. Lay the fabric pieces on top of each other right side to wrong side. Then fold both pieces in half widthwise. Fold with right sides together so that the wrong sides face out.

From the top folded corner, measure your **A** measurement and make a mark (**F**). From **F**, measure straight down your **C** measurement and make a mark (**G**). Draw a line connecting **F** to **G**. Draw a line connecting your **G** to the edge of your fabric. Curve the corner a bit to avoid a 90-degree angle at the waist of the pinafore. This line from the **F** mark through to the end of the fabric is your **FG** line.

Along the folded edge of your fabric, measure down your **C** measurement and then out your **B** measurement. Mark this point on your **FG** line. This is your **H** marking and where you will start your side seam.

Cut out on the lines you have drawn. Open up the fabric widthwise and cut along the top of the pinafore along the fold to create a front and a back piece. Mark which piece you want to be the front of the pinafore with a few stitches or chalk on the wrong side of the fabric.

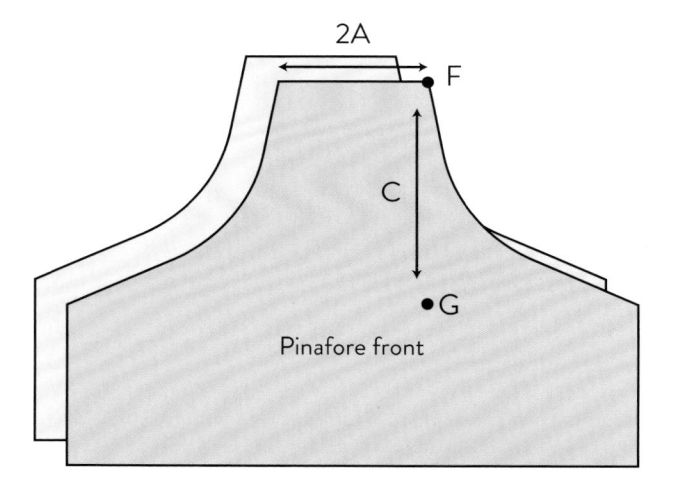

CONSTRUCTION

To Include an Optional Patch Pocket

It is easier to add the patch pocket to the front before you sew the rest of the pinafore. Add the pocket after you have cut out your fabric pieces.

1 Cut out a rectangle of fabric that measures 8" by 16".

2 Fold the long, top edge of the rectangle under ½". Press. Fold under again another ½". Press. Topstitch close to the first fold.

3 Fold the sides and bottom edges of the rectangle under ½" and press.

4 On the right side of the front of the pinafore, position the pocket at the center with the wrong side of the pocket facing the right side of the pinafore. Pin in place.

5 Sew around the side and bottom edges of the pockets near the folds. Make sure to backstitch at the start and end of the seam to secure the stitching. Leave the finished top edge of the pocket open.

Making the Pinafore

1 Sew a ½" seam on the sides starting at the top with a basting stitch. When you reach your **H** side seam mark, switch to a shorter stitch length. Make sure to backstitch at the start of the shorter stitches to anchor the seam.

2 Press the armhole edges under ¼" and then again ¼" above the side seam marking. Topstitch close to the first fold. Open up the seam with a seam ripper to the marking, taking out the basting stitches.

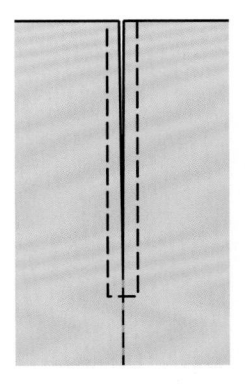

3 Cut four pieces of fabric measuring 8" by 4" for the straps. Fold one piece of fabric in half lengthwise. Sew a ½" seam along one short end and the long edge of the strap. Trim the corners and seams. Turn right-side out. Press. Repeat with the other strap pieces.

4 Sew buttonholes ½" from the finished short end of the strap. Repeat on a second strap.

5 Sew buttons to the finished short ends of the other two straps.

6 With right sides together, match the raw edge of the straps with the buttonholes to the top of the back of the pinafore with the folded edge matched to the side seam. Tack in place.

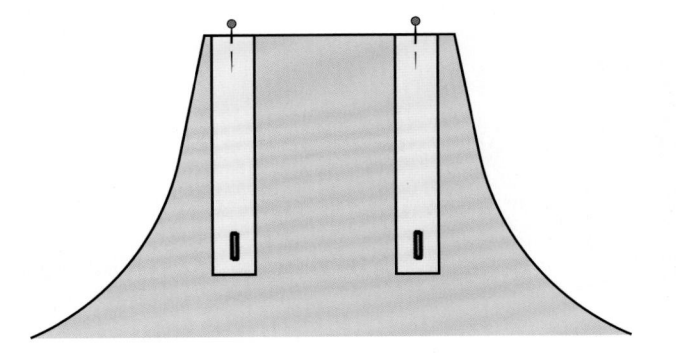

7 Fold the top edge of the back of the pinafore under ½". Press. Fold under another ½". Press. The raw ends of the straps should be encased in the hem.

8 Bring the straps up. Sew near the first fold.

9 Try on the pinafore. Button the straps and bring them over to the front. Adjust the straps so that you are satisfied with their length and mark the placement on the straps.

10 Remove the pinafore. Cut the excess from the front straps.

11 Repeat steps 7 and 8 with the front straps and the front of the pinafore.

12 Add a hem to the bottom sides and front and back edges of the pinafore.

Optional Triple Moon Applique

Using the template on page 176 of the appendix, cut out two crescent moons and one full moon in contrasting fabric. Arrange the moons in a triple moon configuration along the bottom of the front of the pinafore. Hand tack the appliques in place. Sew around the outside of the appliques with a zigzag stitch.

Moon and Magic

The optional triple moon applique featured on the Pinafore taps into the magic of the moon and its phases. Moon magic has been a part of witchcraft for centuries, with its different phases corresponding to subtle energy shifts.

The waxing moon, when the moon is moving from new to full, is seen as a time of growing energy. Spells of increase, strengthening, or drawing things to you are often cast during this time. Healing spells are especially potent during the waxing moon.

The full moon brings energy of completion. It is also a time of stability. This means that spells meant to maintain the status quo—in health, love, and so on—are best cast during this time. Spells for success benefit from full moon energy. The moonlight of the full moon also is useful for charging crystals and other witchy implements.

The waning moon, when the moon is moving from full to new, is the time for banishing spells. Using the waning moon's lessening energy can empower spells that are aimed at reducing and releasing. It's also a good time to get rid of spent spell components or end any ongoing spells you no longer need.

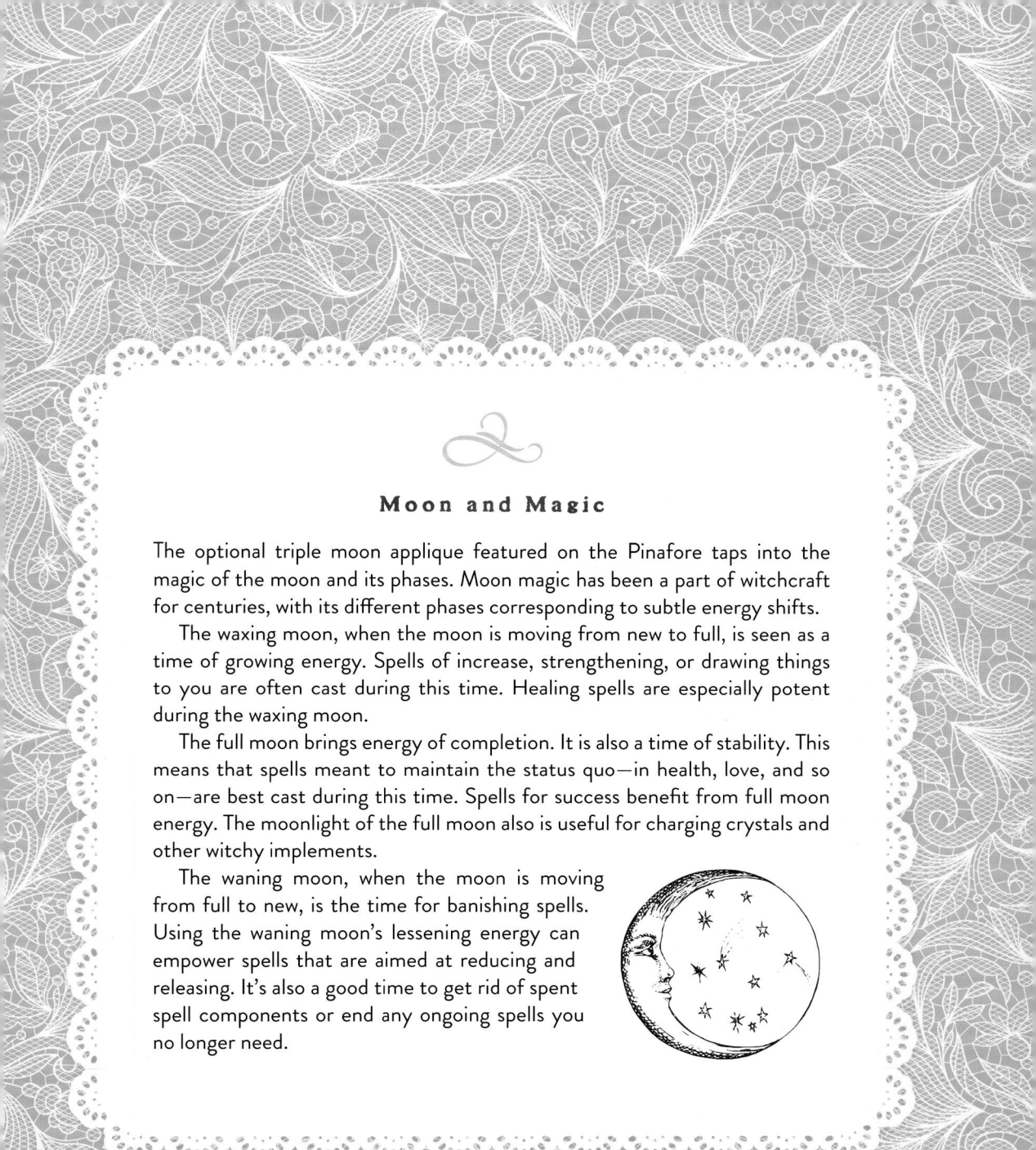

Cape

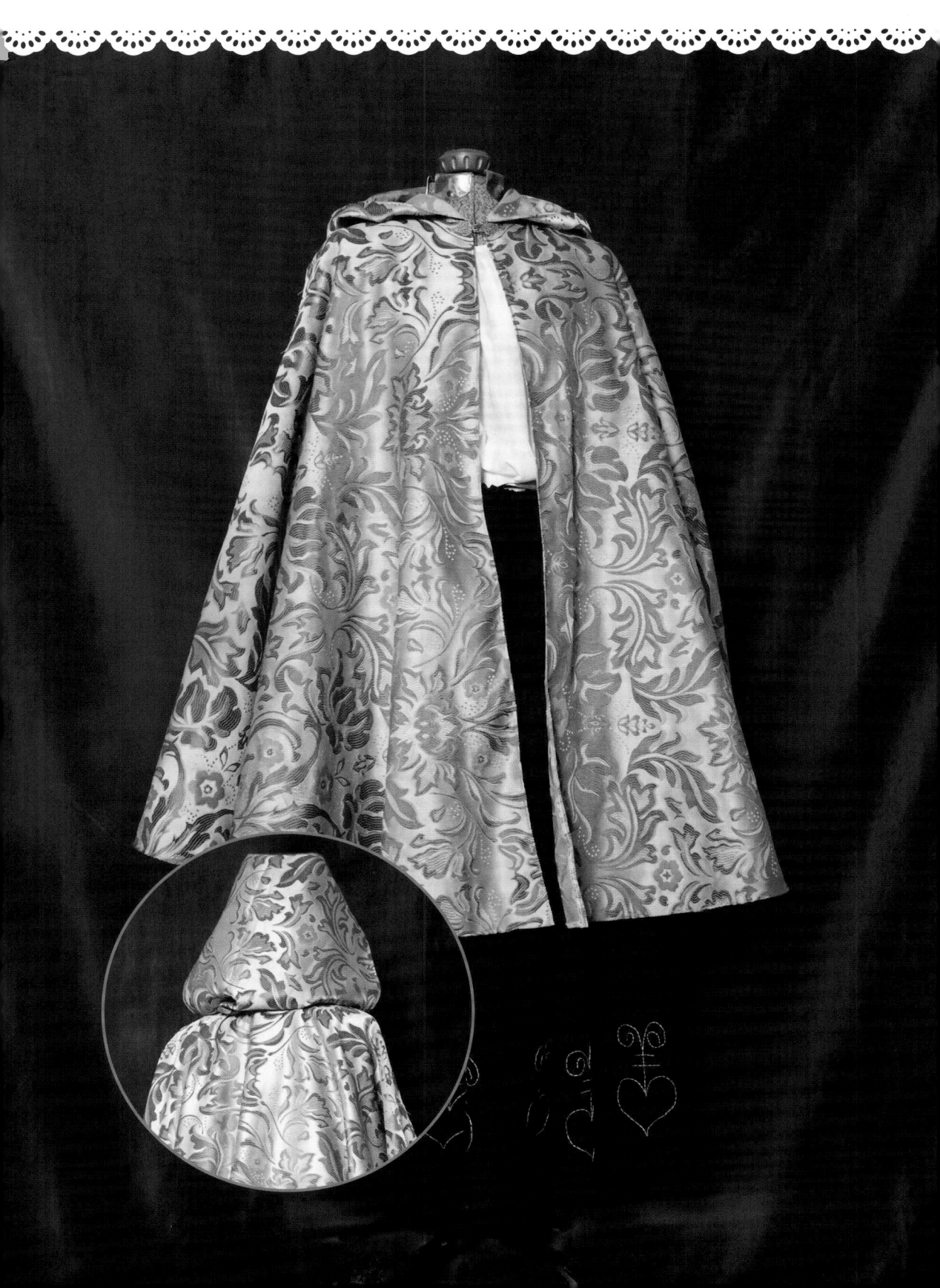

Ah, the cape, the staple of any fantasy, LARP, Renaissance fair, or witchy outfit. Throw on a cape and you immediately feel magical.

This lesson will walk you through making a cape with a drapey hood. I've also included instructions on how to use the pieces to make a capelet and a cowl. Both are useful and fashionable additions to any wardrobe.

This design is meant to be a functional outer layer, so it's recommended that you keep the length to midcalf. If you choose fleece, wool felt, or another thick and heavy fabric, this length cuts down on the final weight of the garment. Capes that reach down to one's feet are very striking, but they are subject to getting snagged. The bottom can also end up caked in dirt and mud, among other things.

What Kind of Fabric to Use

This project takes advantage of the non-fraying nature of **wool felt** and **fleece** to make a warm but not too bulky cloak that will protect you from the elements on your adventures. You can also use **non-felted wool**, as it will likewise resist fraying, but you might want to finish the raw edges with pinking or a zigzag stitch, unless you use a serger. Otherwise, the edges in this project are left unfinished.

Wool, felted or otherwise, isn't cheap, but it is sturdy and long lasting. You can search secondhand shops for wool blankets to use as material. Fleece often goes on sale in the fall at fabric and hobby shops. Both materials come in a range of colors. You can, of course, use other fabrics; however, you'll need to take into account seam, edge, and hem finishes.

How Much Fabric?

You will need a length and width of fabric that measures $2 \times$ **C** in length by $2 \times$ **C** in width. So if you want a cloak that is 48" long, you will need a piece of fabric that is 96" wide and 96" long. You can piece together a square from smaller pieces of fabric by sewing together the selvages of two pieces of fabric. For your 48"-long cape, buy fabric that is 58" and 4 times your **C** measurement. Cut the fabric in half lengthwise and sew the selvages together. This will give a center back seam to your cape. Other sources of fabric such as curtains or blankets might give you all the yardage you need.

MATERIALS

Fabric (see below)

Matching thread

2-part clasp

Self-drafted pieces for cape yoke, body, and hood

TOOLS

Sewing machine and needle

Pins

Iron

Measuring tape

Yardstick

Scissors or a rotary cutter

Thumbtack

Length of non-stretchy string or cord at least 40" long

Seam ripper (just in case)

TERMS & CONCEPTS

You will be **drafting a pattern**, **basting**, **finishing seams**, and making a **standard hem**. See "Methods" on page 6 for more information.

PATTERN DRAFTING

Measurements

You will need the following measurements:

- **A** = The circumference of your neck
- **B** = The length from the base of your neck at your back to the top of your forehead
- **C** = The length you want your cloak to be

The cape has two parts: a hood and the cape. If you decide to make the capelet or cowl or to make a cape without a hood, you won't need all these parts.

The math that follows involves pi (π), which can be shortened to 3.14 when finding circumferences of circles. This is going to give you numbers with decimals that might not be converted to fractions of an inch neatly. Fortunately, cloaks are not exquisitely tailored articles of clothing. You don't have to be precise with your measurements. You have two choices when it comes to dealing with the decimals: you can either round up or round down. My suggestion is to round up or down to the nearest half inch. Thus, if you get a measurement such as 42.39", you can either round up to 42.5" or down to 42". For this project, I'd suggest rounding up, as you can always deepen your seams or cut off any excess material you may end up with. If you end up with the body or hood being too short to fit your cape neckline, there's not a lot you can do to fix the situation other than to start over.

The Cape

1 Divide your **A** measurement by 3.14. Then divide your result by 2.

2 Take your **C** measurement and add 1¼" for the seam allowance to it.

3 Tie the length of cord around the thumbtack. Measure your **A** measurement from the thumbtack along the string. Tie a knot there. Measure your **C** measurement from the thumbtack along the string and tie another knot.

4 Fold your fabric in half lengthwise and then again widthwise. Lay the fabric on a surface you can push the thumbtack into. Position the thumbtack at the point of the folded fabric where the folds meet.

5 Hold the string taut on the fabric, even with the first fold. Mark the first knot's position on the fabric. Move the string in a 90-degree arc, marking the knot's position as you go until you reach the other side of the fabric. You should have a series of points marking out a quarter circle on the fabric. Draw a line connecting the points.

6 Repeat the step above but this time with the second knot. You should end up with two quarter circles marked out on your fabric.

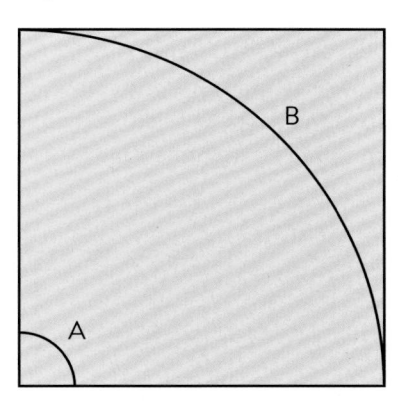

7 Cut on the lines, through all thicknesses.

If your folded fabric is longer and wider than your **C** measurement, you'll end up with a circle of fabric with a circle cut out in the middle. Cut along one of the folds to make the front opening.

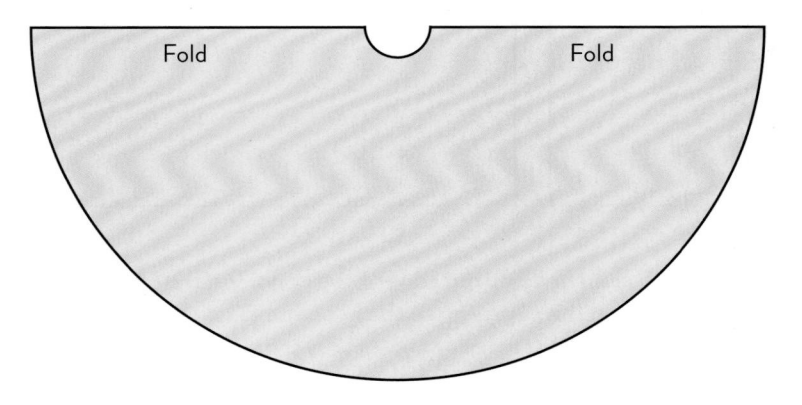

The Hood

1 Take your **B** measurement and add 6" to it. This is your **D** measurement. Take your **A** measurement and add 6" to it. This is your **E** measurement.

2 Cut out a rectangle that measures **D** by **E**.

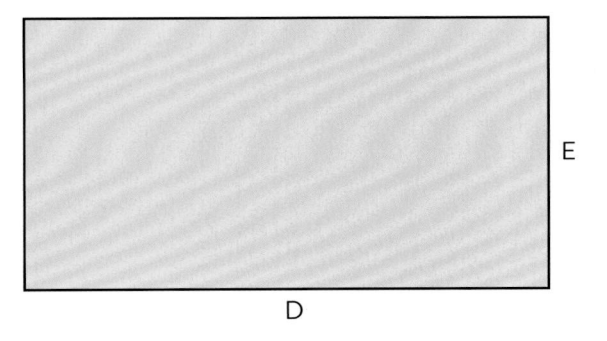

CONSTRUCTION

1 With right sides facing, fold the hood rectangle in half with long sides matching. Sew one side with a ½" seam from the fold to the ends.

2 To shape the top of the hood, we'll be giving it a box corner, so it does not have a point. Cut a 2" by 2" square out of the top of the hood. Unfold the hood so that the opening makes a straight line. Sew the opening closed ½" from the edge.

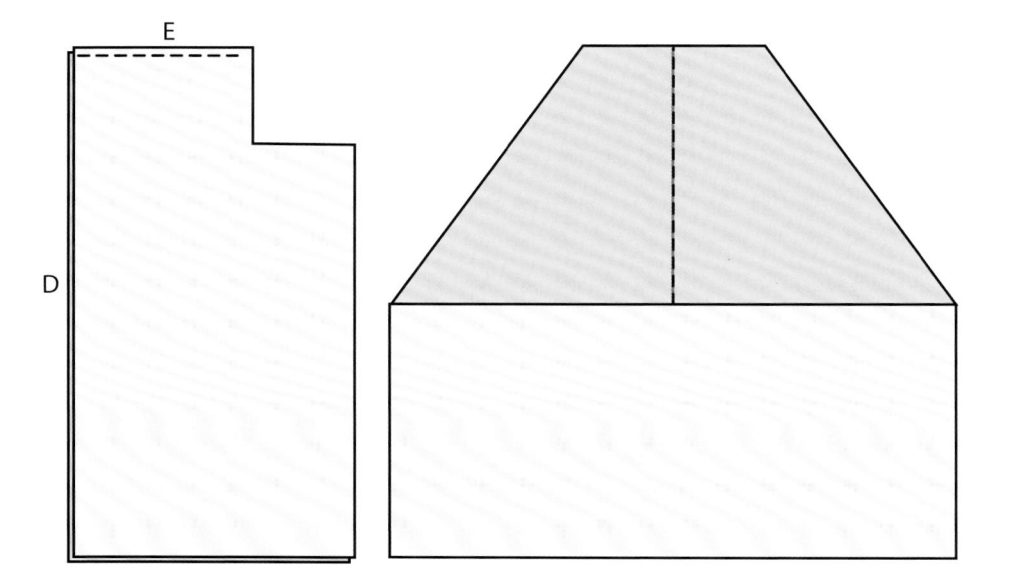

3 Run a gathering stitch along the bottom edge of the hood. Pin the hood to the yoke, matching backs and ends. Pull up the gathering so the hood fits. Baste the hood to the yoke. Stitch the hood to the yoke with a ½" seam allowance. Press the seam up toward the hood.

4 If you are using fabric that unravels (unlike wool or fleece), give the cloak and hood a narrow hem.

5 Sew the clasp to the cloak.

VARIATIONS

Capelet

Draft the cape piece as per the regular cape instructions, but your **B** measurement will be the length of the capelet (usually to midbust). Omit the hood. Give the capelet a narrow hem around all edges and finish with a clasp or a ribbon for the closure. Add trim as desired.

Cowl

Draft the cape piece as per the regular cape instructions, but your **B** measurement will be the length of the cowl (usually to midbust). Do not cut one of the folds for a front opening. Cut 3" on one of the folds, starting from the inside circle. Try the cowl on. If it doesn't fit easily over your head, increase the opening slash another inch. If it still doesn't fit, continue to cut the opening in half-inch increments until it does.

Draft the hood piece as per the instructions on page 103. Follow steps 1–3 in the construction section for making the hood and attaching it to the yoke. Give the bottom of the cape a narrow hem. Give the opening and hood a narrow hem.

Shielding and
Warding Magic

Just as a cape can keep you safe from the elements, you can keep yourself magically safe through shielding and warding yourself. Doing so helps keep negative and malicious energy and magic from attaching to you. One way is to **charge your cape with protective intent**. To do so, you simply need to hold the cape in your hands. Center and ground yourself and then envision white light being pulled from the ground up your legs, into your body, through your arms, and down into your hands. See the light go from your hands into your cape, filling every stitch, every fiber, with brilliant, protective white light. Once you feel the cape is suffused with the light, "turn off the tap" by cutting off the light from coming up your legs from the earth. Your cape is now ready to wear and to keep you safe.

Another way to ward yourself is to **carry a talisman or amulet** to protect yourself. Items like the nazar, usually a bead or piece of jewelry depicting a blue eye, wards off the evil eye. Pentacles and troll crosses are general protection against malevolent magic. You can also carry jet or black tourmaline to protect you psychically.

You can even protect yourself by **creating a magical shield** around yourself. This is as simple as envisioning a bubble of white energy all around your body. As you envision this bubble, you charge it with the task of not allowing anything to enter the bubble that you don't specifically allow. This way anything negative (energies, magic, moods, etc.) cannot pierce through the bubble to attach to you.

Warding or shielding yourself takes only a few seconds and can help keep you magically healthy throughout the day.

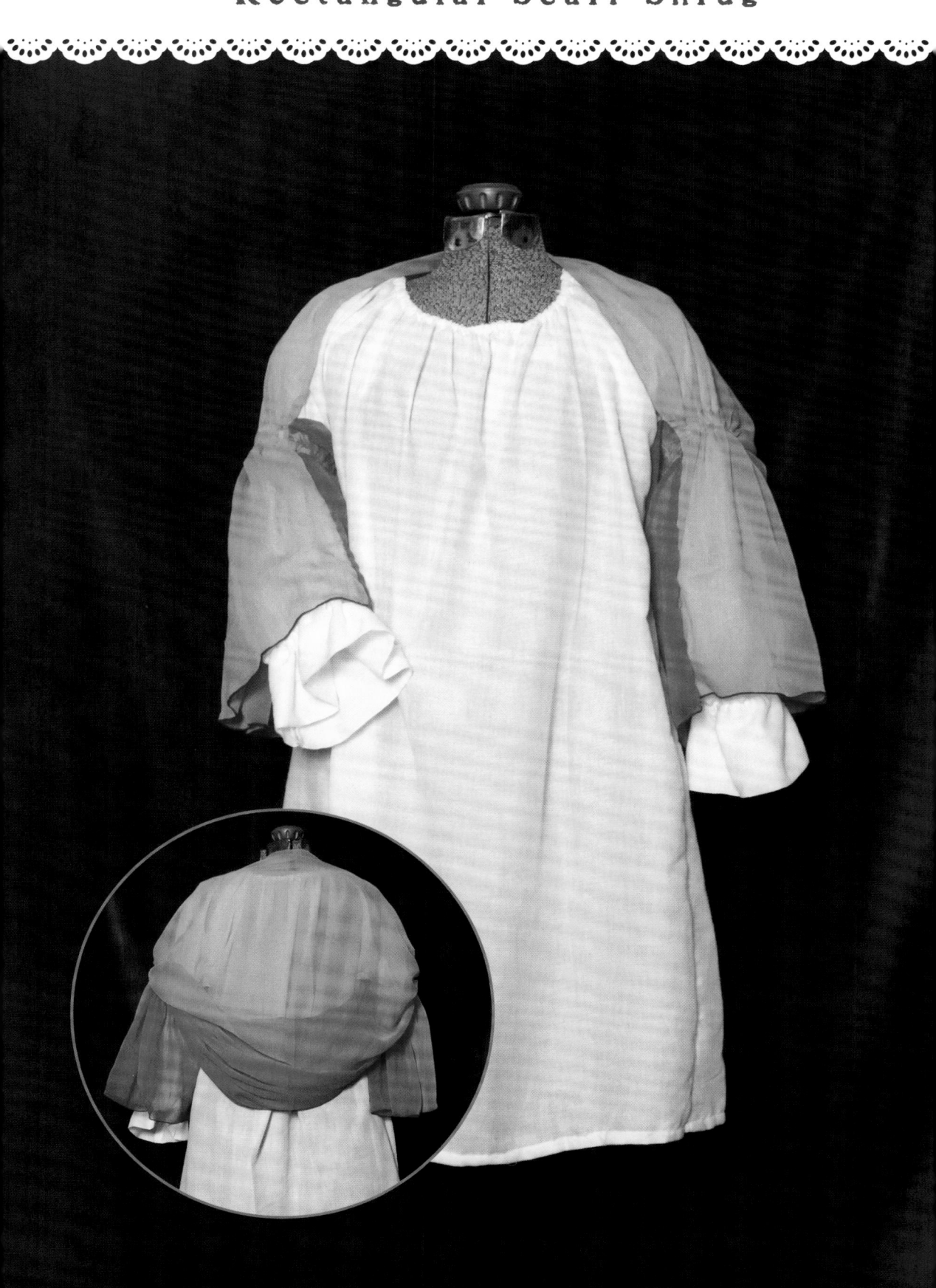

Summer heat often beckons us to bare our shoulders to the sun, only to leave us with chilly skin when clouds play peekaboo. That's where this shrug comes in handy. A simple bit of fabric can provide just the right amount of cover.

Using a rectangular scarf you may already have on hand means less sewing. The elastic at just below the elbows keeps the shrug in place while giving you lots of ease of movement. The whole project takes an hour or less, so you can sew one up in the morning for an afternoon picnic or an evening stroll in the park.

You can embellish your shrug with lace at the sleeve openings and by choosing a complementary or contrasting ribbon for the elastic casing.

What Kind of Fabric to Use

Ideally, you'll want to use a premade scarf that is rectangular in shape. I recommend this just because it minimizes the amount of sewing you'll have to do. This garment is best suited to lightweight, sheer fabrics such as **chiffon**, **cotton lawn**, **crepe**, or **georgette**. You want a fabric that drapes nicely and feels good against your skin.

MATERIALS

1 yard of 58"-wide fabric or a premade rectangular scarf

Matching thread

½"-wide or wider ribbon in a coordinating or matching color

¼"-wide elastic

TOOLS

Sewing machine and needle

Measuring tape

Ruler

Scissors or a rotary cutter

Seam ripper (just in case)

TERMS & CONCEPTS

You will be sewing a **channel** with ribbon to make an elastic casing. See the instructions for more information.

PATTERN DRAFTING

You won't be drafting a pattern for this project.

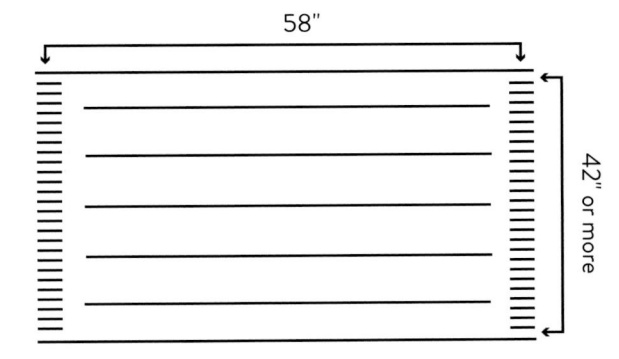

Measurements

You will need the following measurements:

- **A** = Measure from one knuckle up your arm, across the back of your shoulders, and down to your other knuckle to find out how wide the fabric should be.

- **B** = Knuckle to forearm measurement

- **C** = The circumference of your forearm measurement (just below your elbow)

CONSTRUCTION

1 Cut a rectangle that measures your **A** measurement by how far down you want your shrug to hang.

2 Finish the edges of the fabric with a narrow hem if necessary. Add trim if desired.

3 On both ends of the fabric, draw a placement line at the **B** measurement. Draw the line on the outside of the fabric if you want the ribbon to show or on the inside of the fabric otherwise. Repeat on the other end.

4 Sew a ribbon to the fabric along the placement line. Sew close to both edges of the ribbon to make a channel for the elastic. Repeat on the other end.

5 Cut two pieces of elastic to the length of your **C** measurement. Thread the elastic through the channel with a safety pin. Tack both ends of the elastic at the beginning and end of the channel.

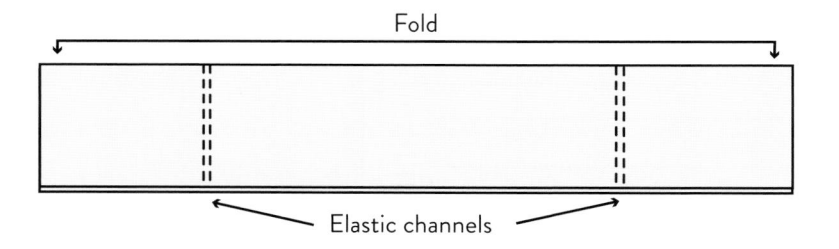

6 With right sides facing, fold the fabric in half lengthwise so that the long sides are together.

7 Sew a ½" seam from the short ends to ½" past the elastic channel. Backstitch to secure the seam. Turn the shrug right-side out.

Types of Divination

The rectangular scarf shrug can be used for ritual and spellwork wear as well as being part of your everyday wardrobe. Make one that you don whenever you engage in divination to get yourself in a mindset of magic and witchery. And whether you are looking to the future, past, or present, you can go beyond just tarot cards. There are so many more ways that witches go about piercing the veil of the unknown.

Witches use **pendulums**, asking questions and then divining the answer from the movement of the pendulum. The pendulums can range from fancy crystals hung from chains to a needle dangling from a thread. They are good for yes-or-no questions and were historically used to help look for water.

Oracle cards are much like tarot decks, but they often carry different messages. Oracle decks come in a variety of themes and do not carry the structured, traditional meanings of tarot decks. Many witches will use oracle and tarot decks together, using the one to clarify and expand on the messages of the other.

Charm casting or **throwing the bones** involves assigning meaning to different objects that are then tossed onto a mat. Answers are divined from how and where the objects lie as well as their position to other objects. This is one of the more personal types of divination tools, as the objects used and the meanings ascribed to them vary from set to set.

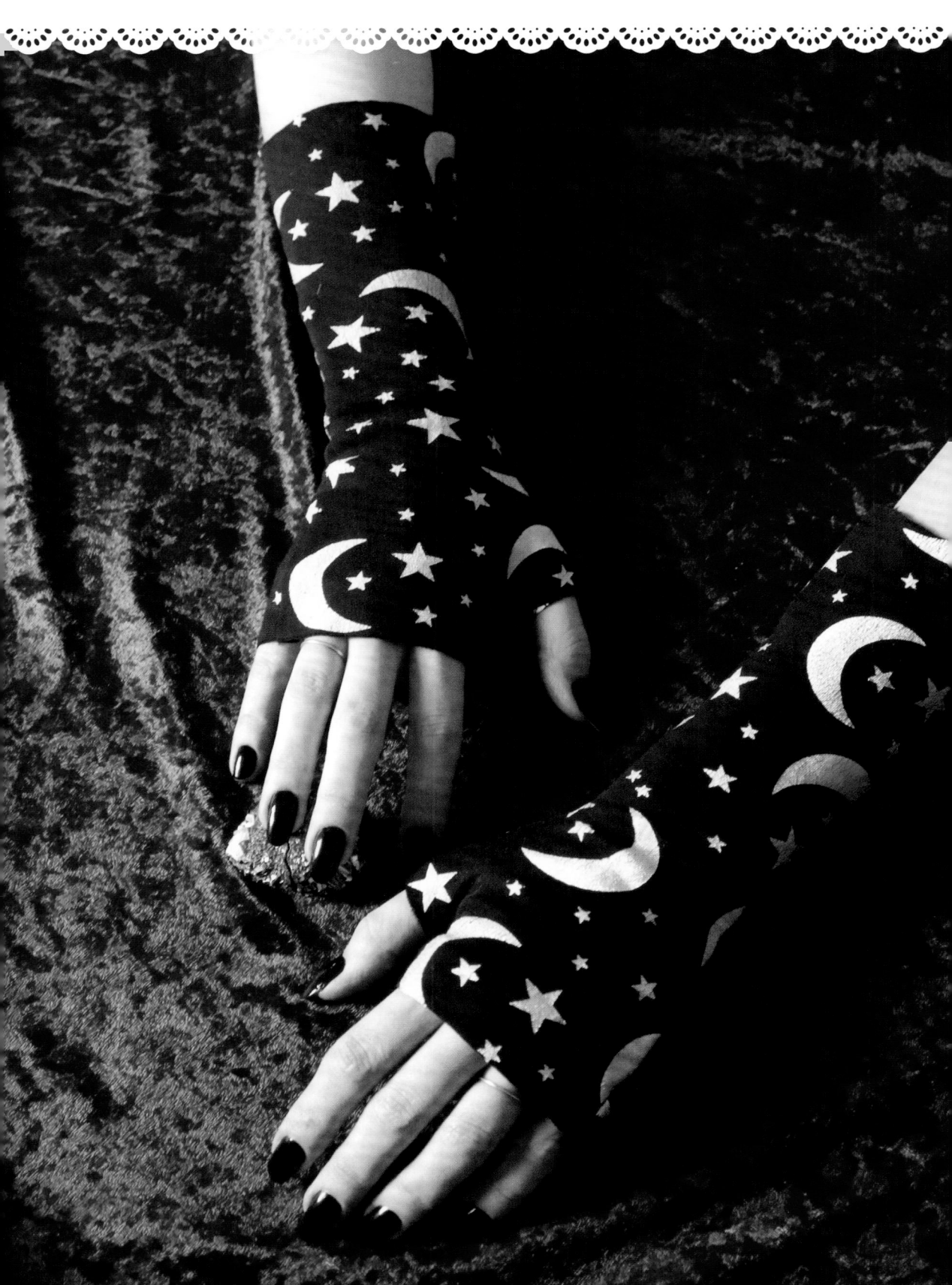

Fingerless gloves are a great way to keep your hands warm while still being able to use your fingers. These gloves will allow you to work your magic outdoors even on cold days without sacrificing dexterity. They will also protect your hands and arms as you forage for materia magica in the forest.

What Kind of Fabric to Use

This project is best suited for a **knit** fabric or **fleece** if you are making gloves to keep you warm during the colder months. You want a stretchy fabric, as the gloves will need to be pulled over your hands. As the openings of the gloves will not be hemmed, using knit fabric ensures they don't fray.

PATTERN DRAFTING

1 Lay your non-writing arm down on your pattern paper. Keep your fingers together with your thumb pointed away from your hand. Starting at just below where your pinky finger joins your hand, or higher if desired, trace the outside of your arm to just above your elbow. Repeat on the other side, starting from where your thumb joins your hand to just above your elbow.

2 Trace the curve between your fingers and thumb.

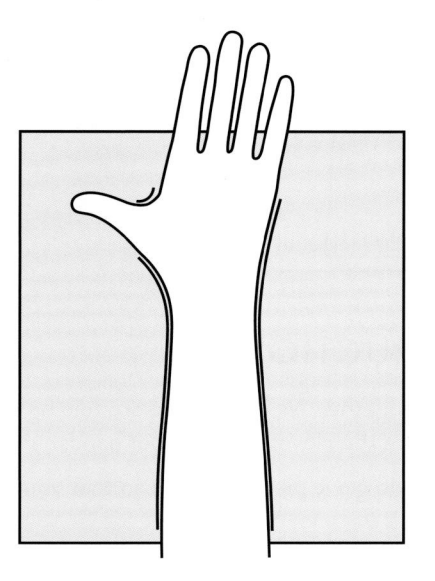

MATERIALS
½ yard of fabric
Matching thread

TOOLS
Pattern paper
Sewing machine and needle
Scissors
Ruler
Pencil
Seam ripper (just in case)

TERMS & CONCEPTS
You will be **drafting a pattern**. See "Methods" on page 6 for more information.

3 Using a ruler, mark a line ½" out from the lines you traced. This is to add ease and the seam allowance.

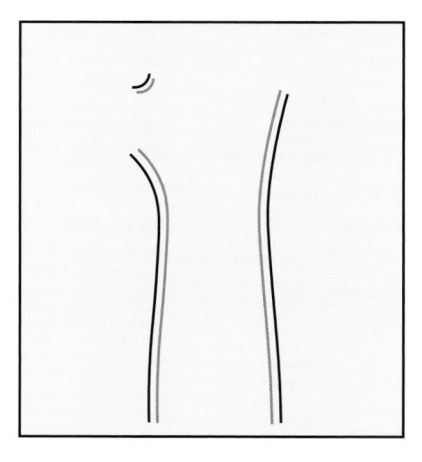

4 Close up the lines at the top and bottom of the pattern. Cut out the pattern.

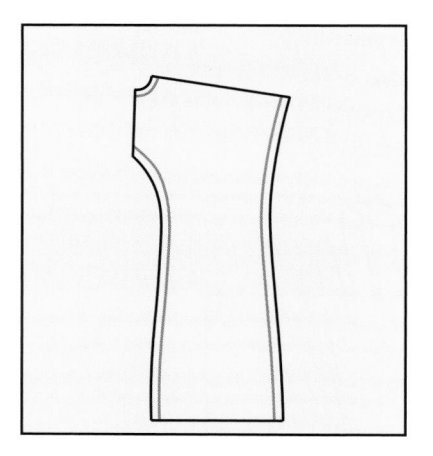

CONSTRUCTION

1 Fold your fabric widthwise, with right sides together. Make sure you are folding the fabric in the direction of the stretch, as this will ensure the gloves go over your hands.

2 Lay your pattern on the fabric and cut out two glove pieces. Repeat so that you have four glove pieces from the fabric.

3 With right sides facing, sew a ¼" seam along the long sides of the gloves.

4 Sew the curved line between the fingers and the thumb of the gloves using a ¼" seam. Sew the seam again to reinforce it.

5 Clip the curves, making sure not to cut the stitches. Turn the gloves right-side out.

Tincture Magic

I usually wear my fingerless gloves during colder weather, which is when I also get my tea drinking on. And while tea can be magical all on its own, I like to include tinctures to give it a boost. **Tinctures** are a great way to work the energies and properties of plants into your magic. You can add tinctures to your tea, coffee, smoothies, or other culinary spellwork. The best part? Tinctures are easy to make. While the instructions below use vodka, you can use vegetable glycerin instead, although the resulting glycerite will have a shorter shelf life (twenty-four months) than alcohol tinctures (six years).

To make a tincture, you will want to fill a small jar with your herb matter. Then fill the jar with 80–120-proof vodka so that it covers the herbs. Place the jar in a dark place for two weeks. Shake the jar every two days. After the two weeks, strain the herbs and store the tincture in a dropper bottle.

The standard use for tinctures is 10–20 drops for adults (5–10 for children) to ¼ cup of liquid.

Better Sleep Tincture

When you need restful sleep, add 10 drops of this tincture to a cup of lemon balm tea.

3 Tbsp. dried catnip
4 Tbsp. dried chamomile flowers
3 Tbsp. dried lavender blossoms
1 tsp. dried licorice root

Divination Tincture

Add 13 drops of this tincture to Earl Grey tea and drink before engaging in any kind of divination to help tap into your psychic powers.

3 Tbsp. dried dandelion leaves and flowers
3 Tbsp. dried orange peel
3 Tbsp. dried creeping Charlie leaves and flowers

Prophetic Dreams

Unlike the Better Sleep Tincture, which gives you a restful night's sleep, this tincture is meant to help you with prophetic dreams. Add 10–20 drops of the tincture to a tea of your choice and drink before you head to sleep. Make sure to have your dream journal at hand for when you wake up.

4 Tbsp. dried mugwort leaves
3 Tbsp. dried marigold leaves
2 Tbsp. dried rose leaves

Ribbon Skirt

There is something magical about ribbons. They bring to mind maypoles, we see them tied around trees, and they make neat little bows in braids. This project captures a bit of that magic in an accessory you can tie over your existing outfit. It is also very easy to make and can use up your extra ribbons and even fabric scraps. If you have sheer or brocade fabric, cut it into strips no more than 2" wide. Finish the raw edges with a serger or zigzag stitch, or you can cut the edges with pinking shears.

What Kind of Fabric to Use

This project uses ribbons and fabric scraps. Choose ribbons that have a similar color scheme or ones that coordinate for a put-together look. Or go with a rainbow of colors for something more fanciful. Vary the width and texture of the ribbons to give the skirt depth. For the waist, choose a ribbon that is around 3" wide.

PATTERN DRAFTING

You will not need to draft a pattern for this garment.

Measurements

You will need the following measurements:

- **A** = Your waist circumference measurement

CONSTRUCTION

1 Cut two lengths of ribbon measuring your **A** measurement + 40".

2 Mark 20" in from each end of one of the ribbons.

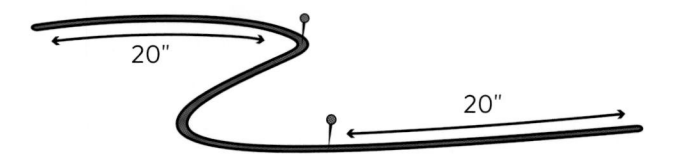

MATERIALS
3"-wide ribbon

Various ribbons and strips of fabric 1–2" wide

TOOLS
Sewing machine and needle

Pins

Measuring tape

Yardstick

Marking pen or chalk

Seam ripper (just in case)

TERMS & CONCEPTS
You will be **drafting a pattern**, **basting**, making a **narrow hem**, and adding a **pocket**. See "Methods" on page 6 for more information.

3 Arrange the ribbon strips between the two marks, basting them in place to the wrong side.

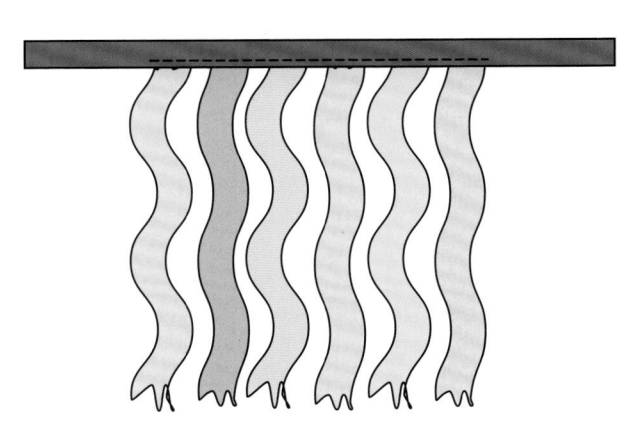

4 With the right sides together, sew the short ends of the two waist ribbons together, creating a loop. Turn it right-side out.

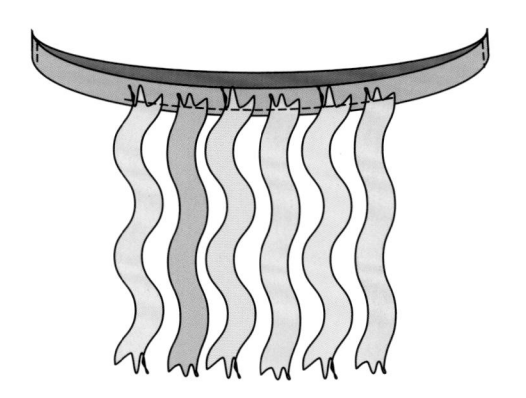

5 Flatten the loop to make one long ribbon, sandwiching the skirt ribbons between the waist tie ribbons. Topstitch ⅛" from the edge all around the waist tie through all layers.

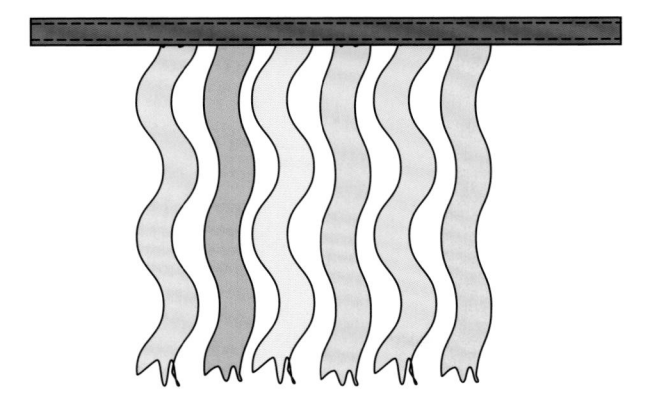

Glamour Magic

Clothes like the ribbon skirt can be magical tools. The act of choosing what to wear and why can be turned into a glamour spell. In its simplest form, glamour magic's goal is to attract something to a person. While this could be the attention of someone, that's not the only way the magic can be used.

Glamour magic is more akin to an illusion spell. The witch is trying to make something or someone, usually themselves, look different from their reality. There are many different reasons a witch might want to present themselves in a different way. They might want to exude self-confidence at work or seriousness in an interview, or they might be a trans person trying to deal with body dysmorphia. No matter the reason, clothing can be a big part of one's glamour spellwork.

One way to use it is to charge your clothing with your intentions. You can do so by holding the clothing and envisioning a white light full of what you want the clothes to radiate washing over them. Speak your intention out loud or in your mind. You can go with something like **"When I wear these clothes, I appear professional"** or **"People see me as a beautiful person."** Fill the clothes with the white light until they take on a glowing aura. Then get dressed.

Another way to seep your clothing in the energies you wish to convey is to place crystals, herbs, and other items that correspond to your intentions with the clothing as it sits in your drawers or hangs in your closet. If, for example, you need for people to see you as loving, tuck rose quartz in with your clothes, along with a sachet of dried rose petals. Your clothes will soak up the loving energies, and when you get dressed, you can visualize that you are projecting a gentle and loving aura.

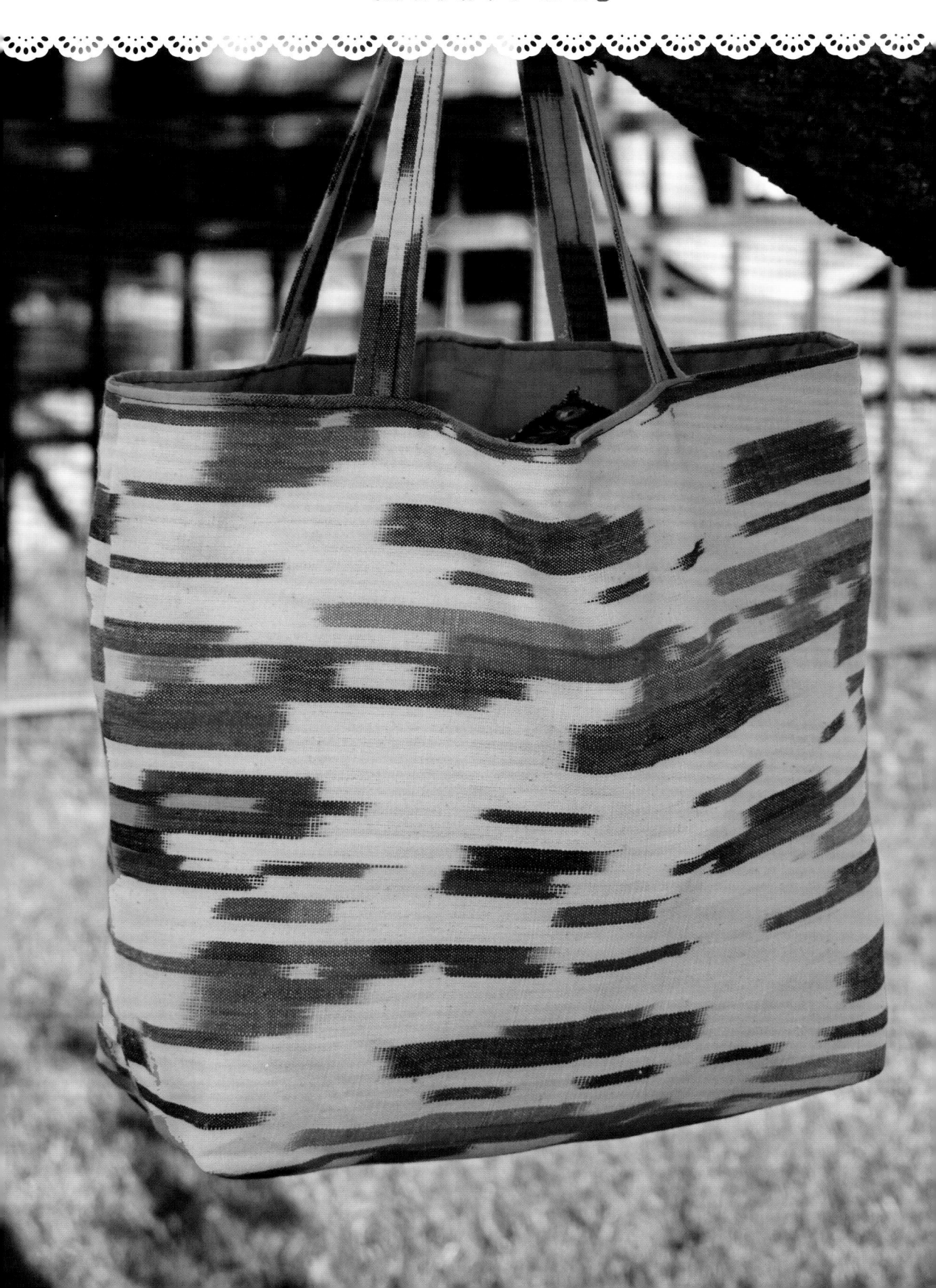

This bag isn't fancy, but it is a workhorse. You can use it to pick up your groceries from the farmer's market or when you go into your local park or forest to collect various items for crafting and witchcraft.

What Kind of Fabric to Use

Cotton or linen fabric is best for the market bag. You can use upholstery fabric, duck cloth, denim, and other heavyweight fabrics for the outside to give the bag structure.

The lining should use a lighter-weight fabric like broadcloth.

PATTERN DRAFTING

You will not need to draft a pattern for this project. All the pieces can be marked right on the fabric and cut out.

CONSTRUCTION

1 Cut out two rectangles measuring 18" long by 3" wide from the outside fabric. These will be the straps. Set aside.

2 Cut out two rectangles measuring 17" by 15" from the outside fabric. Cut two more rectangles measuring 17" by 15" from the lining.

3 With the right sides together, sew the short sides and one long bottom side together with a ½" seam of the outside fabric. Repeat for the lining.

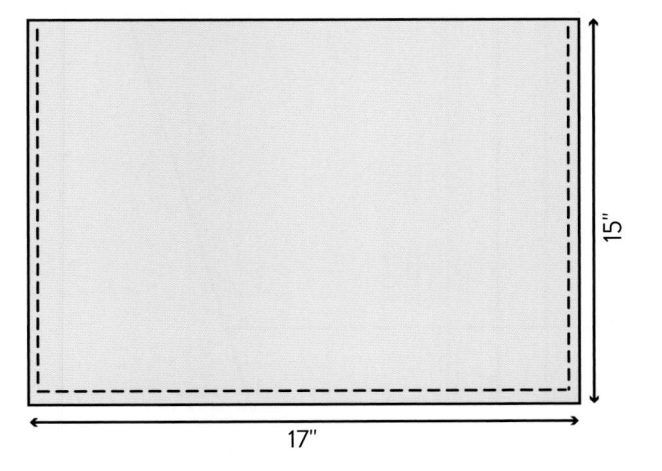

15"

17"

MATERIALS

½ yard of fabric for the outside of the bag and straps

½ yard of fabric for the lining

Thread

TOOLS

Sewing machine and needle

Pins

Iron

Hem gauge

Measuring tape

Yardstick

Marking pen or chalk

Seam ripper (just in case)

TERMS & CONCEPTS

You will be topstitching. See "Methods" on page 6 for more information. This project also includes box seams, the instructions for which are on page 122.

4 To make the box seams, do the following:

    a Cut a 2½" by 2½" square from the bottom left and right corners of the outside.

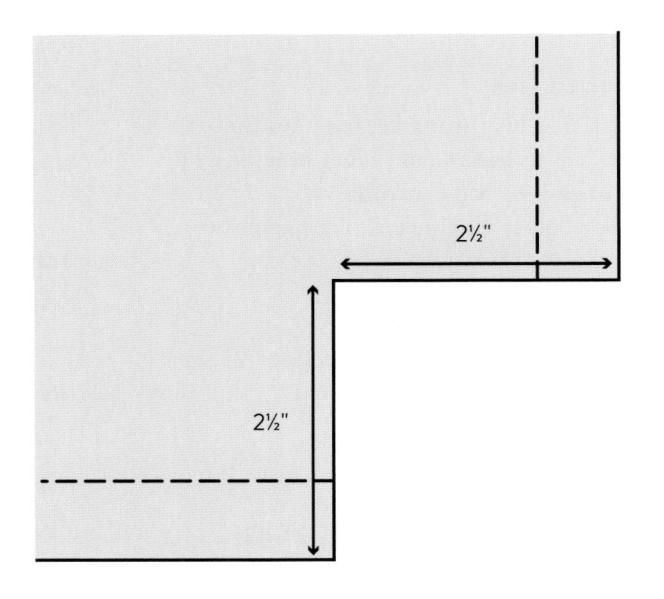

    b Bring the side and bottom seams together and sew ½" from the edge. Stitch back and forth over the seams to reinforce them.

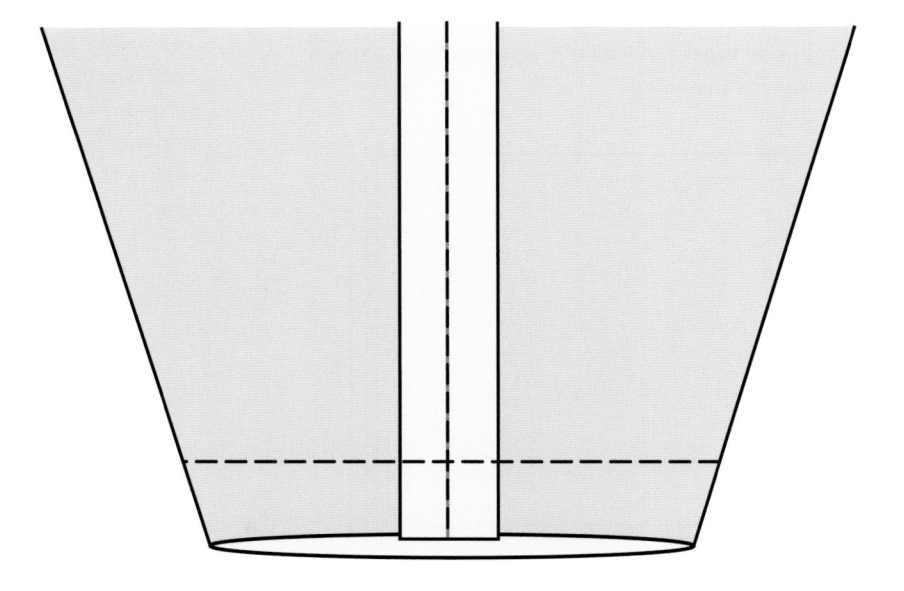

    c Repeat steps 4a and 4b with the lining.

5 Take one strap piece. With right sides together, fold in half widthwise, so that it measures 18" long by 1½" wide. Sew a ½" seam down the long side of the strap. Turn right-side out. Repeat with the other strap fabric.

6 Press the straps. Topstitch along each long side.

7 Pin one strap to the right side of the outside fabric, with each end 4" in from the side seam. Repeat with the other strap on the other side.

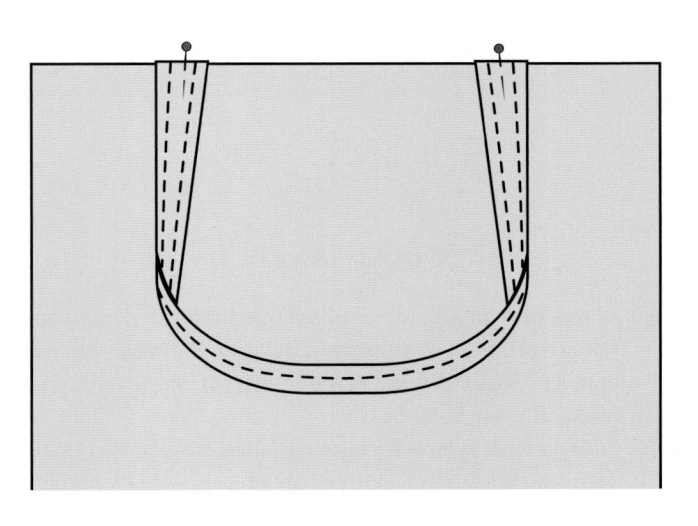
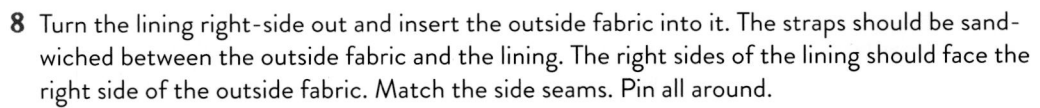

8 Turn the lining right-side out and insert the outside fabric into it. The straps should be sandwiched between the outside fabric and the lining. The right sides of the lining should face the right side of the outside fabric. Match the side seams. Pin all around.

9 Sew a ½" seam all around the opening of the bag, leaving a 3" gap for turning.

10 Turn the bag right-side out. Press the opening of the bag. Topstitch all around the opening, closing the gap.

Color Magic

Color magic is not just limited to candles in witchcraft. The various correspondences that are assigned to colors can be utilized in your wardrobe. Need a boost of creativity? Wear yellow. Want to attract money your way? Wear clothes with gold and silver buttons.

Keep this in mind when you are choosing fabric for your various garments. Think about what you want your clothing to promote, not only in your own mind but how it presents to the outside world. A patchwork skirt, for example, can be a hodgepodge of leftover fabric, or you could take time in choosing what fabric will go into it. You could focus on shades of blue and purple to help enhance your psychic abilities. Or you could use oranges (for breaking down barriers) and red (for assertiveness) and wear it to your job to help you get ahead in your career.

Color magic goes beyond just fabric choices, however. The thread you sew with can be put into service to support your magical aims.

When you take into account things like the ways in which color can be used for magic, you open up a whole new toolbox packed just as full as Grandma's cookie tin.

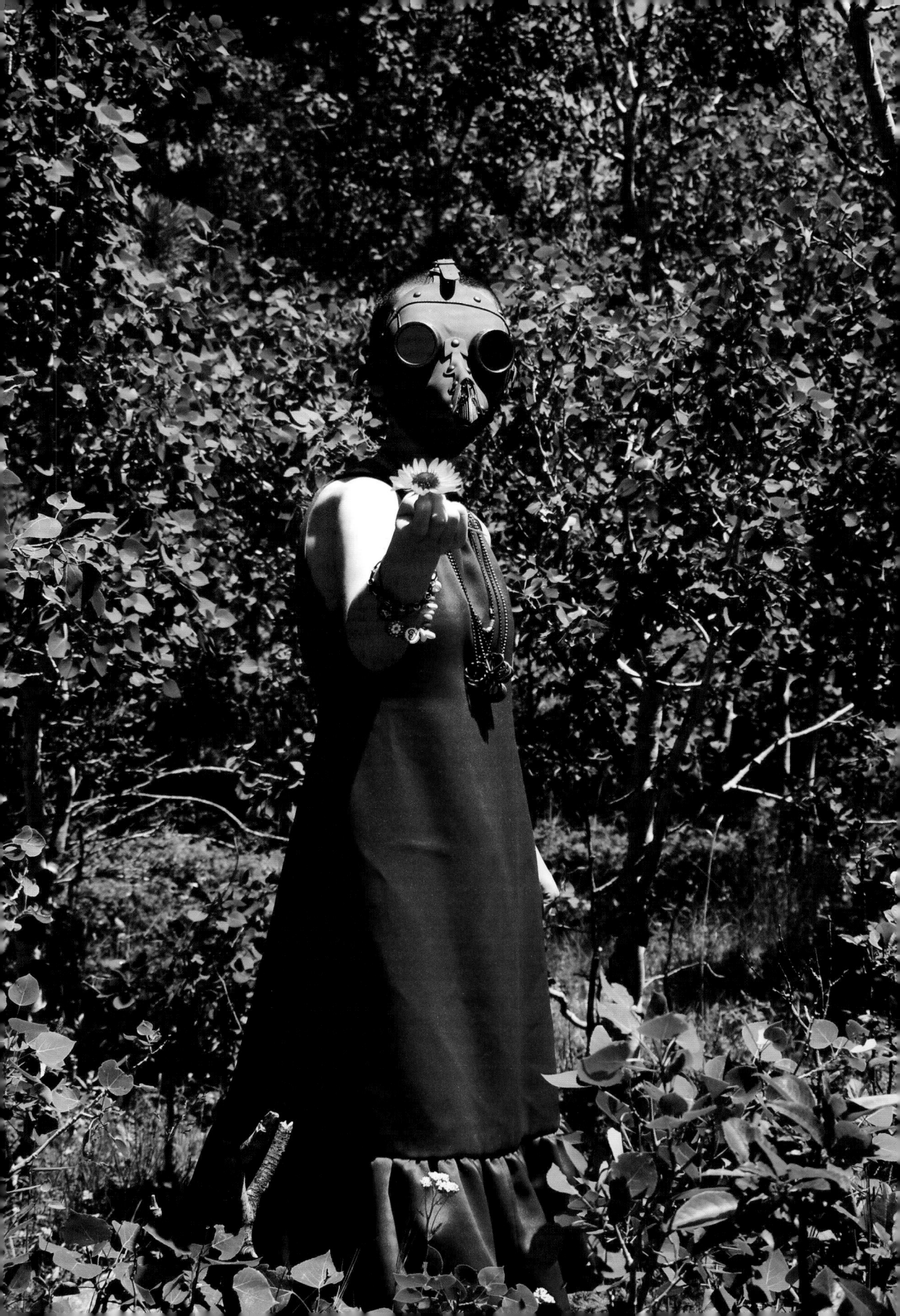

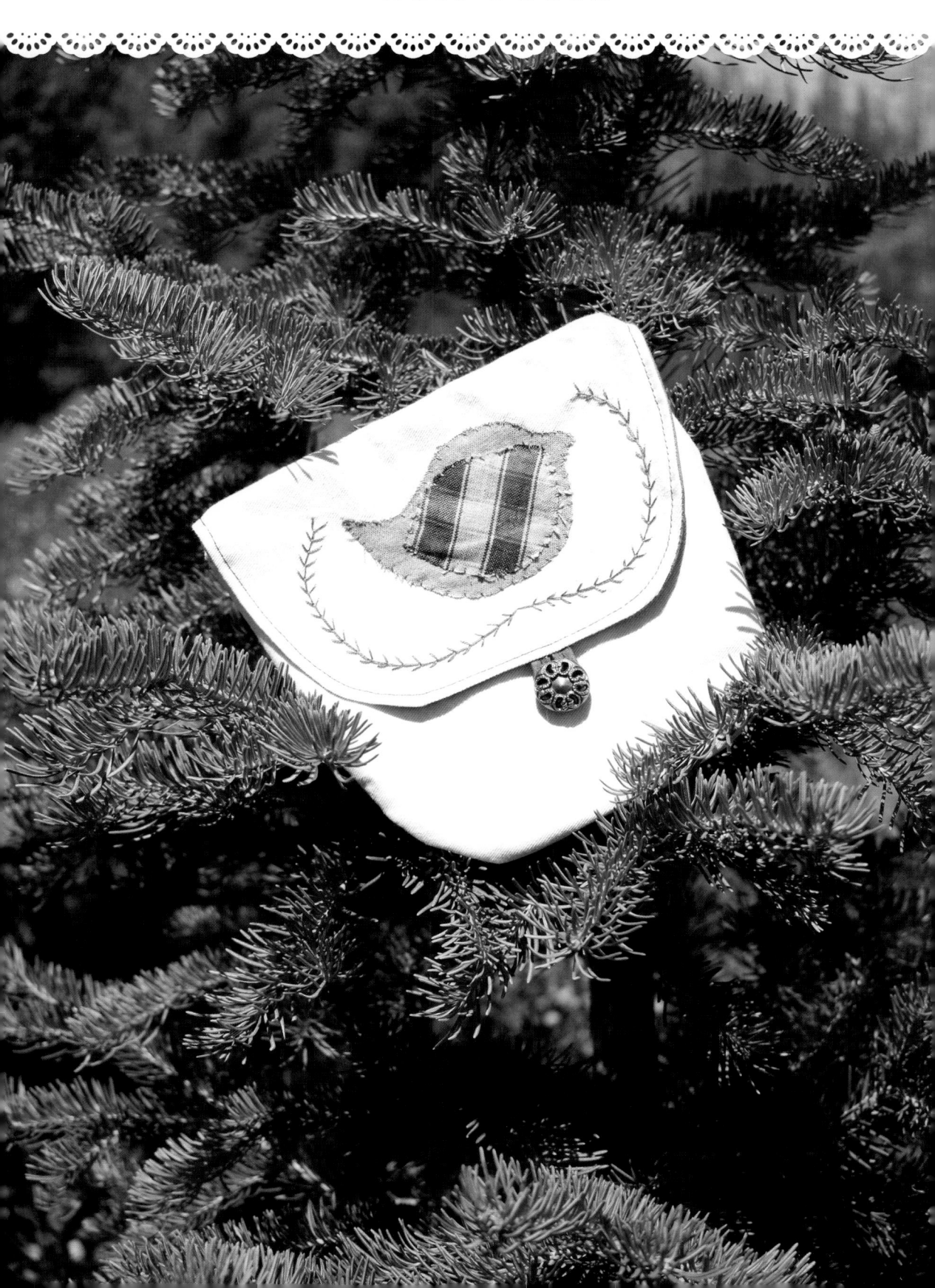

A belt pouch is a useful accessory for carrying witchy materials, use in foraging, or just carrying your cash and ID.

The flap of the pouch allows you to flex your creative muscles and pay homage to whatever spirits, deities, or branches of witchcraft you are aligned with. Use one of the templates in the appendix or create your own designs on the flap using trims, notions, and embroidery. This is also a good project to use up that really pretty leftover fabric that has been languishing in your stash.

What Kind of Fabric to Use

Use materials such as **moleskin**, **canvas**, **linen**, **denim**, and other heavier materials for the outer fabric of the pouch.

The lining can be made using any **lightweight material**.

CONSTRUCTION

Making the Belt Pouch Flap

If you want to have a decorated flap for your belt pouch, start with the uncut fabric and follow the instructions below. Once you have decorated the fabric, you can center the flap pattern piece over the design and cut out the flap. Make sure that when you are placing the pattern piece, you are leaving ½" all around for the seam allowance.

TO MAKE THE FLOWER BELT POUCH

1 Make three fabric yo-yos following the instructions on page 166.

2 Sew the yo-yo flowers onto the belt flap as shown:

3 Embroider stems and leaves with two strands of green embroidery thread using a **backstitch** (see page 130).

TO MAKE THE BIRD BELT POUCH

1 Cut out the bird body and wing using the templates on page 181.

2 Sew the bird body and wing using a **whipstitch**.

3 Trace the **fern stitch** design from page 181 underneath the bird. Using two strands of an embroidery thread in a coordinating color, work the fern stitch (see page 131).

MATERIALS

½ yard of fabric for the outside of the pouch

Trim, buttons, embroidery thread, and other notions for making the flap design

½ yard of fabric for the liner of the pouch

3" of double-fold ¼"-bias tape

1⅞" button

Coordinating thread

TOOLS

Pattern from page 175

Scissors

Pins

Sewing machine (or hand-sewing needle)

Steam iron

Seam ripper (just in case)

TERMS & CONCEPTS

You will be sewing **curved seams** and **edge stitching**. See "Methods" on page 6 for more information.

TO MAKE THE TRIPLE MOON BELT POUCH

1 Cut out the moon pieces from scrap fabric using the template on page 176.

2 Lay out the moon pieces on the belt flat fabric and stitch them down using a **zigzag** or **whip-stitch** around the edges.

Making the Belt Loops

1 Cut two rectangles of fabric 4" in length and 3" in width.

2 Fold one rectangle in half widthwise with right sides together so that you now have a rectangle that is 4" in length and 1½" in width. Sew ¼" seam around the raw edges, leaving a gap for turning.

3 Trim the seam and cut the corners. Turn the loop right-side out through the gap, using a chopstick or wooden skewer to push out the corners. Press.

4 Top stitch around the loop, closing the gap.

5 Repeat with the other rectangle of fabric. Set both aside for later use.

Making the Button Loop

1 Take a piece of ¼"-wide double-fold bias tape measuring 3" long. Sew close to the edge on the open end of the tape through all thicknesses.

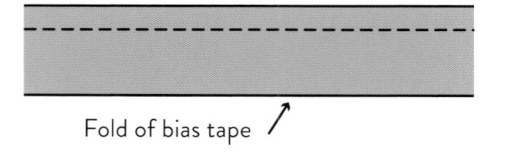

Fold of bias tape ✏

2 Fold the bias tape as illustrated to make the loop.

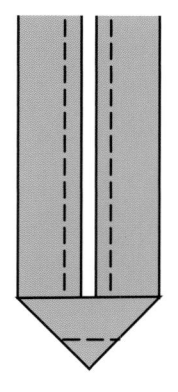

Making the Pouch

1 Decorate the flap fabric as desired and then cut out the flap fabric with the pattern centered over the design. Decorate the flap as desired, making sure to leave a gap of ½" around the flap fabric for the seam allowance.

2 Cut out the flap liner, pouch fabric, and pouch lining fabric.

3 Tack the button loop to the center of the bottom of the flap fabric with raw edges of the loop and fabric matching.

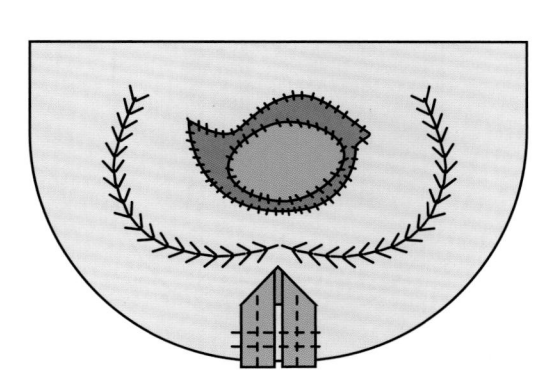

4 With right sides together, sew the flap lining to the flap fabric along the curved edge. Trim the seam and clip the curve.

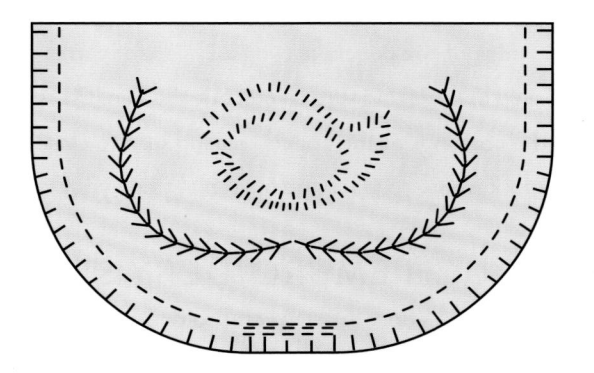

5 Turn the flap right-side out and press. Topstitch the curved edge and baste the straight edge closed.

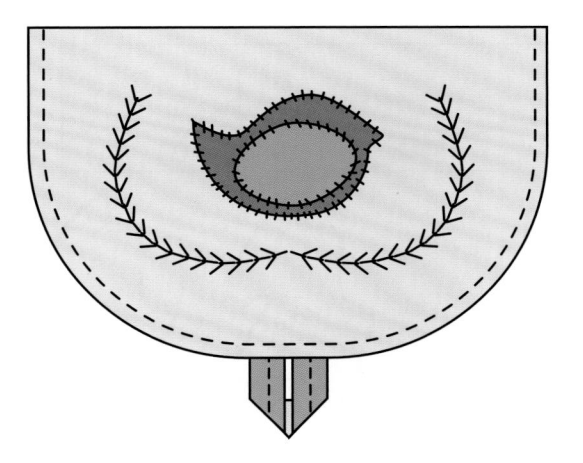

6 Position the belt loop straps onto the back pouch fabric piece where indicated on the pattern. Sew the top and bottom of each belt loop strap to the back pouch fabric piece.

7 With right sides together, sew the pouch front and back fabric pieces together along the curved edge. Repeat with the pouch lining pieces. Trim the seams and clip the curves.

8 Pin the flap to the back of the pouch with right sides together. Baste.

9 Insert the lining into the pouch with right sides facing and side seams matched up. Pin.

10 Sew all around the top edge of the pouch, leaving a 2" gap for turning.

11 Turn the pouch right-side out, making sure to pull out the flap. Press all seams.

12 Top stitch all around the openings of the pouch, making sure to close the gap.

13 Close the pouch and mark where to place the button. Attach your button.

BELT POUCH EMBROIDERY STITCHES

The belt pouch flap designs employ three different embroidery stitches: the backstitch, the whip-stitch, and the fern stitch. Learn how to make all the stitches here.

Backstitch

A backstitch is a simple embroidery stitch for making lines.

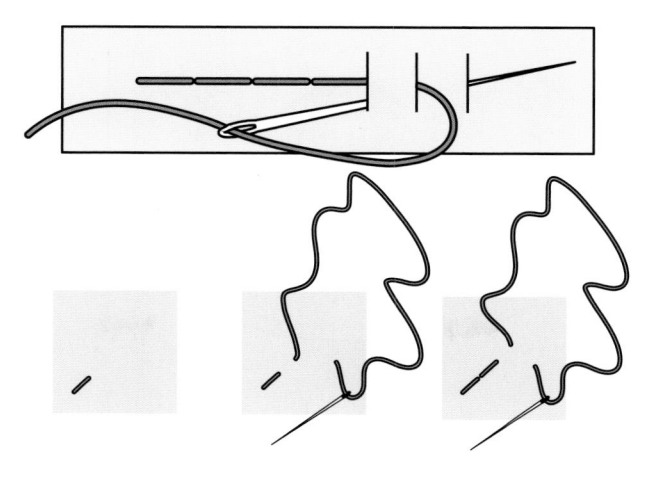

Whipstitch

A whipstitch is worked with two strands of embroidery thread, making stitches perpendicular to the edge of an applique.

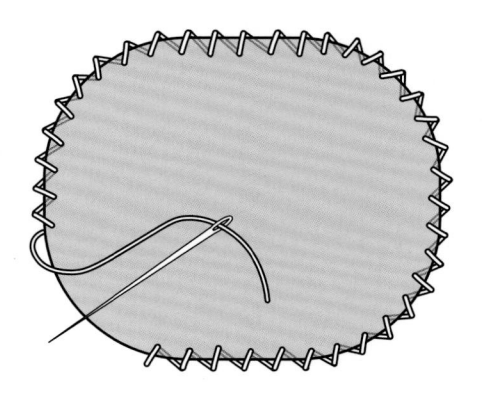

Fern Stitch

The fern stitch may seem complicated, but once you get the hang of it, you will see how simple it really is.

Come up through the fabric at **A** and then bring your needle just to the right of **A** at **B**. Don't pull your needle all the way through the fabric before coming up again at **C**, keeping the thread underneath the needle. Pull your needle all the way through, creating a V shape.

Bring the needle down into the fabric a short distance vertically from **C** at **D**, and then bring the needle up to the left a little below **A**. Repeat the first steps, making another V shape, with the needle coming up at **D** to create a chain.

Continue stitching until you have a fern stitch the desired length.

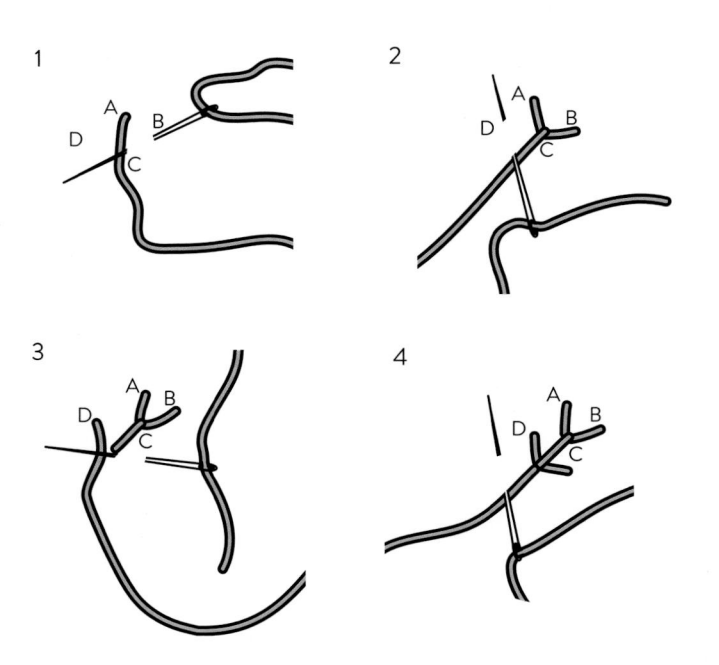

Money Magic

Ah, money. Is there a more vexatious topic? People have been casting money spells, using divination to find hidden treasure, and generally trying to get rich with witchcraft for ages.

Folk magic tells us to keep a basil leaf in our purse to keep money flowing toward us. Other plants like goldenrod and mint and grains like rice and oats are also associated with money and money spells. Ringing a bell is also said to bring in money, as the sound resembles coins falling.

Once you've made your new belt pouch, how about making a little money spell bag to keep inside to attract money to it? To make the spell pouch, you'll need a pinch of rice, a pinch of dried mint leaves, a penny, a small piece of green fabric, and green thread. Place the rice, mint, and penny in the middle of the green fabric and say, **"From sources varied and diverse, bring in money to my purse."** Secure the fabric around the items with the green thread. Keep the spell bag in your pouch or purse.

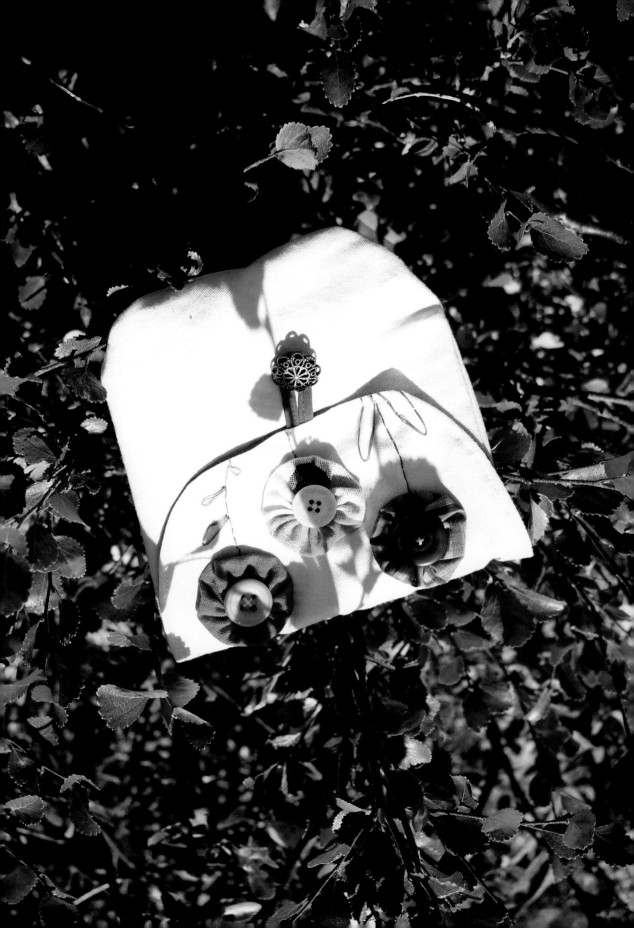

Waist Cincher

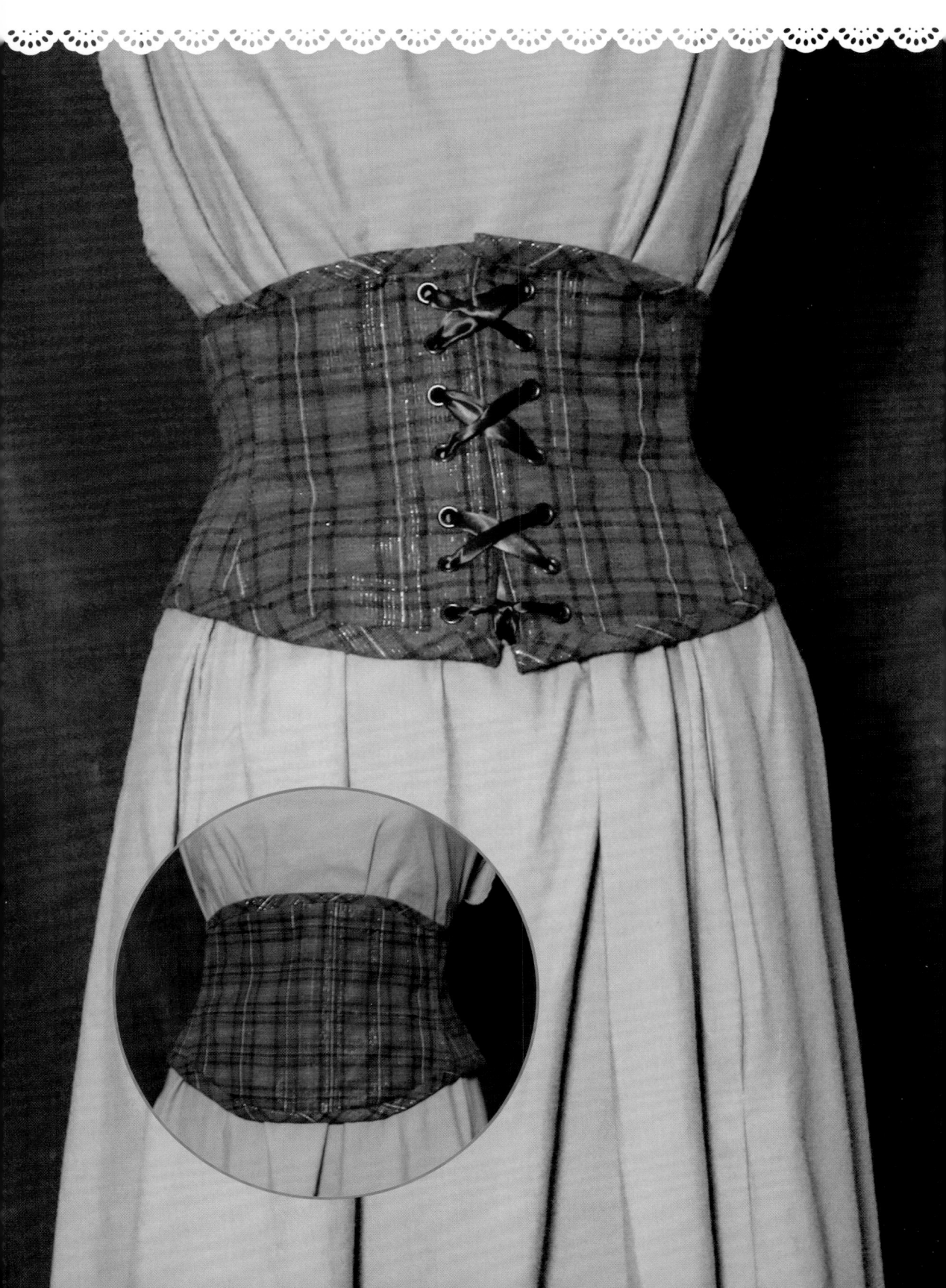

A waist cincher is more of a boned belt than a true piece of corsetry. However, it can be a versatile item in your wardrobe. Making one introduces you to many concepts and techniques involved in corset construction, and it can offer a bit of waist shaping.

Grommet Setting

Grommets are circles of metal, much like eyelets, but they consist of two parts: a male side and a female side. The male side has a protruding part that goes through the fabric and the female part. Usually, the male side is set on the right side of the fabric and the female on the wrong side. You use a grommet setter and a rubber mallet to set the grommets into the fabric. Some sets will come with a round metal tube with a sharp edge to cut circles in the fabric before inserting the grommet. You can also use an awl to poke holes into the fabric in which to set the grommets.

Boning

Steel and plastic boning can be purchased from several places online, like Etsy. You can purchase the boning cut into various lengths that are already tipped (meaning a cap or plastic coating has been applied to the ends of the boning) and finished. Steel boning comes in two varieties: spiral and flat. Spiral steel is flexible and suitable for front and side seams, whereas flat steel is used on either side of the grommets to provide support and structure. Steel boning should be tipped and plastic ends should be rounded so there aren't any sharp edges to cut through the fabric.

For the waist cincher, you will need:

- 3 spiral boning measuring 7" in length
- 2 spiral boning measuring 4½" in length
- 2 spiral boning measuring 4" in length
- 2 spiral boning measuring 5" in length
- 4 flat steel boning measuring 7" in length

What Kind of Fabric to Use

The kind of fabric you use is limited only by your imagination with this project. The fashion fabric can be anything from lace to vinyl to linen to any kind of blend. This is due to the interlining and the structural fabric providing the support so that the fashion fabric can hold up to repeated stress of cinching.

For the interlining, you will want a tightly woven fabric like broadcloth.

MATERIALS

½ yard of fashion fabric

½ yard of interlining fabric

½ yard of structural fabric

2 packages of extra-wide double-fold bias binding (or an equivalent amount of self-made bias binding)

Thread

Flat and spiral boning (see "Boning")

14 two-part grommets

5 yards of satin ribbon

TOOLS

Sewing machine and needles

Scissors

Pins

Hand-sewing needle

Rubber mallet

Awl

Iron

Measuring tape

Pattern pieces from pages 177–80

Seam ripper (just in case)

TERMS & CONCEPTS

You will be **basting** and optionally making **bias binding**. See "Methods" on page 6 for more information. You will also be making **boning channels** and adding **two-part grommets** (see "Grommet Setting").

For the structural fabric, you will want something heavier like **duck cloth** or even **coutil** (a specialty cotton that is made primarily for corsetry).

PATTERN DRAFTING

No pattern drafting is necessary. Use the patterns from pages 177–80 in the appendix in your size based on waist measurement. Choose a pattern size that is closest to your waist measurement without going over. The waist cincher should be smaller than your waist so that it can provide the "cinching" part of its name.

Measurements

You will need the following measurement:

- Your waist circumference

Cutting Instructions

1 Make copies of the pattern pieces in your size. You will need a center front, side front, side back, and center back piece.

2 Fold your fashion fabric in half widthwise. Place your center front pattern piece on the fold and pin. Pin the rest of the pieces to the fabric. If you are using fabric with a design, try to position your pattern pieces in a line across the fabric so that the design stays consistent.

3 Cut out your pattern pieces. You will have one center front piece, two side front pieces, two side back pieces, and two center back pieces.

4 Repeat steps 1–3 with your interlining and lining fabric.

CONSTRUCTION

1 With the right side of the interlining facing the wrong side of the fashion fabric, baste the panels together. Treat them as one panel going forward. The fashion fabric side will be the right side and the interlining side will be the wrong side. Do this with the center front piece and the side front, side back, and center back pieces.

2 With right sides together, sew the side front panels of the fashion fabric to the center front panel.

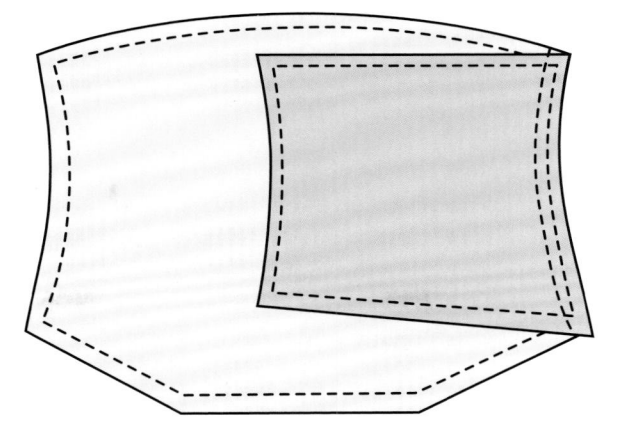

3 With right sides together, sew the side back panels to the side front panels.

4 With right sides together, sew the back panels to the side back panels.

5 Clip the curves and press the seams open.

6 Repeat steps 2–5 with the structure fabric panels.

7 Place the fashion fabric and structure fabric together, right sides facing and raw edges of the center back facing. Sew a ½" seam down both center back edges.

8 Turn the waist cincher right-side out and press the center back seams.

9 Mark a ½"-wide channel down the length of the center front panel. Mark two similar channels on either side of the first. Sew along the marked lines through all thicknesses.

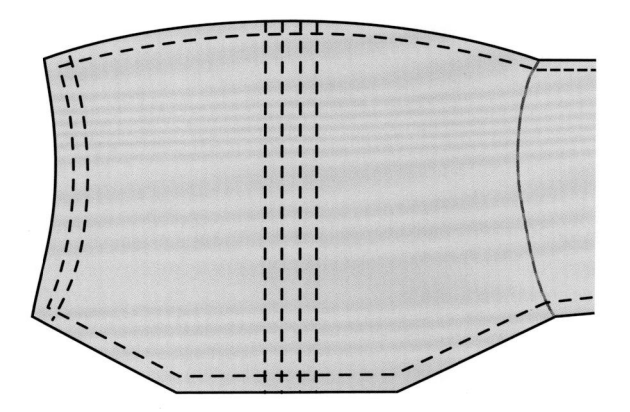

10 Mark a line ¼" on either side of the center front and side front seam. Sew along those lines through all thicknesses. Repeat for all other seams except for the center back seams.

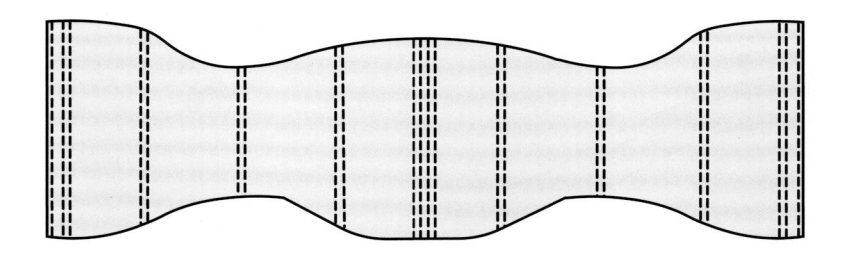

11 Mark a line ½" from the center back seam. Sew along that line. Make another ½" channel on the center back panels ¾" in from the center back channel. Sew those lines through all thicknesses.

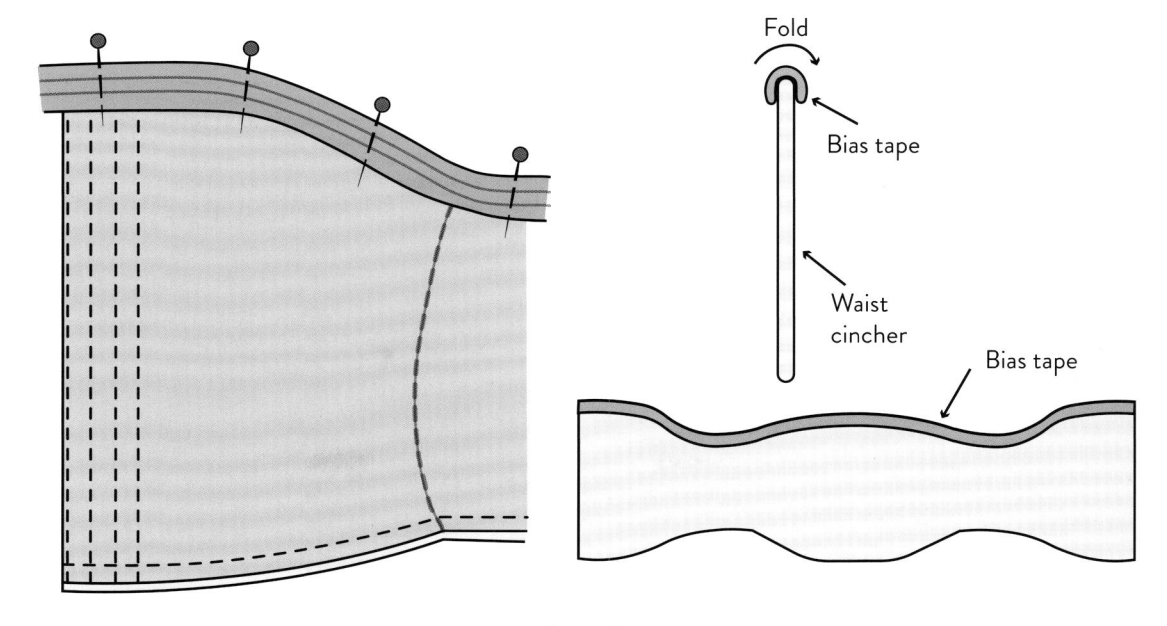

12 Mark the gromment placement as follows: In between the two channels on the center back panels make eight marks, starting ¾" from the top of the waist cincher and with 1" between each mark. The eighth mark should be ¾" from the bottom of the waist cincher. Attach grommets at the marks following manufacturer's instructions.

13 Attach the bias binding to the top of the waist cincher by unfolding the bias tape and placing one long edge against the top of the waist cincher with edges even and right sides together. Sew a ¼" seam along the edge. Fold the bias tape to the inside of the waist cincher so that the raw edge is inside the folded edge and lies flat against the structural fabric. Hand-sew it to the structural fabric. To finish the ends of the bias binding at the ends of the waist cincher, fold the raw edges to the inside of the waist cincher and then tack in place.

14 Insert your boning by slipping it into the channels between the structure fabric and the fashion fabric.

15 Attach the bias binding to the bottom of the waist cincher following the same instructions in step 13.

16 Lace your ribbon through the grommets.

Corset History

The corset has had a lot of myths and misconceptions tied to it, but when you look at its history, you see that it was simply an undergarment. The corset provided support, not only for the human form wearing it but also for the clothing worn over it. Many past fashions would not work without a corset providing the proper base and shaping for the gowns, blouses, and skirts that went over it.

The move from corset as underwear to outerwear began in the mid-nineteenth century. First viewed as subversive, corsets have gained acceptance and even popularity as outerwear.

Waist cinchers, or boned belts, were in fashion in the Victorian era. They were used to enhance the small waists even further. The waist cincher was also referred to as a "waspie" due to the resemblance of the cinched waist to that of a wasp.

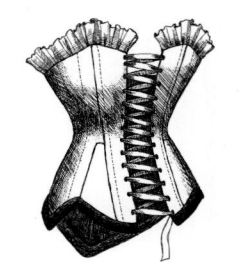

Bustle

While historically bustles were found underneath skirts and gowns to provide a particular silhouette and structure, this one is worn over the skirt or dress. As it ties around the waist, it is most often paired with the waist cincher from the previous chapter to hide the ties. You can also tuck them under the waistband of your skirt, however.

What Kind of Fabric to Use

You will need a heavyweight fabric for the bustle base. This can be **denim**, **duck cloth**, **twill**, and the like.

For the fashion fabric, you can use any **light- to medium-weight fabric**. I've even used **upholstery fabric** in some bustles.

This project also calls for a sheer fabric like **gauze**, which will provide a nice contrast to the fashion fabric.

PATTERN DRAFTING

No pattern drafting is needed for this project. Use the pattern pieces on pages 182–83 in the appendix for the bustle pad.

CONSTRUCTION

Making the Flounces

Flounces can be as large or small as you want. I've used platters, wreath forms, and even a cheap Halloween witch's hat to draw the outside flounce circle. The important part of the flounce is the inside circle, which should be at the center of the outer circle and 2" in diameter. For this bustle, cut four different flounce templates measuring 8½", 10½", 12½", and 15½" in diameter. Cut a straight line from the outside of the circle to the inner circle, and then cut out the inner circle.

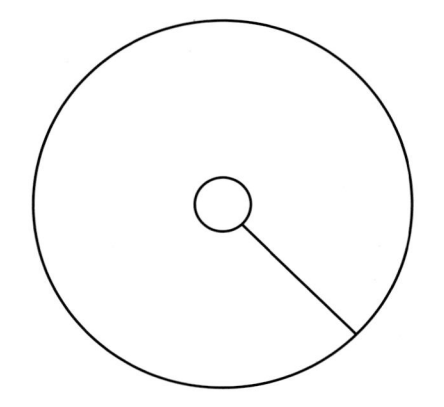

MATERIALS

1 yard of a structural fabric

1 yard of a solid fashion fabric

1 yard of a sheer fabric

Thread

4 yards of ⅞"-wide grosgrain ribbon in a matching color

Bustle pad pattern on pages 182–83

TOOLS

Scissors

Sewing machine and needle

Chalk

Pins

Seam ripper (just in case)

TERMS & CONCEPTS

You will be making flounces with **finished edges**, sewing **darts**, and marking line placement. See "Methods" on page 6 for more information.

Cut out **four** of each of the following flounces:

STRUCTURAL FLOUNCE: 8½" in the structure material

LARGE FASHION FLOUNCE: 15½" in the fashion fabric

LARGE GAUZE FLOUNCE: 15½" in the gauze fabric

MEDIUM FASHION FLOUNCE: 12½" in the fashion fabric

MEDIUM GAUZE FLOUNCE: 10½" in the gauze fabric

SMALL FASHION FLOUNCE: 8½" in the fashion fabric

SMALL GAUZE FLOUNCE: 8½" in the gauze fabric

1 Take two of the 8½" structural flounces. With right sides together, sew the short straight edge together with a ½" seam. Repeat with the other two pieces of structure fabric, and then sew together the resultant two flounces to make one flounce piece.

2 Finish the straight edges and the curved outer edge of the flounce. You can do this by pinking the edges, giving them a narrow hem, using a zigzag stitch, or serging them.

3 Repeat steps 1 and 2 for each other batch of flounces.

Sewing the Bustle

1 Cut out four bustle pad pieces from the structure fabric.

2 Place two bustle pad pieces together, right sides facing each other, and sew the center seam. Repeat with the other two bustle pad pieces. Press the seams open.

3 Sew darts along the waist on the front and back pad pieces.

4 Mark lines for flounces on the front pad.

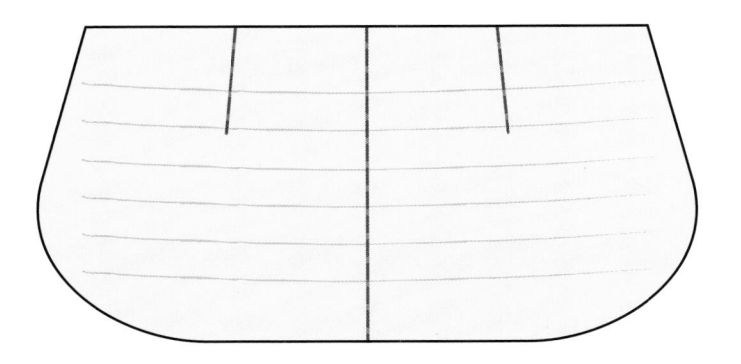

5 Pin the unfinished edge of the structural flounce to the bottommost line marked on your bustle pad. Sew ¼" from the edge, attaching the flounce to the pad. Create tucks and folds where needed to make the flounce fit to the line.

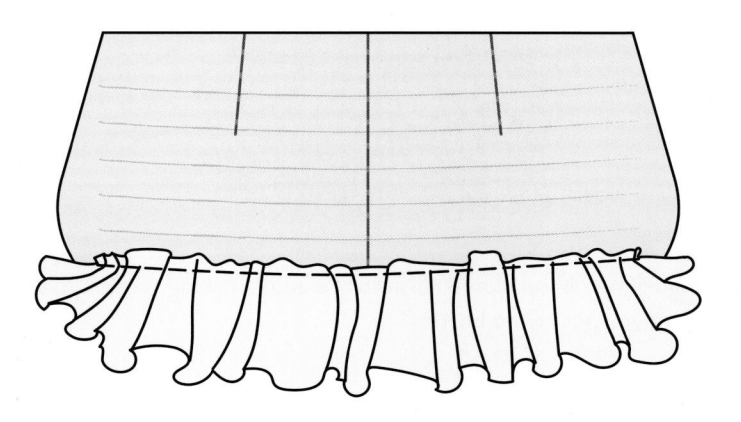

6 Repeat step 5 with the other flounces, moving upward in this order: large fashion flounce, large gauze flounce, medium fashion flounce, medium gauze flounce, small fashion flounce, small gauze flounce.

7 With right sides together, sew the sides and bottom of the bustle pads together with a ½" seam, making sure not to catch the flounces in the seam. Clip the curves.

8 Turn the bustle right-side out. Baste the opening closed.

9 Sew the short ends of grosgrain ribbon together to make a long loop. Turn right-side out.

10 Flatten the loop so that it makes one long ribbon. Sew along the top long side of the ribbon a scant ⅛" from the edge to close the loop.

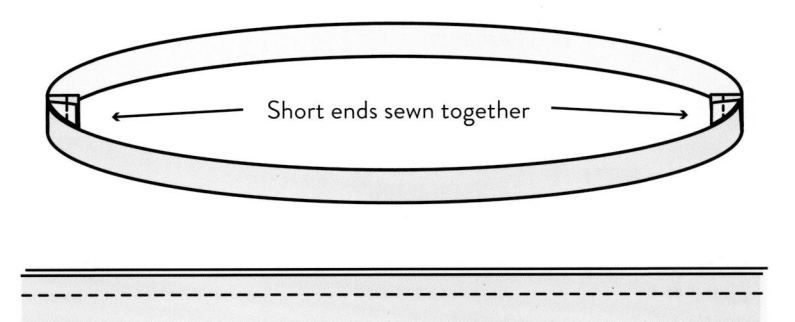

Short ends sewn together

11 Mark the center of the ribbon and match that with the center of the top edge of the bustle. Sandwich the top of the bustle between the open edge of the ribbon.

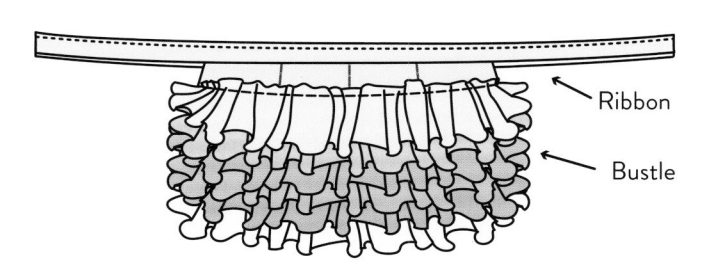

Ribbon

Bustle

12 Sew the opening of the ribbon closed close to the edge, making sure to go through all layers of the fabric when you get to the bustle.

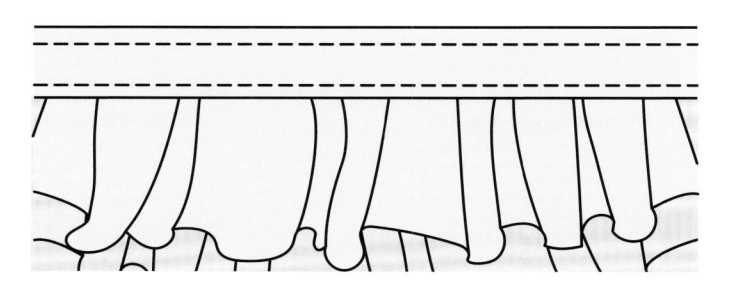

Bustle History

The bustle is often associated with the Victorian era, when it gained popularity, but it has its roots in various support structures of previous centuries. As long as there has been fashion, there has been the need for undergarments to help give the fashion the correct shape. From the panniers of the seventeenth century to the bum roll of the eighteenth century, fashion needed something underneath gowns and skirts.

Part of the reason for this is the amount of fabric used in said skirts. The volume of fabric needed support to keep from dragging in the mud. In the case of the bustle, skirts of the Victorian era were drawn up, or "bustled," at the rear and would droop without the proper rigging underneath. Bustles of those days were as simple as a pillow-shaped item tied around the waist and as complex as the lobster tail bustle, which was a contraption that looked like the tail of a lobster and included steel boning to bear the weight of all the fabric.

The bustle fell out of fashion around the start of World War I, as cotton was needed for wartime. Much like the corset, the bustle has made a comeback in various niche interest groups such as historical reenactment societies and steampunk enthusiasts. It has also become an accessory used as an overskirt, enhancing the silhouette again but this time from the outside.

Infinity Scarf

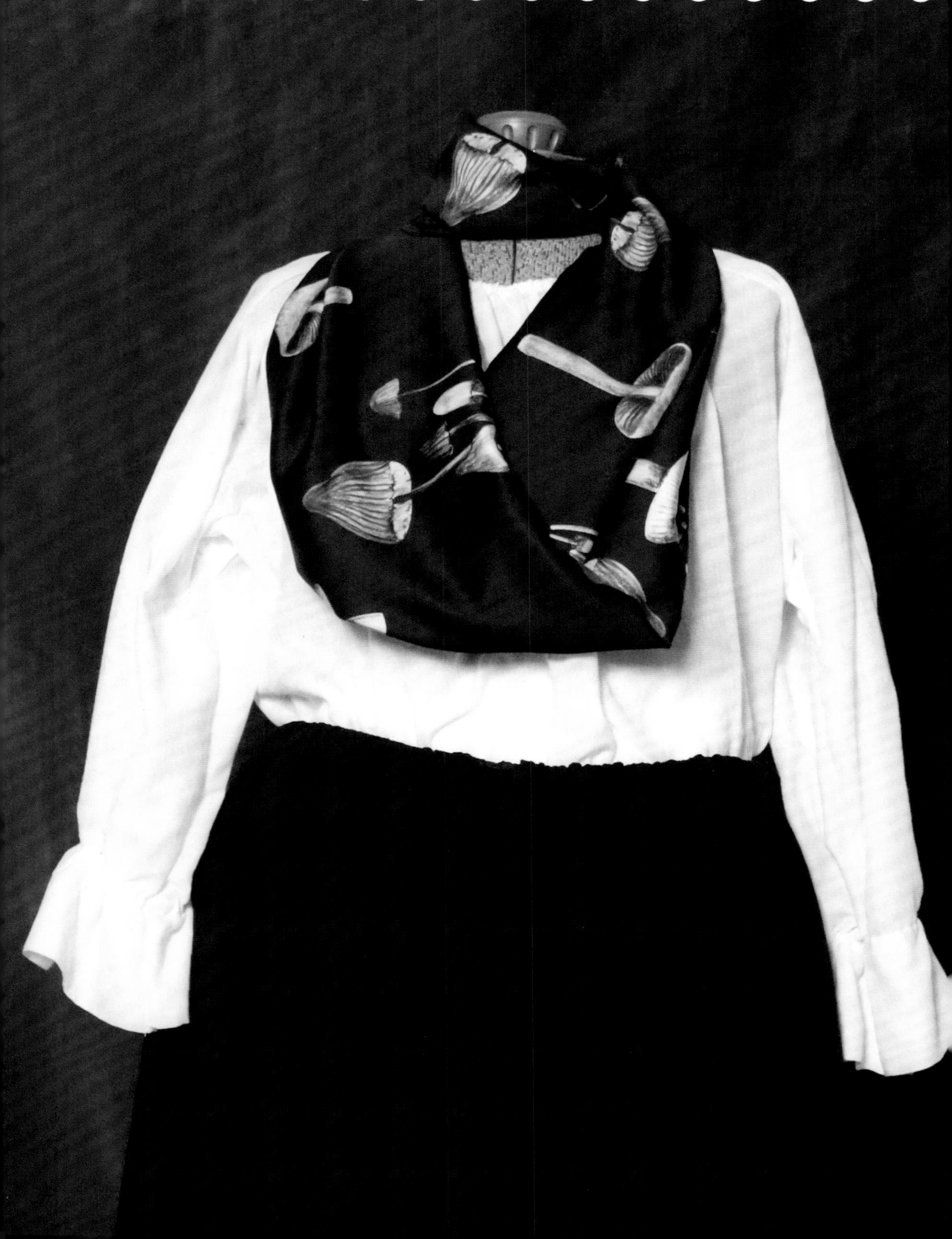

The infinity scarf is a bit of a misnomer. It is actually a circle of fabric. The length of the scarf, however, allows one to wrap it twice around one's neck, thus making an infinity symbol. The infinity symbol is a powerful one of manifestation. Wear your infinity scarf when you are looking to make things happen, to give your words confidence, or to wrap yourself in intentions of fulfillment and completion. Choose fabric that feels good to the touch, as the skin around your neck is some of your most delicate.

What Kind of Fabric to Use

Any **light- to medium-weight fabric** is well-suited to this project. Choose **silk**, **cotton lawn**, or **synthetic fabric** for a spring or summer scarf. For fall or winter, go with a **fleece** or **medium-weight knit fabric** to keep you warm.

PATTERN DRAFTING

There is no pattern needed for the infinity scarf. You need only to cut a rectangle that is 21" wide by 72" long. Depending on the width of your fabric, you can just cut it in half lengthwise. This will give you material for two scarves.

CONSTRUCTION

1 With right sides together, sew short ends together in a ½" seam.

2 Fold the resulting fabric circle in half lengthwise, with right sides facing. Pin.

3 Mark your start and end points 2" on either side of the short seam to leave a gap for turning.

4 Sew a ½" seam, backstitching at the start and stop.

5 Turn the scarf right-side out. Close the opening either with a slip stitch or by topstitching the seam.

MATERIALS

2 yards of fabric

Thread

TOOLS

Sewing machine and needle

Ruler

Scissors or a rotary cutter

Pins

Seam ripper (just in case)

TERMS & CONCEPTS

You will be **slip stitching** or **topstitching** a seam closed. See "Methods" on page 6 for more information.

Giving Your Voice
a Magical Boost

Scarves like the infinity scarf offer a lot of magical possibilities. They cover your throat, the source of your voice, and you can sew a garment that will help you achieve your goals magically.

You can use different colors to help enhance your voice and words. Choose red colors to imbue your speech with passion. Orange is good for speaking creatively. Blue and green colors can help when you need to speak words of healing and compassion.

Prints in your fabric also are useful to consider if you are looking to give your scarf a magical kick. Choose various animal prints to tap into the powers of the animal kingdom. Zebra stripes provide protection from harmful words just as they protect zebras from noxious flies. Cheetah spots can grant your words speed. Floral designs help the words you speak promote growth and abundance.

Even the type of fabric you use can give your speech certain properties. Cotton, with its association with fire, will add a little oomph to what you say, while silk will give your words elegance and grace.

Button Magic

Buttons are associated with the direction of north and the element of earth, meaning they can be used to connect with earth-based magics, protective energies, and even abundance and prosperity spellwork.

The shape, color, and composition of buttons should be considered when working sewing magic. Metal buttons can be used on wallets and purses to imbue them with prosperity and wealth energies. Heart-shaped buttons can be used to bring loving intentions to projects. Novelty buttons are available in a multitude of styles so that you can work good luck, protection, and glamour magic, and so much more.

If you are sewing on a button as part of spellwork, take a moment to ground and center yourself before you start. Keep your intention in mind as you work. When you tie off the thread, visualize your magic being fixed in place.

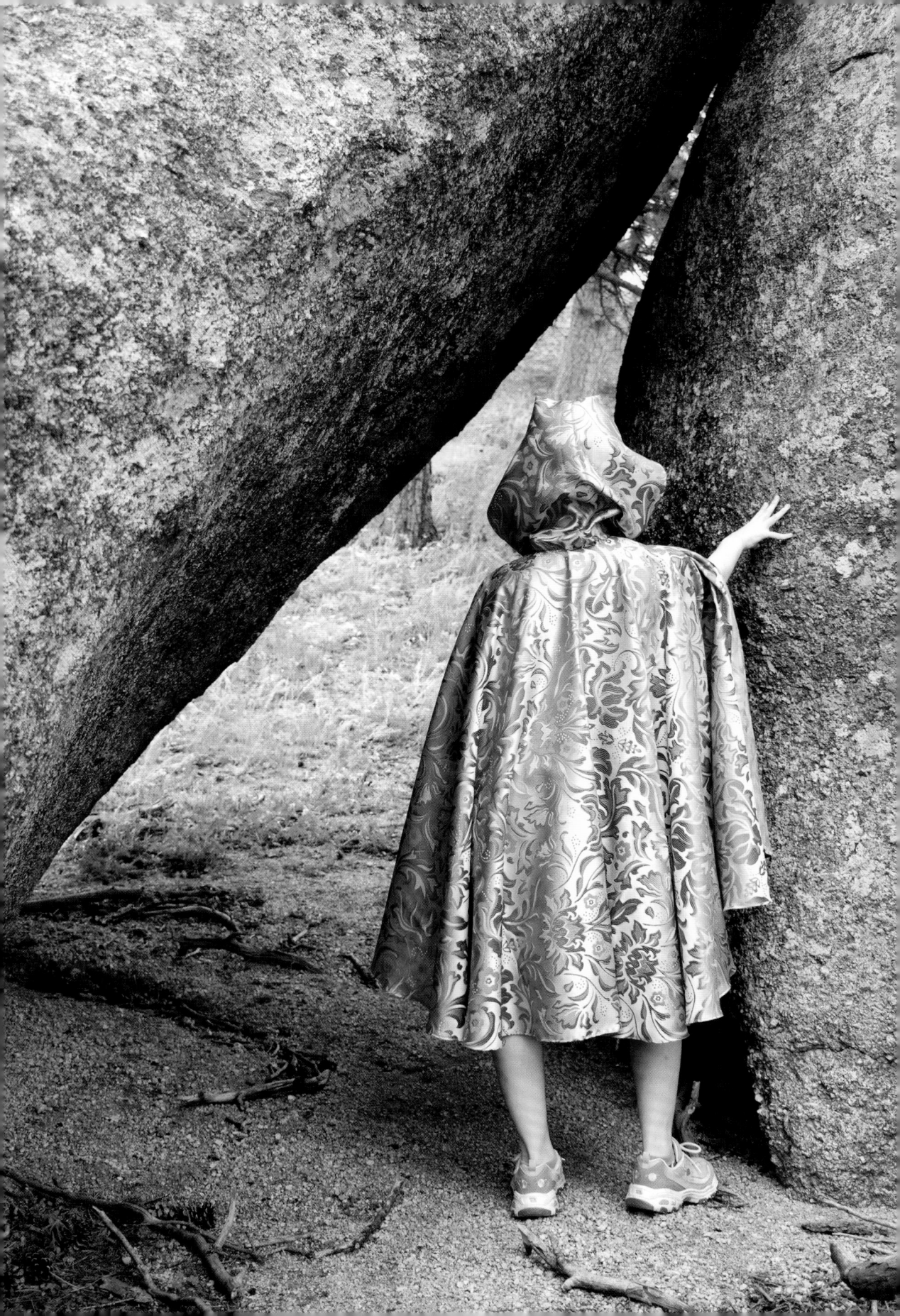

Neck Warmer

Magically, the throat is one of your most important tools. You use your voice to recite and sing incantations. You can literally speak your intentions into reality via your words. With that in mind, sew this neck warmer as a piece of protective clothing. After you have made it, dedicate it to protecting yourself and your words.

This project is one where you could use a fabric like fleece or even buy sweater knit material from your local fabric store. However, it also presents an opportunity to upcycle a sweater that you no longer wear. Even if the sweater has been damaged or stained, you can still put it to use as a neck warmer since you only need a rectangle of fabric measuring 25" by 18". You can make a thinner neck warmer by reducing the width of the rectangle from 18" to 16" or even 14" if there isn't quite enough to use from the sweater. The buttons are optional but provide a nice decorative touch.

What Kind of Fabric to Use

The neck warmer can be made out of any stretchy material, although fabrics like **fleece** and **heavyweight knits** are often used as they provide more warmth than thinner fabrics. You can also use **sweaters** or **sweatshirts**, as they are made of the same material.

PATTERN DRAFTING

You will not need to draft a pattern for this project. All you will need to do is cut a 25" by 18" rectangle of fabric.

CONSTRUCTION

1 Fold the long sides of the fabric together with right sides facing. Sew a ¼" seam on the long edge.

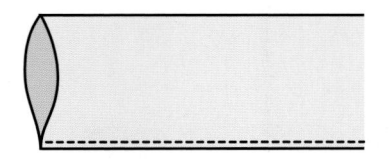

2 Start turning the neck warmer right-side out inward with the long-edge seam on the outside, stopping halfway, with the open ends matched up. Sew a ¼" seam around the open side, leaving a 3" gap for turning.

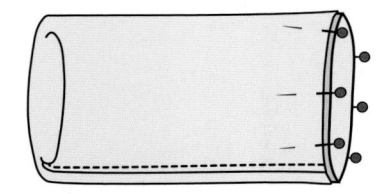

3 Turn right-side out. Close the opening either with a slip stitch or by topstitching the seam.

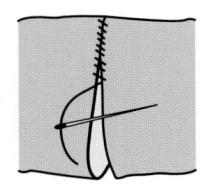

4 Add button accents to the outside of the neck warmer if desired.

MATERIALS

25" by 18" rectangle of fabric

Two 1" buttons (optional)

TOOLS

Sewing machine and needle

Pins

Measuring tape

Yardstick

Marking pen or chalk

Seam ripper (just in case)

TERMS & CONCEPTS

You will be sewing a **slip stitch**. See "Methods" on page 6 for more information.

Cross-Over Apron

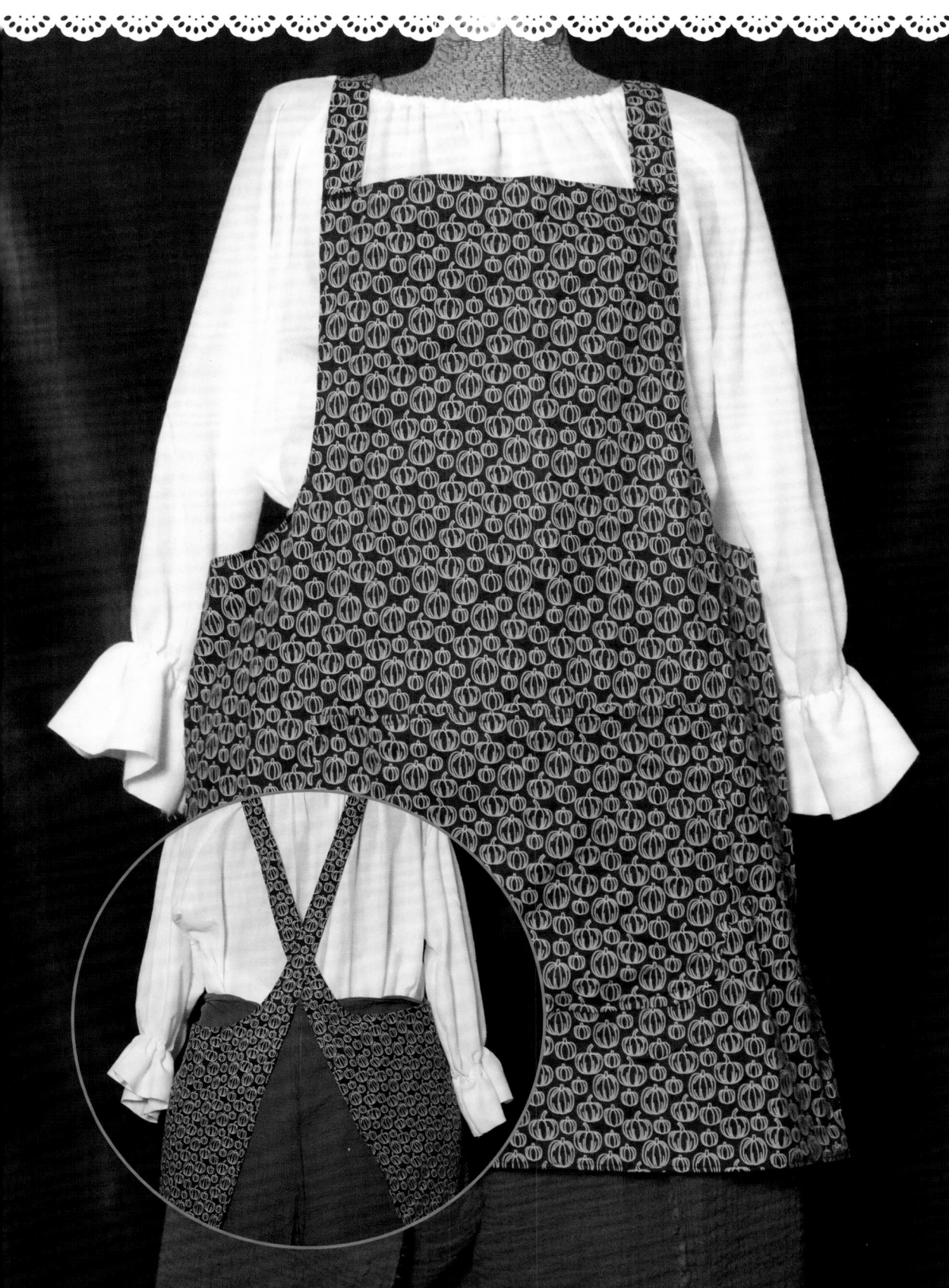

Aprons were a vital garment for all people when clothes were handsewn. Aprons protected against stains and some wear and tear, helped carry items, and acted as rags to wipe up spills or to dry hands. In the 1950s the apron took on a decorative function for many American housewives. It was an accessory, signaling women's work but often not actually used in that work. In the age of fast fashion, aprons aren't in use outside of specific occupations and chores.

Magically, aprons are useful in that you can have one that is specifically for your spellwork. Putting on the apron signals to yourself and the universe that you are going to be engaging in magic.

I believe aprons need to make a comeback. Their utility—in the garden, the kitchen, the apothecary, and more—makes tasks easier. And with how quickly you can put this project together and how little fabric it uses, I think you'll find yourself making up two or three to have on hand.

This apron features two variations on the pockets—either one center front pocket or two side ones—because every apron should have pockets.

What Kind of Fabric to Use

Choose **cottons** and **linens** for this project. You want a fabric that is medium weight and that can stand up to wear and tear, as well as repeated washings.

How Much Fabric?

You will need fabric measuring your **D** measurement plus **E** measurement in length and your **C** measurement in width. If the **C** measurement is less than 44", you will use fabric that is 44" wide. Otherwise, you will need fabric that is 58" wide.

MATERIALS
Fabric (see below)
Thread

TOOLS
Sewing machine and needle
Measuring tape
Ruler
Scissors or a rotary cutter
Paper for pattern making
Pins
Seam ripper (just in case)
Iron

TERMS & CONCEPTS
You will be **drafting a pattern**, **basting**, making a **narrow hem**, and adding a **pocket**. See "Methods" on page 6 for more information.

PATTERN DRAFTING

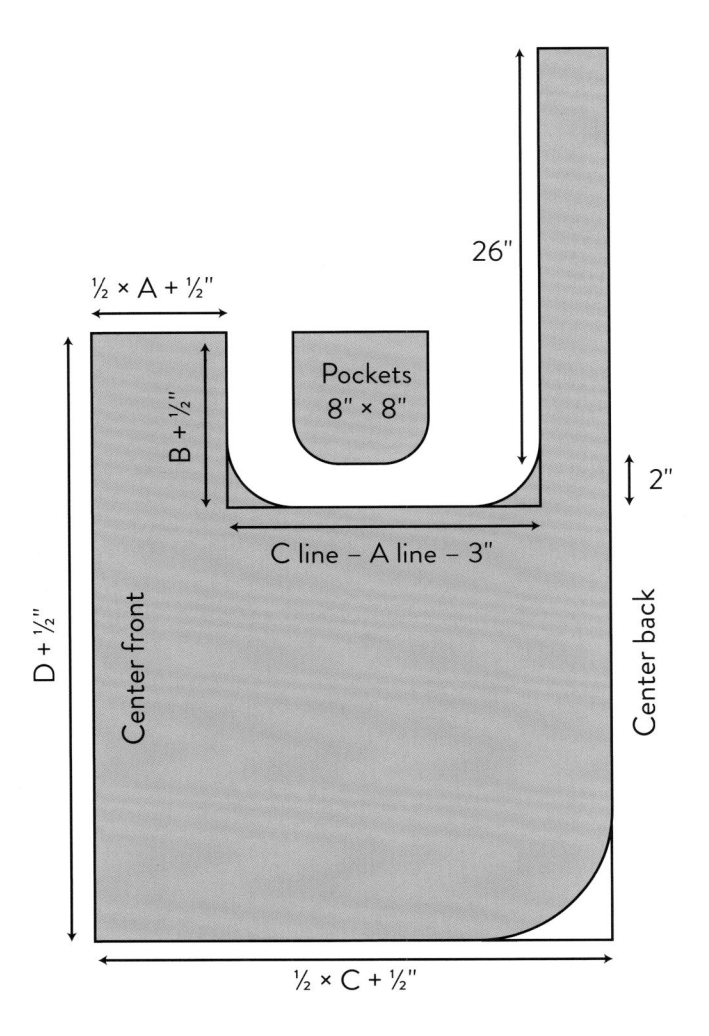

Measurements

You will need the following measurements:

- **A** = The distance from shoulder to shoulder across your front
- **B** = The distance between your overbust and underbust down your center front
- **C** = The circumference of your hips (or largest part of your body, if not hips)
- **D** = The desired length (bust to hem)

Optional: For the straps, you can either use the default length of 26" or measure from your overbust over your shoulder and down to the middle of your back to get the strap length. Call this measurement **E**.

Refer to the diagram as you follow the instructions to draft your apron pattern.

On a piece of pattern paper, brown paper, or wrapping paper, draw your pattern. Start at the lower left and corner of the paper and draw a vertical line from the bottom up your **D** measurement + ½".

At the bottom of your **D** line, draw a perpendicular line out to the right that measures half your **C** measurement + ½". At the top of your **D** line, draw a perpendicular line out to the right that measures half your **A** measurement + ½".

Starting at the unconnected end of your **A** line, draw a perpendicular line down your **B** measurement + ½".

Here's where we get into some advanced math. You will need to draw a line from your **B** line that measures your **C** line – your **A** line – 3". Draw that line from the unconnected end and perpendicular to your **B** line. Draw a line 2" long up from the end of this line.

Measure 3" over to the right from the end of your 2" line and mark a point. Draw a line from that point down to the unconnected end of your **C** line.

Add the straps to your pattern by extending the two unfinished lines at the back of the apron. Extend the lines upward either 26" or by your **E** measurement. At the top connect the two ends of those lines with a perpendicular line.

Round the corner at the lower right of the apron as well as the inner corners of the sides.

For the Pocket(s)

For two side pockets, draw a square that measures 8" by 8". For a large middle pocket, draw a rectangle that measures 8" by 16". Round the corners of the bottom of the pocket.

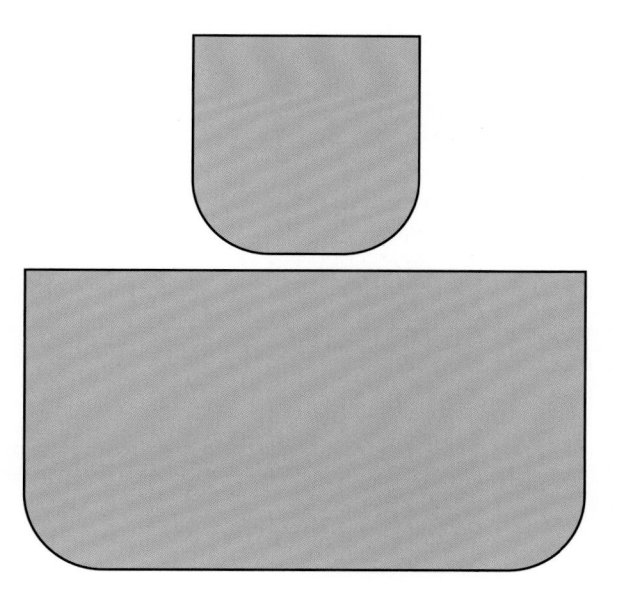

CONSTRUCTION

1 Fold your fabric and place your pattern with the center front on the fold. Cut out the apron and pockets from your fabric. Cut out your pocket pieces from the remaining fabric. You will need two square pockets or one rectangular pocket.

2 Finish the curved edges of the apron with a narrow hem.

3 Try on the apron. Pull the straps over your shoulders, crossed at the back, and pin them in place to the front. Adjust to a comfortable fit. Make sure the straps aren't twisted.

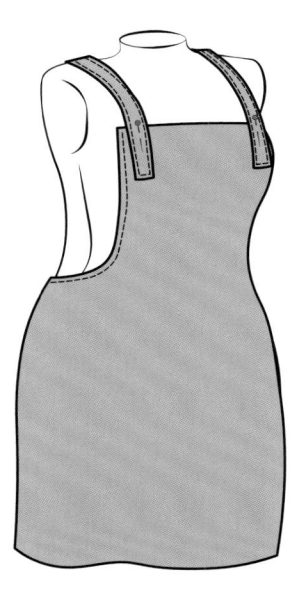

4 Remove the apron and mark where the straps meet the top of the apron. Unpin the straps and cut off excess material from them.

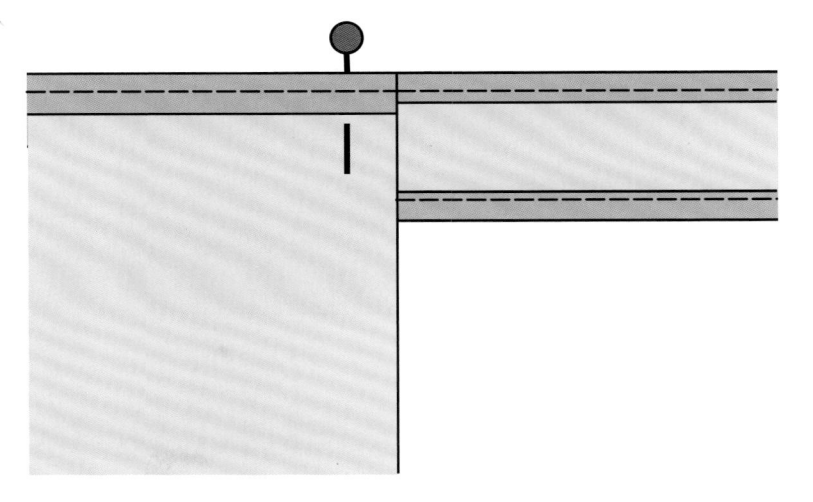

5 Fold the top edge of the apron to the inside ¼" and then in again another ¼". Press.

6 Fold the raw edge of the apron straps to the outside ¼". Press.

7 Cross the straps over the back of the apron so that the left strap reaches the right top of the apron and the right strap reaches the left top of the apron. With the outside of the strap facing the inside of the apron top, slip the folded edge of the straps under the folded edge of the apron top. Match outer edges. Baste in place.

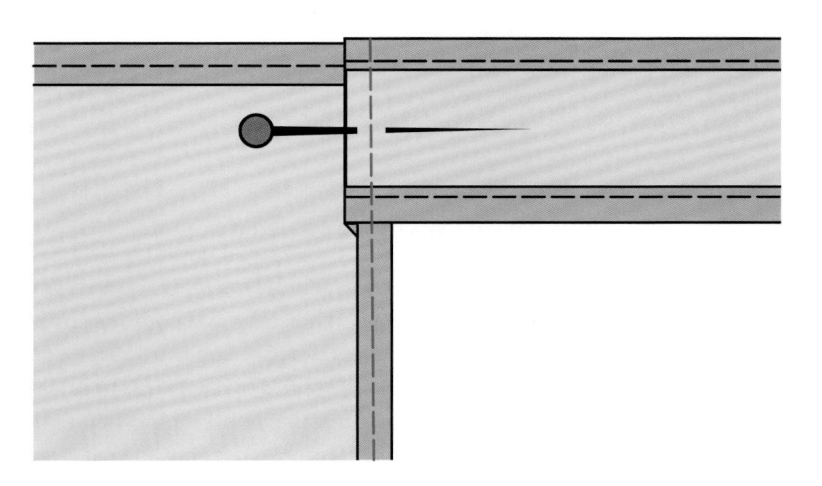

8 On the outside, stitch along the top of the apron near the first fold, through all thicknesses of fabric. If desired, secure the straps with a bar tack by sewing a zigzag stitch with a short stitch length over the point, backstitching to secure the threads. Remove basting.

9 Try on the apron once more and mark where you want the pockets to be.

10 Finish the top edge of the pocket with a narrow hem.

11 Fold the raw edge of the sides and bottom of the pocket ½" to the inside. Press.

12 Position the pocket(s) where you marked and sew them in place.

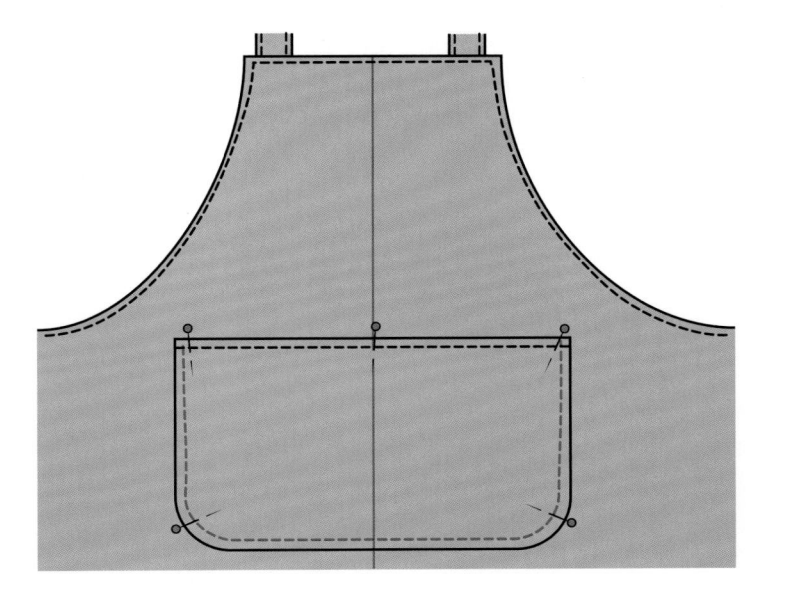

Kitchen Witchery Tips

Kitchen witchery is one of the most recognizable forms of all modern witch-craft. The image of a witch baking up magic in her oven is a common trope. It isn't surprising that it is such a popular way to practice spellwork. The kitchen is a confluence of the elements—fire, water, air, and earth—as well as the source of transformation from raw ingredients to something new and differ-ent. If you are new to magic, kitchen witchery is an accessible and easy way to try your hand at casting a spell and engaging in ritual.

Some ways to engage in kitchen witchery are as follows:

- Bless your tools. Spoons and spatulas are the kitchen witch's wands.

- Label your spices and herbs with the planets, elements, and powers they are associated with.

- Keep a culinary book of shadows. Write down recipes with the corre-spondences of each ingredient.

- Keep a kitchen altar. Something as simple as a mortar and pestle and a picture of a deity associated with the kitchen (like Demeter, Hestia, or Brigid) can help remind you that magic can be found in the mundane.

- Add moon water to your kitchen chores. Yes, washing the dishes isn't the most magical of all activities, but adding moon water to the soapy water will help energetically cleanse and bless your dishes while you clean them.

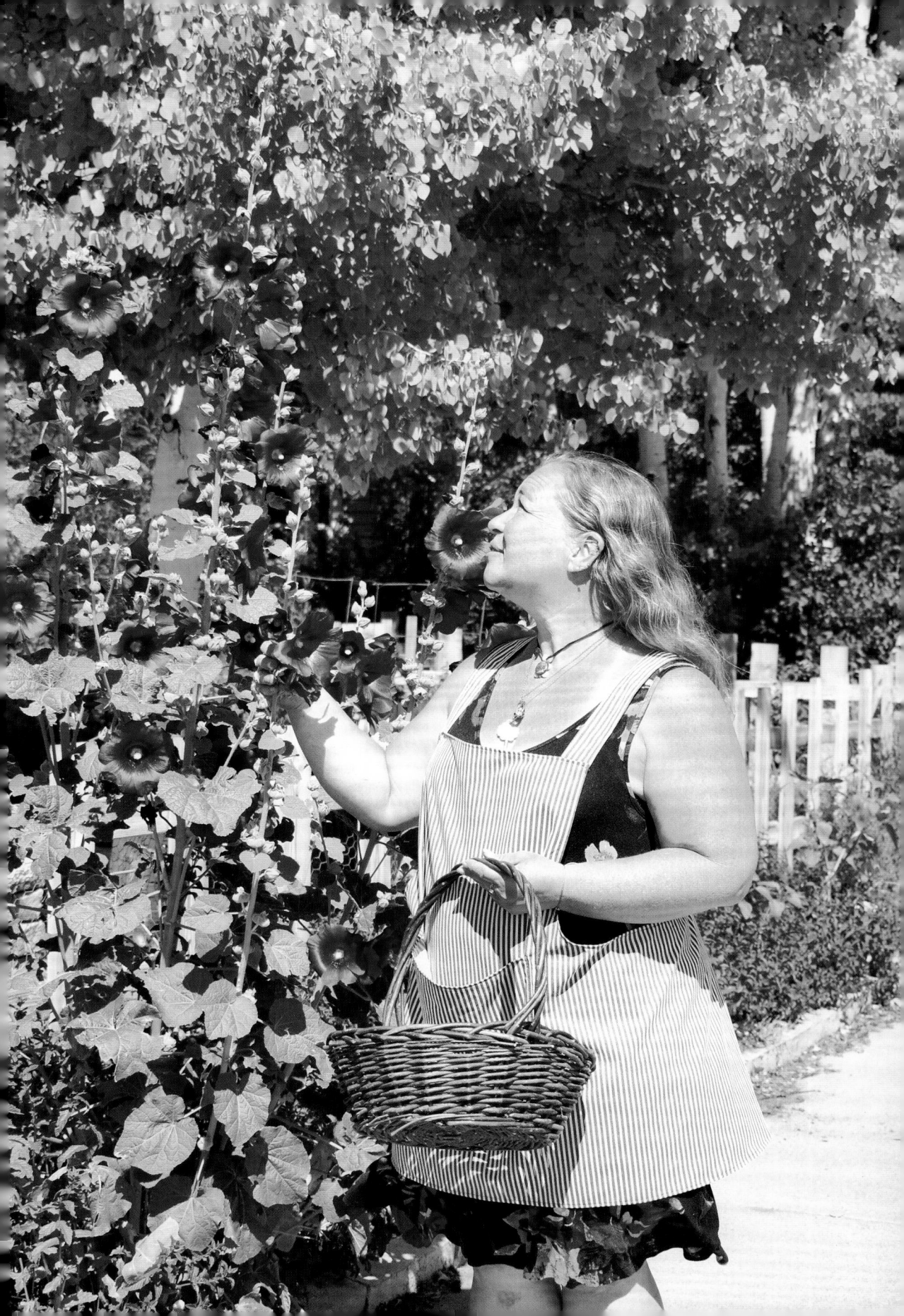

Gathering Apron

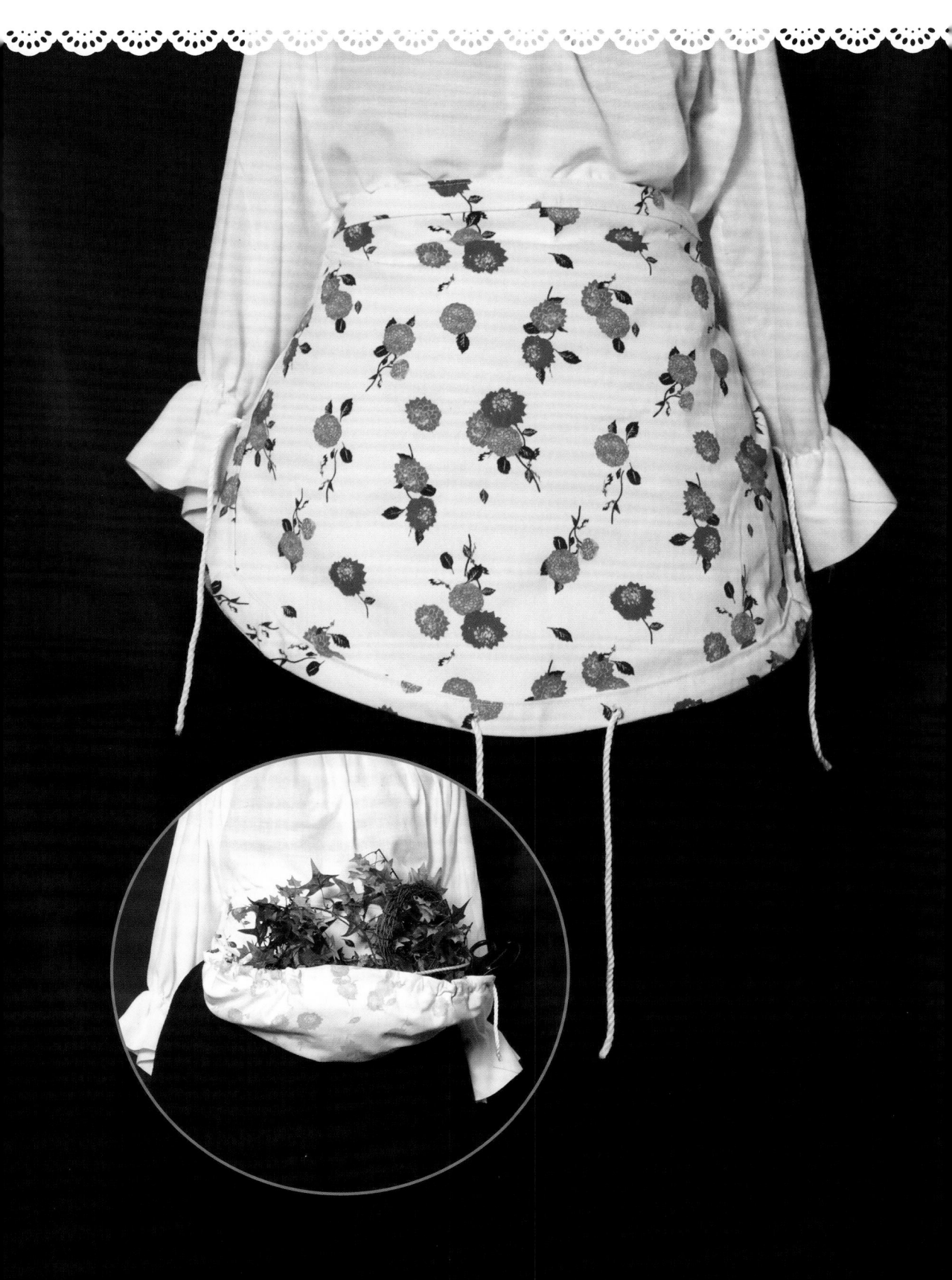

This project is based on vintage aprons used by many gardeners in the early twentieth century. The idea behind this apron is to pull on the cording that runs through the bias binding channels so that the apron is gathered into a basket shape. Tying the cording together maintains the shape, leaving your hands free to gather tomatoes, herbs, pinecones or whatever else you are collecting. Untying the cording and letting it slip back into the channels allows the apron to flatten out again and serve as a covering in the kitchen.

As with other projects in this book, such as the market bag, the gathering apron is useful for all types of witches but especially the kitchen witch. Use the bucket design to carry any ingredients, crystals, or other materia magica you need, and leave your hands free for the actual spellwork.

To use the gathering apron, pull the cording on the right-side top and bottom of the apron so that the fabric gathers and tie the cording together. Repeat on the left side so that the apron creates a bowl or basket. When you no longer need the apron to be gathered, untie the cording, let it slip back into the channels, and flatten the apron out.

What Kind of Fabric to Use

I recommend using a **medium-weight cotton** or **linen** for your apron. You want a fabric that will stand up to frequent use, especially when it will be gathered up to carry your goods. As the bias binding will be visible on the apron, pick a color that you like. Or you can make bias-binding from the same fabric as the apron so that it matches.

DRAFTING THE PATTERN

The pattern for the gathering apron is essentially a square with rounded bottom corners.

½ × A

B + 1"

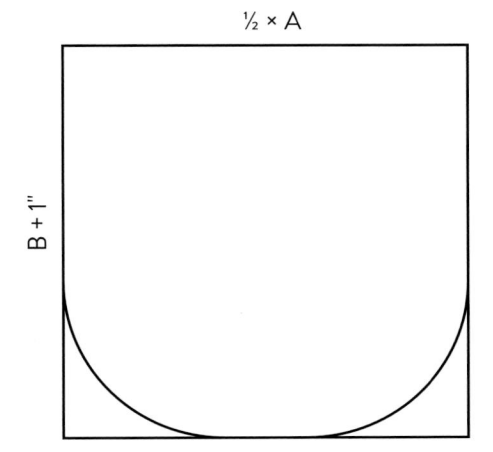

MATERIALS

1 yard of cotton or linen fabric

2 packages of bias binding (or the equivalent amount of self-made bias binding)

Cording such as cotton cording

TOOLS

Sewing machine and needle

Pins

Iron

Measuring tape

Yardstick

Marking pen or chalk

Bodkin or small safety pin

Seam ripper

TERMS & CONCEPTS

You will be **drafting a pattern**, making **bias binding** (optional), and sewing **buttonholes**. See "Methods" on page 6 for more information.

Measurements

You will need the following measurements:

- **A** = Your waist circumference
- **B** = The length from your waist to the tops of your knees

Draw a square that is ½ your **A** measurement by your **B** measurement + 1".
Round the bottom corners of the square.
Cut out one piece of the apron using the pattern.

CONSTRUCTION

1 Make the waist tie for the apron by cutting a piece of fabric that measures your **A** measurement + 10" by 4". If you can't cut the waist tie in one piece, cut two pieces that measure ½ your **A** measurement + 6" in length. With the right sides together, sew the two halves of the waist tie together with a ½" seam. Set aside.

2 Measure around the length of the apron's two sides and bottom. Cut a piece of double-fold bias binding equal to that length. Open out the bias binding and match one long edge to the edge of the fabric with the right side of the bias binding to the wrong side of the apron. Sew the bias binding to the apron with a ¼" seam.

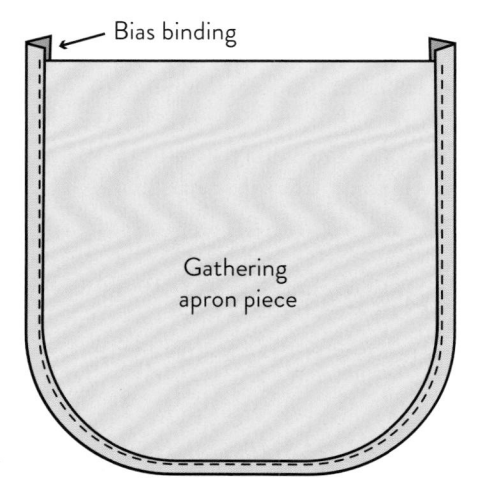

Bias binding

Gathering
apron piece

3 Press the bias binding out away from the apron with the seam edge pressed in toward the apron.

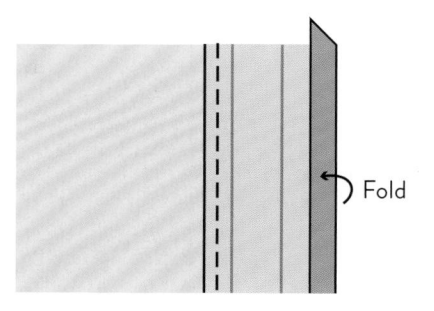

Fold

4 Make four marks on the right side of the bias binding: two marks 7" from each end of the bias binding and then two marks on either side of the center of the apron's bottom edge 2" from the center.

5 Sew ¼" buttonholes at the marks and open them up with a seam ripper.

6 Clip the rounded corners of the apron.

7 Fold the bias binding over the right side of the apron. You may have to tuck the bias binding around the curve. Make sure the unsewn edge of the bias tape is folded in. Press.

8 Sew along the folded edge of the bias binding to make the drawstring channel. Make sure not to sew through the buttonholes.

9 Using a bodkin or small safety pin, thread your cording in one side buttonhole and out one bottom buttonhole. Leave a good 5–6" of cording on either side of the channel openings. Tie knots or add beads to the ends of the cording to keep them from pulling back into the channel. Repeat on the other side.

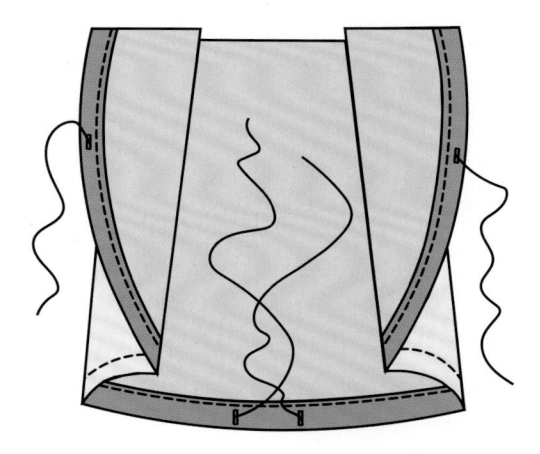

10 Fold the waist tie in half lengthwise and press. Open up the waist tie and fold each edge in to meet at the middle. Fold the waist tie in half again and press.

11 Open out the waist tie and center it over the top of the apron, with right sides together and edges matching. Baste in place.

12 Fold the short ends of the waist tie in to the wrong side of the fabric ½".

13 Fold the waist tie over, enclosing the top of the apron in the folds. Sew all around the waist tie ⅛" from the edge, making sure to go through all layers.

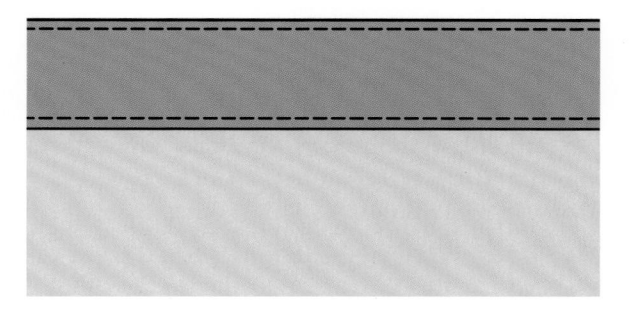

Fabric Flowers

There are many ways to embellish your garments. One way—fabric flowers—makes use of the scraps, reducing the amount that gets thrown out. There are countless ways to make flowers from fabric. Here are some of my favorites.

CIRCULAR FLOWERS

Cut circles of fabric to sew together into petals. Fill in the center with colorful buttons. Use **lightweight fabrics** for this project, as the diameter of the hole in the middle of the flower is affected by the weight of the fabric: the heavier it is, the bigger the hole.

Construction

1 Cut out four, five, or six circles of the same size (or use the pattern on page 184).

2 Fold a circle in half with the right side of the fabric facing out.

3 Sew a gathering stitch around the curved edge of the semicircle. Pull the thread tight so that the fabric forms into a petal shape.

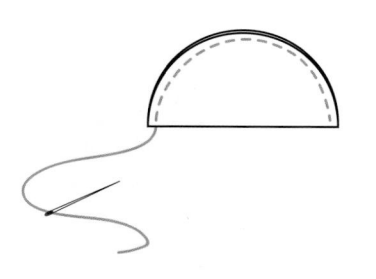 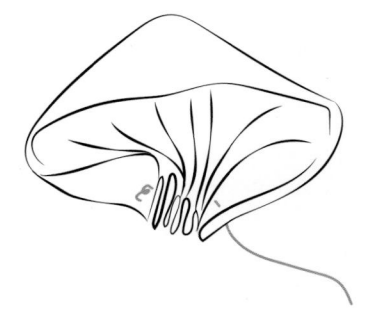

4 With the same needle and thread, repeat steps 2 and 3 with the rest of the fabric circles.

5 Arrange the petals into a circle with the gathered edges facing in toward each other. Sew a stitch on the back of the first petal to secure the flower.

YO-YOS

These little abstract flowers make charming additions to the belt pouch on page 126. They can also be turned into pins or barrettes. All they require is a circle of fabric, thread, a needle, and a button. Choose buttons without a shank and in colors that coordinate with the fabric. They can be made out of nearly any weight of fabric with the exception of very stiff material.

Construction

1 Cut out a circle measuring 3" in diameter (or use the pattern on page 184).

2 With the wrong side of the fabric facing up, run a gathering stitch around the outside of the circle ⅛" from the edge. Start and end the stitch on the wrong side of the fabric.

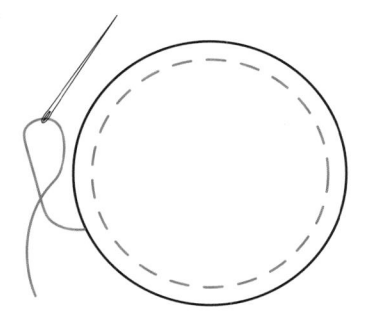

3 Pull the thread up so that the outside edge gathers into the middle.

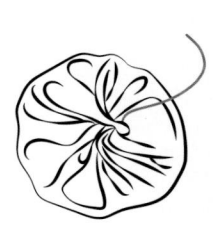

4 Flatten the circle and tie off the thread.

5 Sew the button onto the yoyo, covering the gathered edges.

FRAYED FLOWERS

For a less polished-looking bloom, create these frayed flowers to decorate bodices and skirts. One 5" by 5" square creates one flower, making this an easy way to use up the last fabric scraps. This project is also perfect for using up odd buttons at the bottom of your sewing basket. Use the template on page 184 to draw the petals, or freehand it for a more primitive look.

Construction

1 Cut a 5" by 5" square of fabric.

2 Cut the square into three equal rectangles.

3 Stack the three rectangles on top of each other. Using the template on page 184, trace the petals on the fabric.

4 Cut out the petals on all three rectangles.

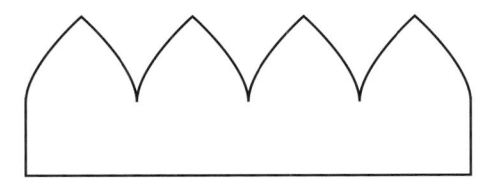

5 Using a needle with a long piece of thread, run a gathering stitch along the straight edge of one of the rectangles ⅛" from the edge.

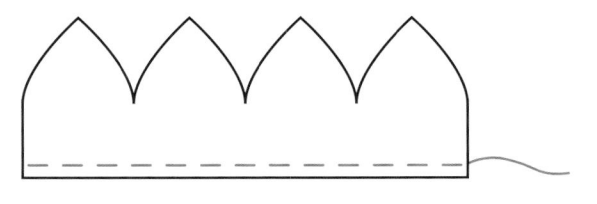

6 Pull the thread, gathering the rectangles into a circle.

7 Continue to make a gathering stitch on the other two rectangles with the same thread. Pull the thread, gathering the rectangles into a circle.

8 Make a small stitch securing the first set of petals to the third.

9 Tie off the thread.

10 Add a button to the center.

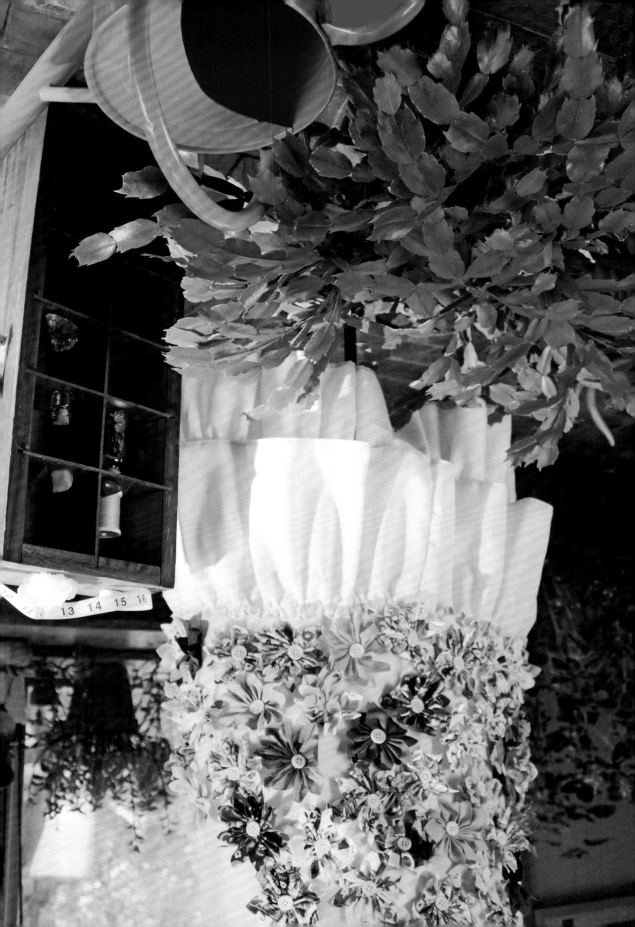

Conclusion

The projects in this book are a culmination of years of dreaming and planning. It took decades to get a handle on my style. Like a magpie, I took inspiration from other looks—from the *mori* fashion trend from Japan to prairie grunge (think Holly Hobbie + combat boots) and even Ren fair shopping spree. Being a self-taught sewist and clothing designer, I felt self-conscious about what I was making and wearing. But after so many years of practice, I am proud when someone compliments my clothing and I can say, "Thank you, I made it!"

I hope that you have found some designs that inspire you to break out the sewing machine and play around with that weird fabric you picked up and then stashed away. I also hope that you have been inspired to check out your local thrift stores for craft supplies and linens that could be made into beautiful garments. The more we salvage, upcycle, and remake, the less ends up in a landfill.

And when you do make your garments, please feel free to tag me on social media so that I can see your creations. I am on Instagram at @idiorhythmic. I would love to see what you come up with.

Until then, happy sewing and blessed be.

~Raechel

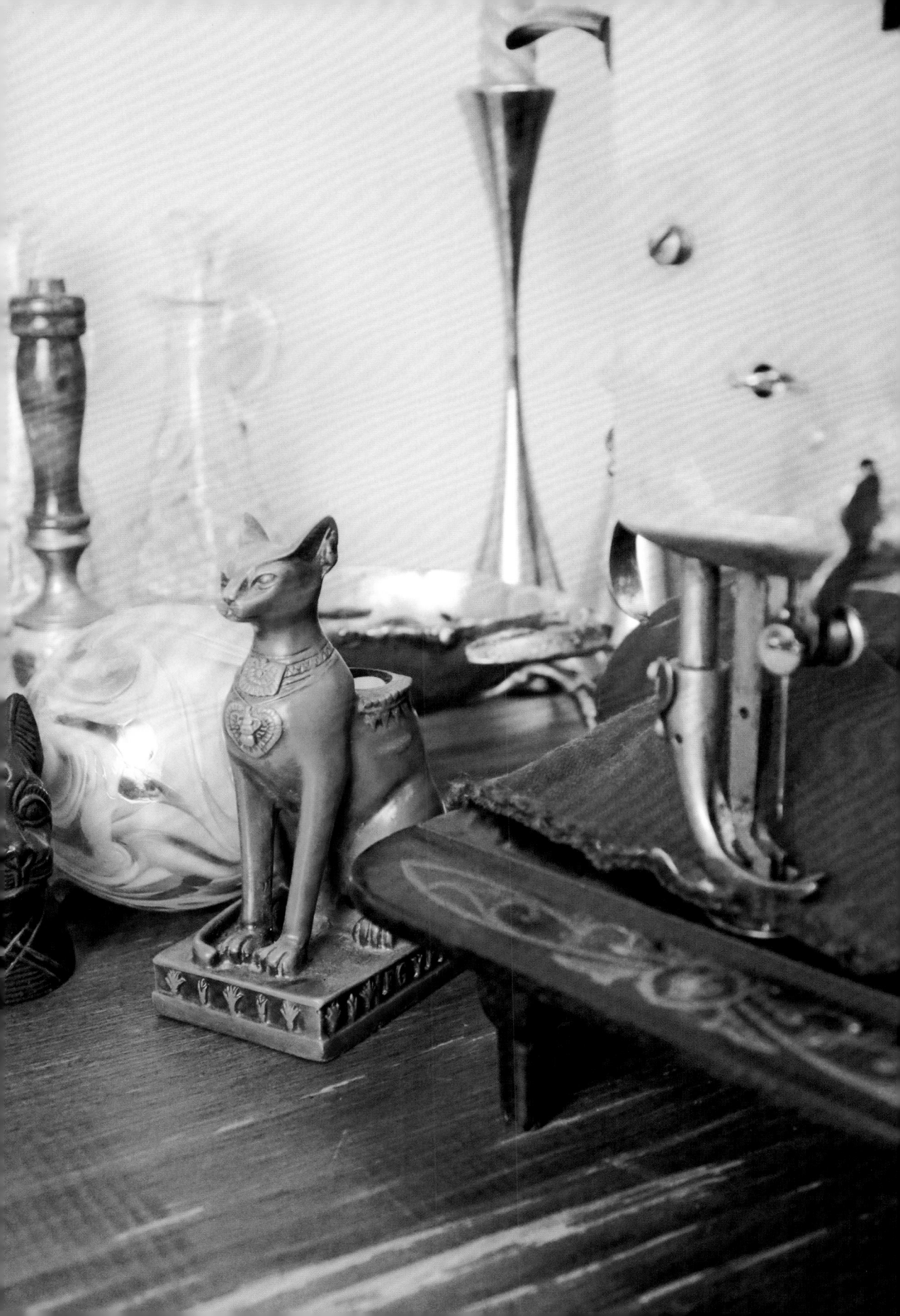

APPENDIX: PATTERNS

Walking Skirt Sigil

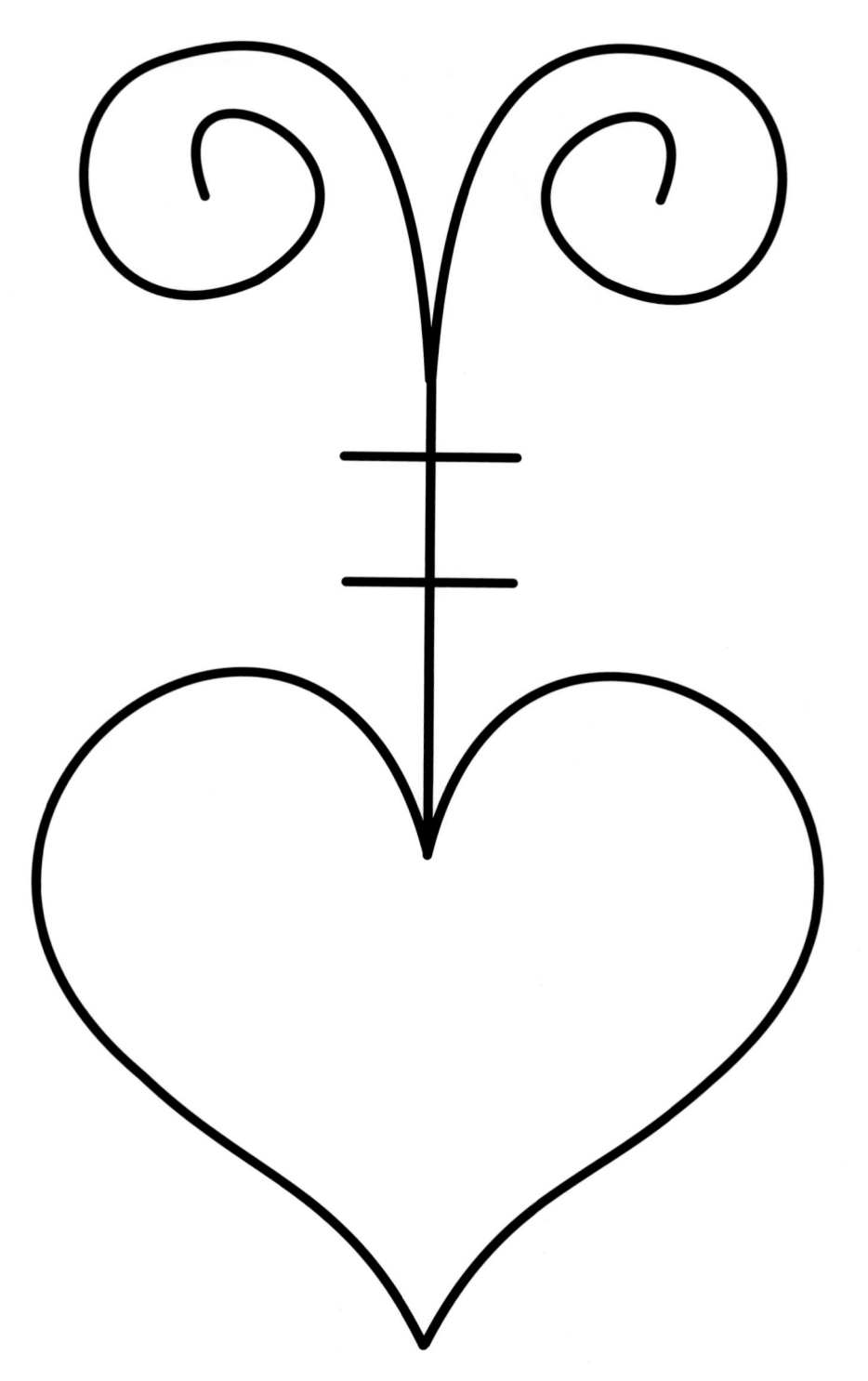

Walking Skirt Pocket
Scan and increase this piece to 157% for accurate sizing.

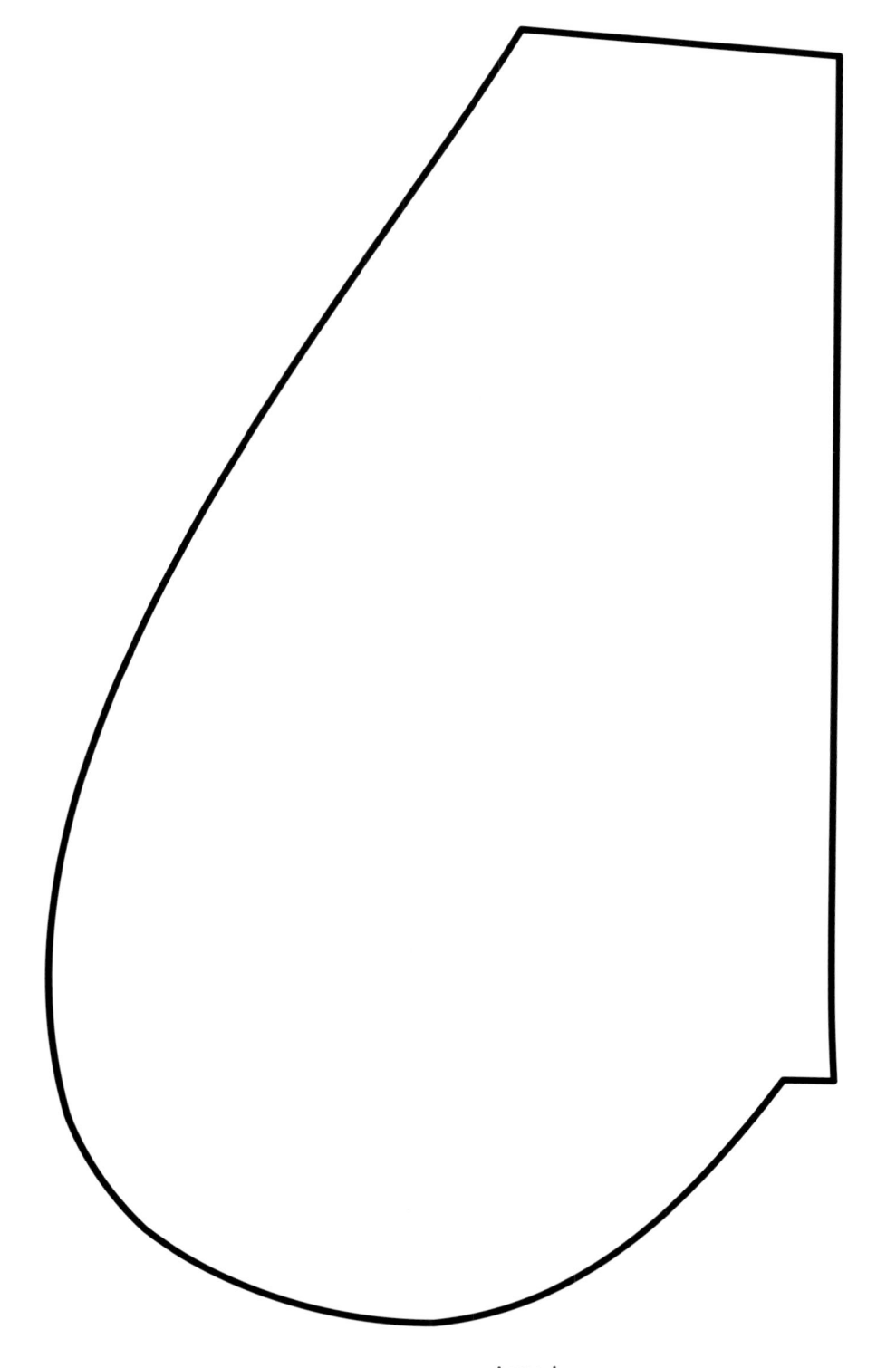

Belt Pouch Pattern Piece

Scan and increase this piece to 149% for accurate sizing.

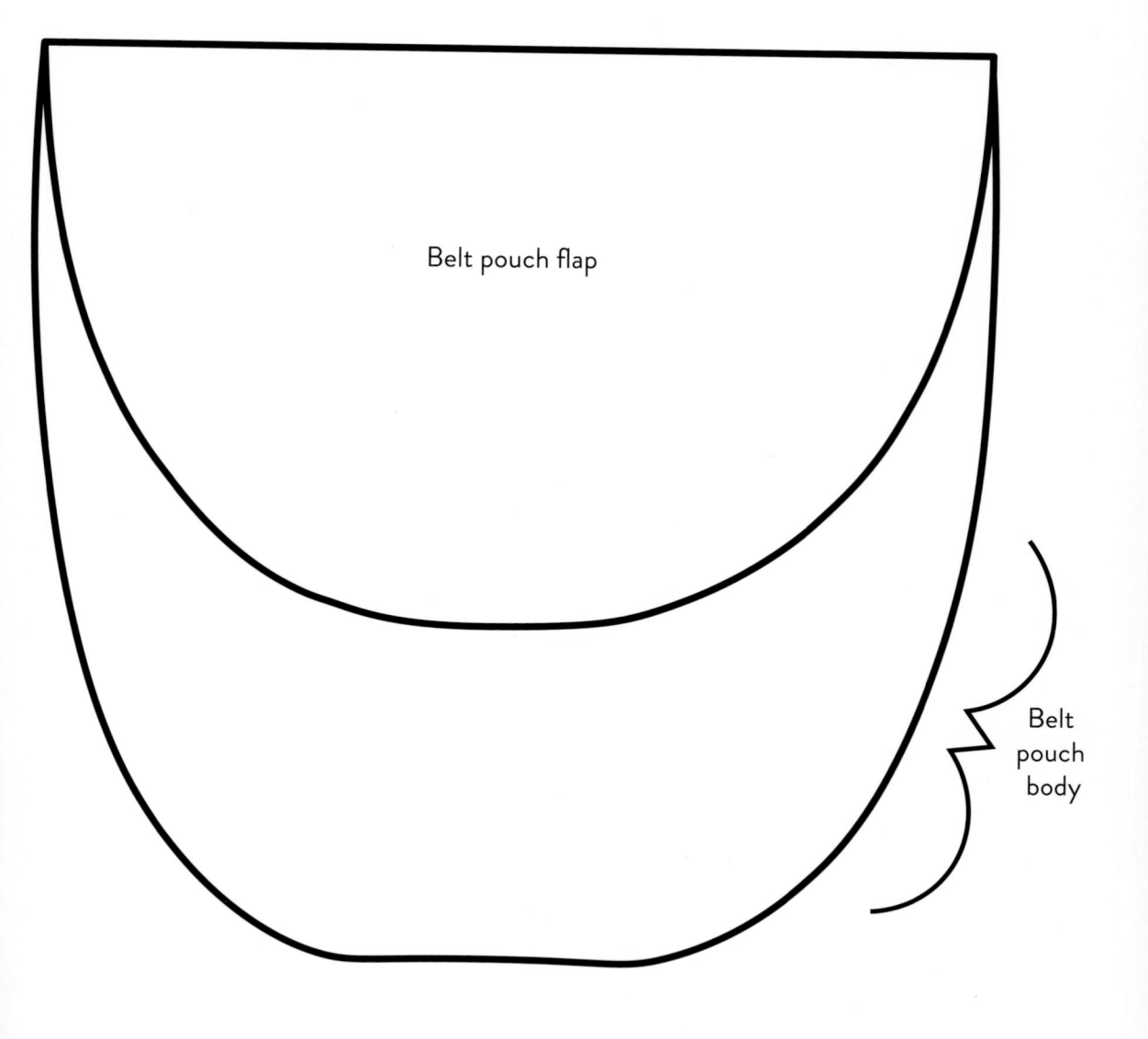

Belt pouch flap

Belt pouch body

Triple Moon Template

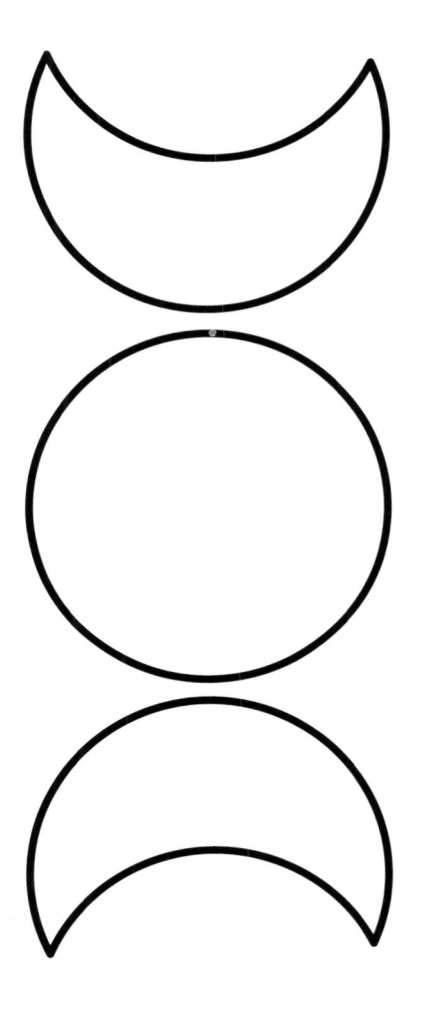

Waist Cincher: Front Center Pattern Piece
Scan and increase this piece to 150% for accurate sizing.

Center Front
Cut 1 fashion fabric
Cut 1 interlining
Cut 1 structure fabric

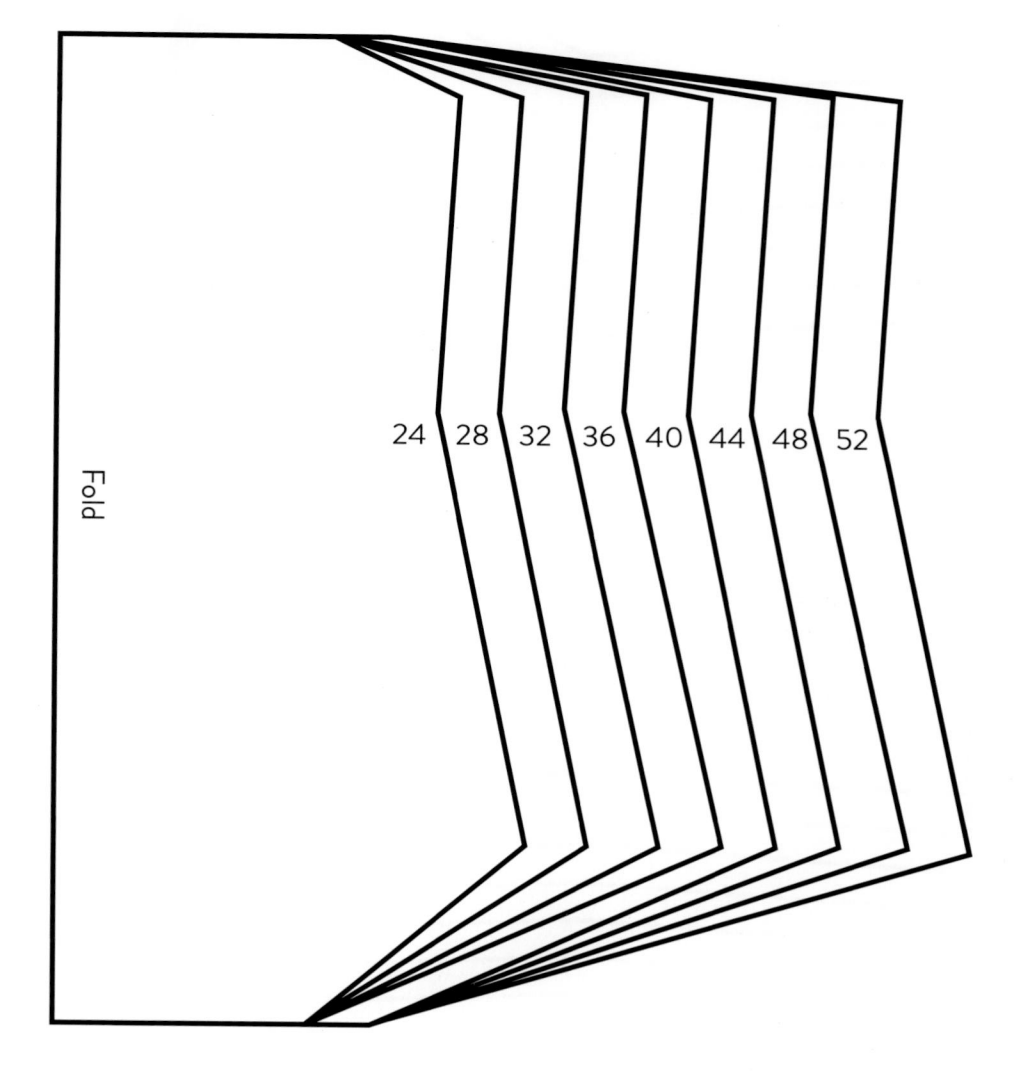

Waist Cincher: Side Front Pattern Piece

Scan and increase this piece to 150% for accurate sizing.

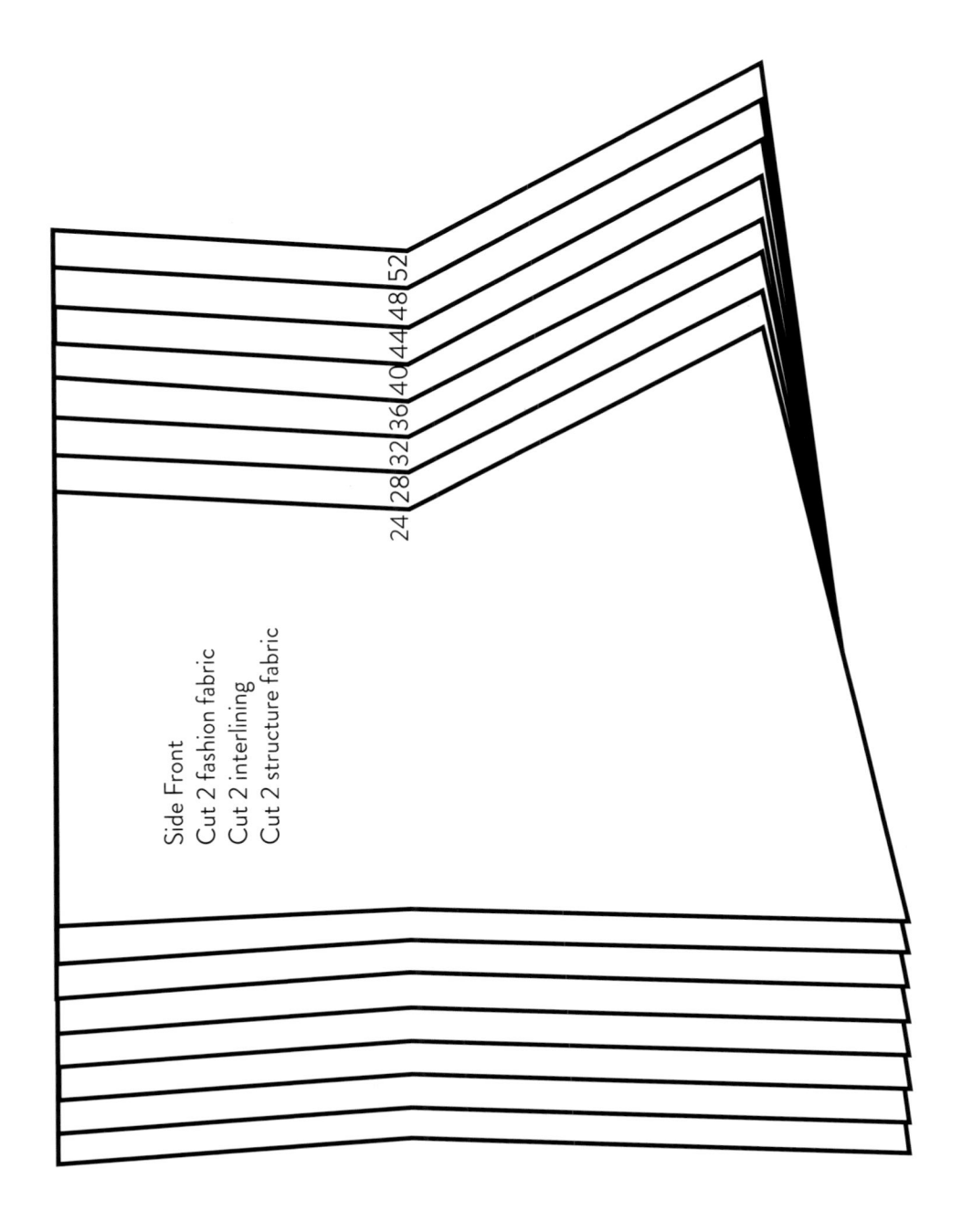

Waist Cincher: Side Back Pattern Piece
Scan and increase this piece to 124% for accurate sizing.

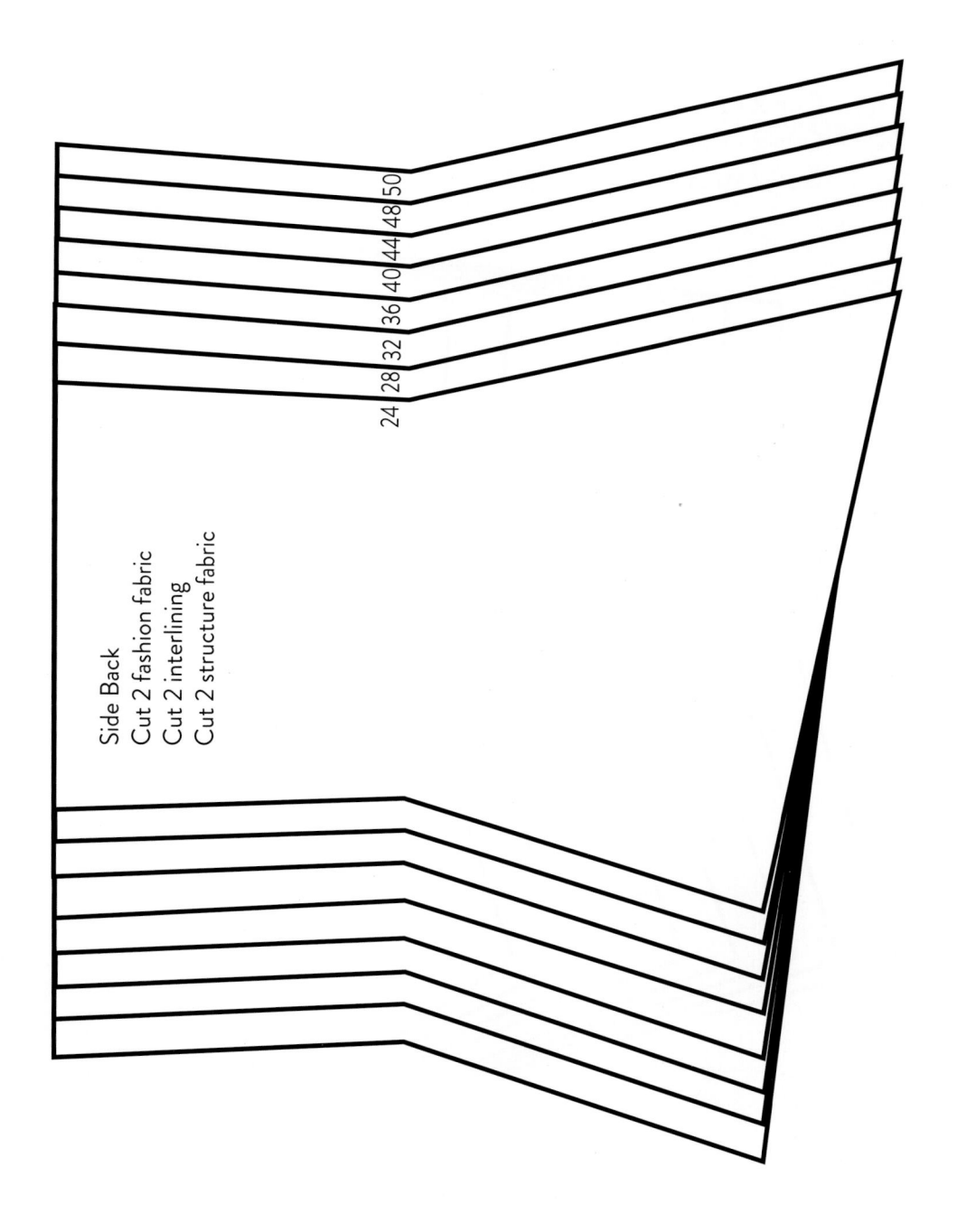

24 28 32 36 40 44 48 50

Side Back
Cut 2 fashion fabric
Cut 2 interlining
Cut 2 structure fabric

Waist Cincher: Center Back Pattern Piece

Scan and increase this piece to 156% for accurate sizing.

Center Back
Cut 2 fashion fabric
Cut 2 interlining
Cut 2 structure fabric

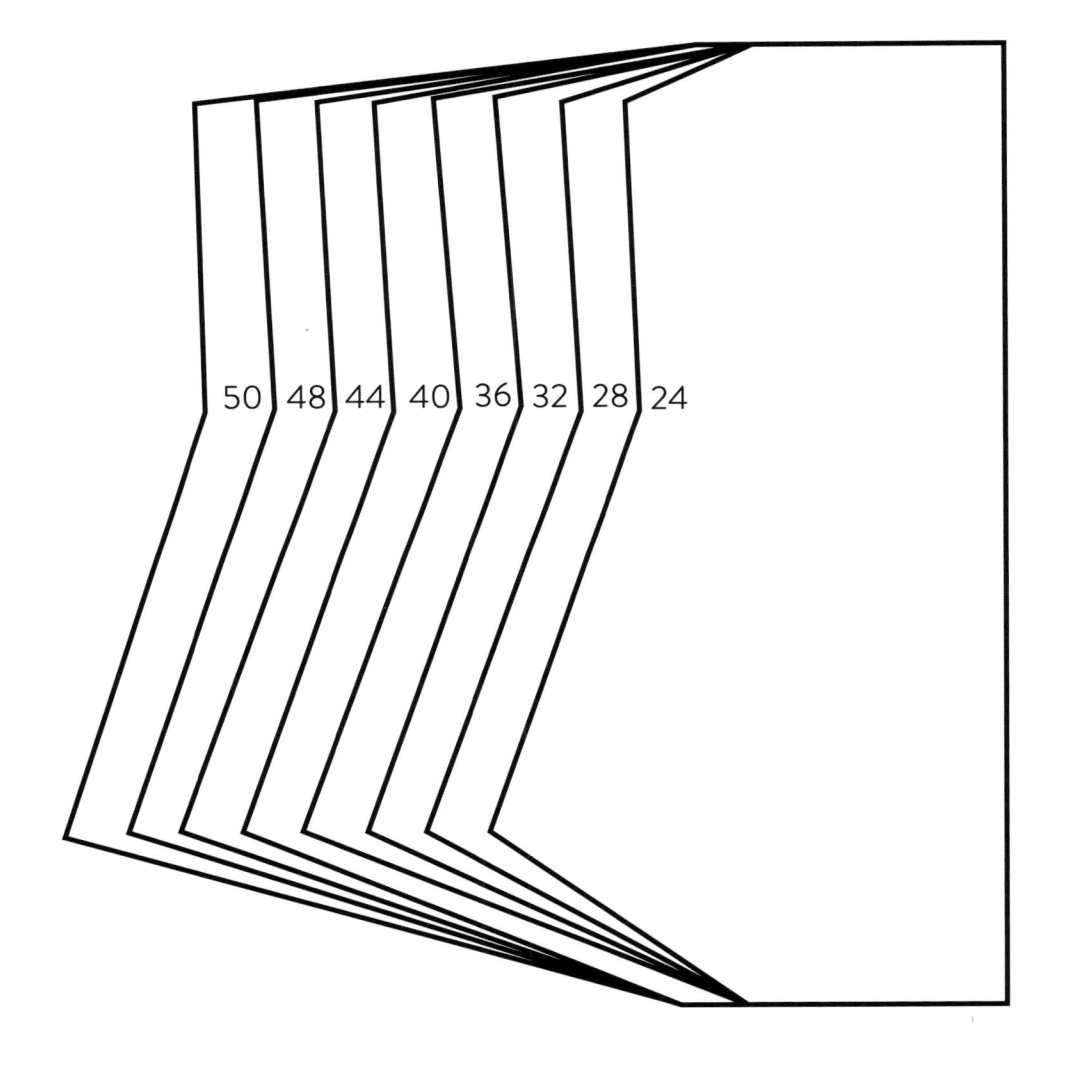

50 48 44 40 36 32 28 24

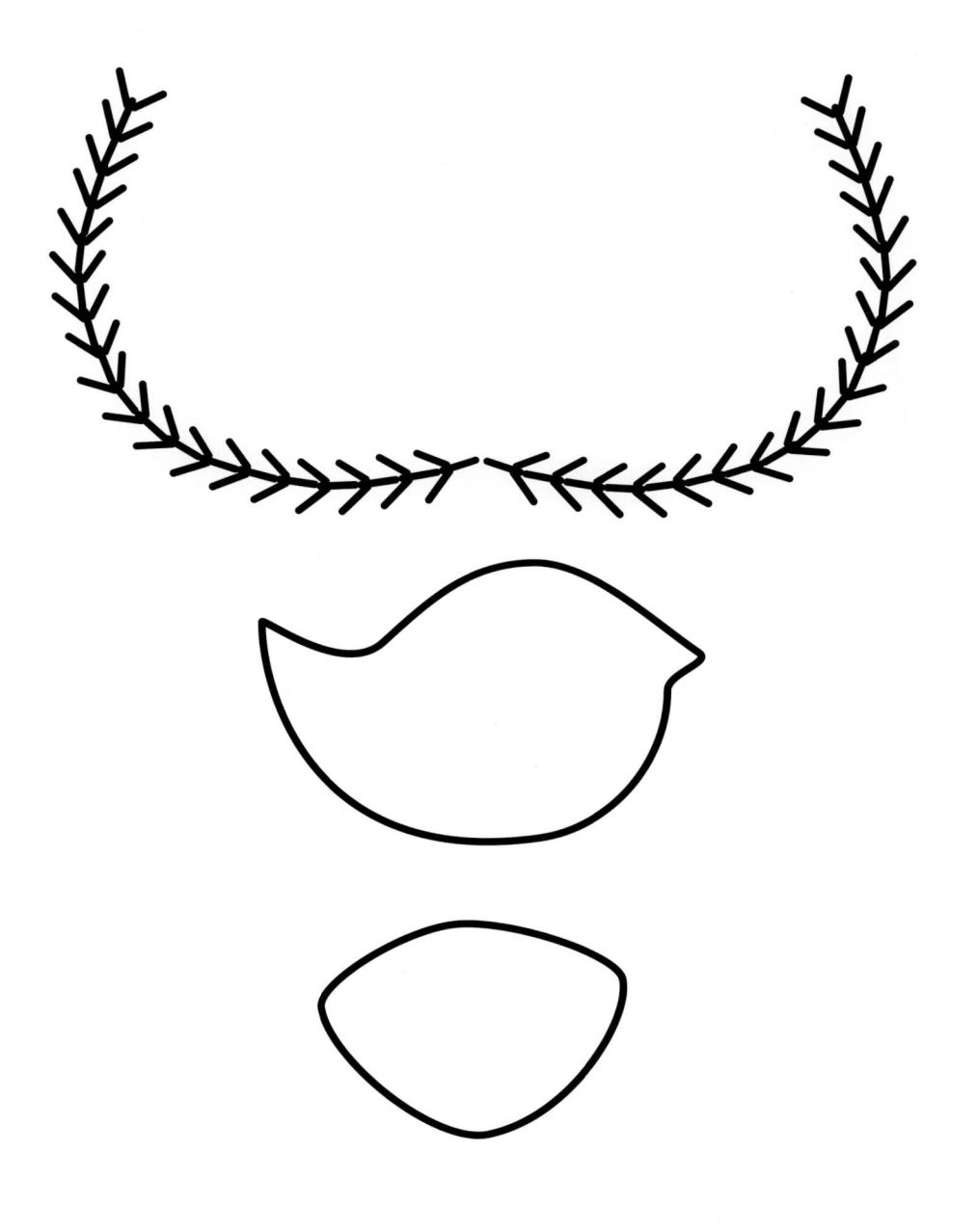

Bustle Pad Pattern Piece

Scan and increase each half to 130% for accurate sizing,
then combine them at the dotted line to complete the bustle pad.

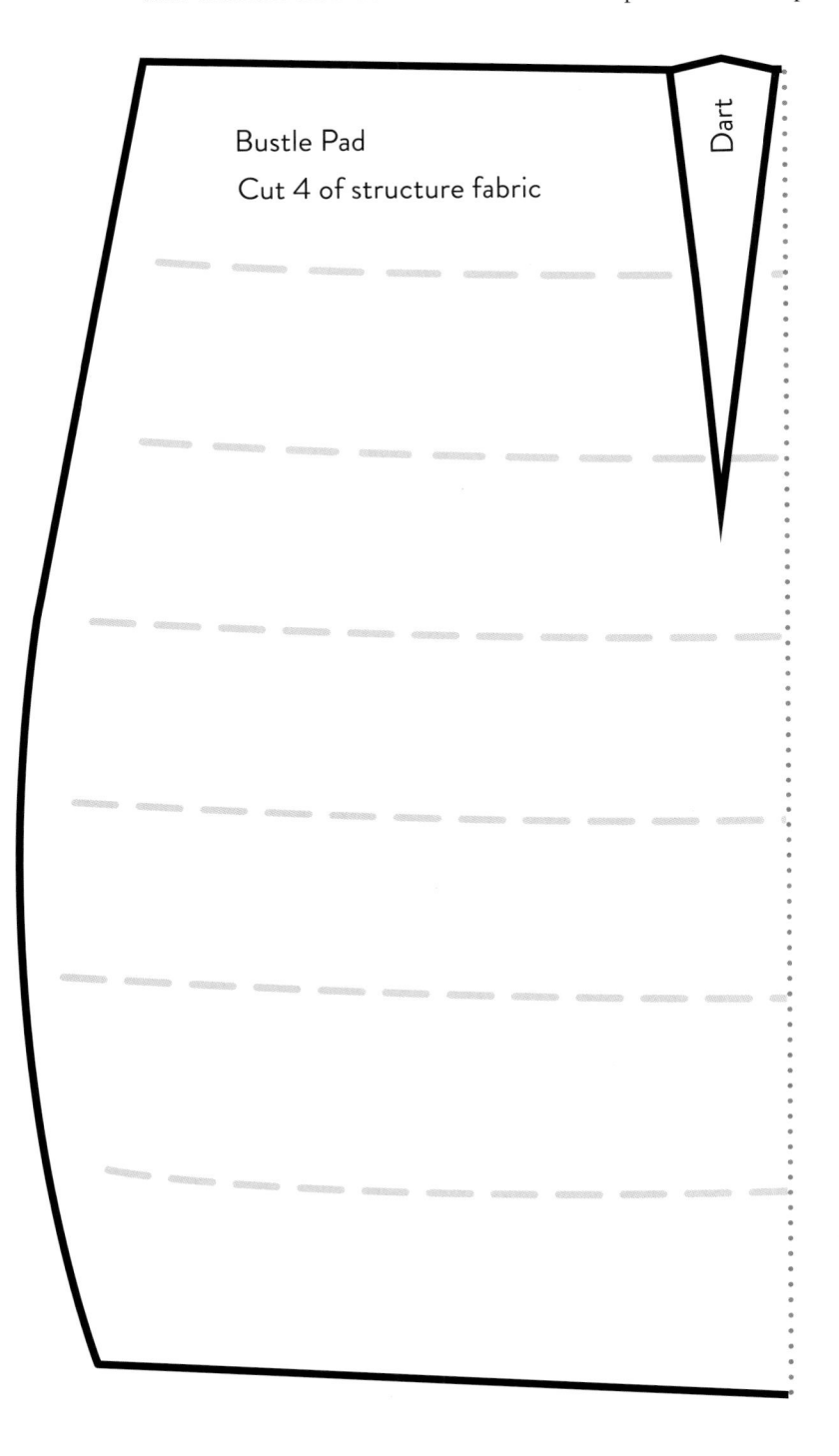

Bustle Pad

Cut 4 of structure fabric

Dart

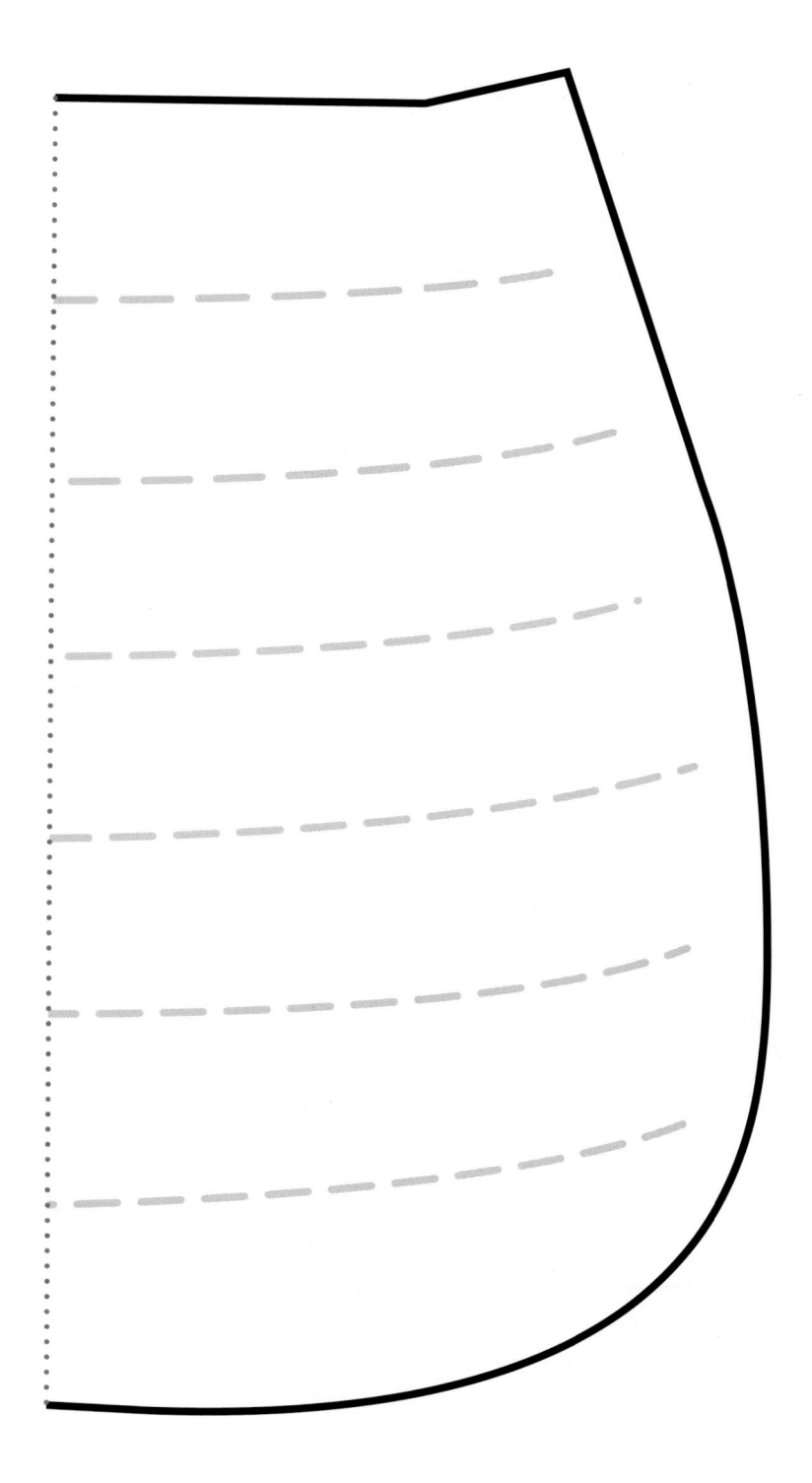

Circular and Yo-yo Flower Template

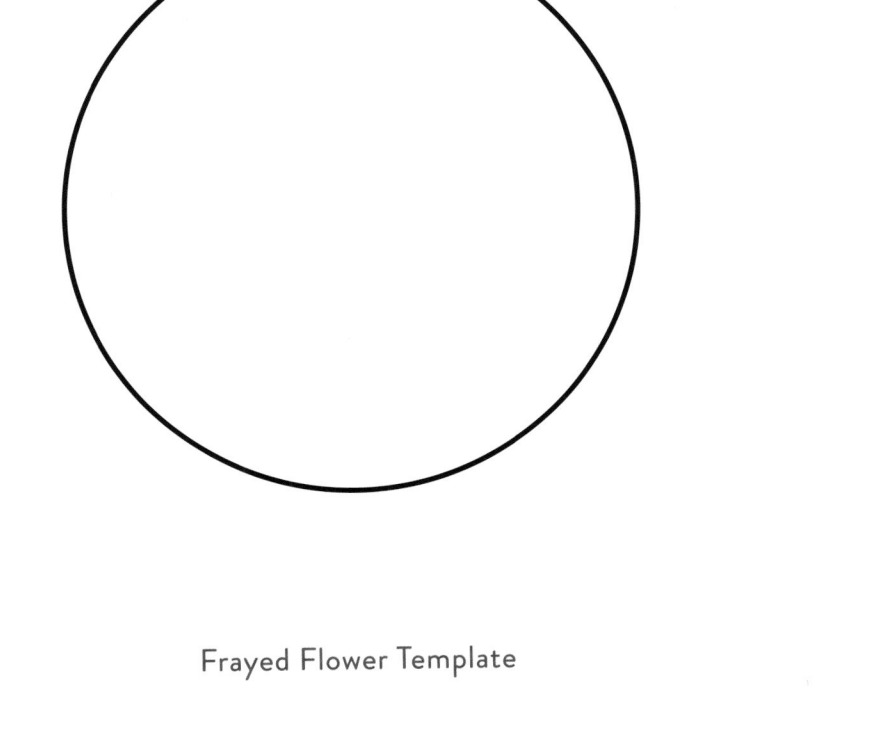

Frayed Flower Template

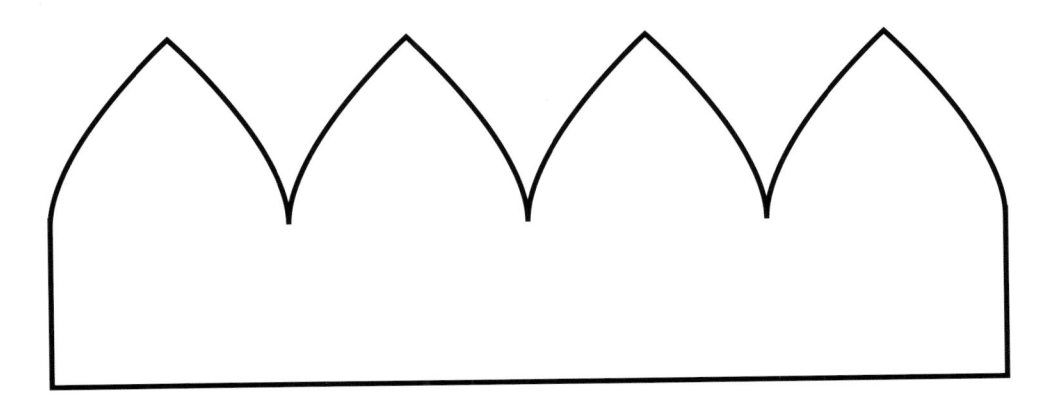

TO WRITE TO
THE AUTHOR

If you wish to contact the author or would like more information about this book, please write to the author in care of Llewellyn Worldwide Ltd. and we will forward your request. Both the author and the publisher appreciate hearing from you and learning of your enjoyment of this book and how it has helped you. Llewellyn Worldwide Ltd. cannot guarantee that every letter written to the author can be answered, but all will be forwarded. Please write to:

Raechel Henderson
℅ Llewellyn Worldwide
2143 Wooddale Drive
Woodbury, MN 55125-2989

Please enclose a self-addressed stamped envelope for reply, or $1.00 to cover costs. If outside the U.S.A., enclose an international postal reply coupon.

Many of Llewellyn's authors have websites with additional information and resources. For more information, please visit our website at http://www.llewellyn.com.

MW00667553

Praise for *The Witch's Wardrobe*

"*The Witch's Wardrobe* guides you through the process of filling your closet with layers of witchcore fashion. Even those new to sewing will find it easy to get started. Each garment comes with tips for infusing magic into your creations. This book truly resonates with me and should be a part of every crafty witch's library."
—**OPAL LUNA,** author of *Fiber Magick*

"Not only is *The Witch's Wardrobe* a total delight to read, but it is also a very much-needed resource for today's witch. . . . This book is the answer to all my witch wardrobe requirements, and I can put my own personal spin on it with the fabric I choose. The book includes all kinds of garments from skirts to dresses and even accessories to zhuzh up any outfit. The instructions are clearly laid out with detailed photographs, which is really helpful. I am just about to dust off the sewing machine and create myself a stunning, unique, made-to-fit-me wardrobe."
—**RACHEL PATTERSON,** witch, podcast host, and bestselling author of over twenty-five books

"Got flounces? Raechel Henderson had me at 'Curtains make great walking skirts' (don't worry, there's a pants project, too) and kept me through the history of the petticoat and kitchen witchery tips. The patchwork skirt, ribbon skirt, and fabric flower crafts will finally use up all those odds and ends you've been keeping in the closet. So get that stack of IKEA curtains down from the shelf and start sewing!"
—**LINDA RAEDISCH,** author of *The Secret History of Christmas Baking*

"Raechel Henderson has inspired me to dust off my sewing machine and give making another go. Her easy-to-follow instructions (with pictures!) and down-to-earth and genuine encouragement will remove all intimidation (and excuses) for making your own garments. There are projects in *The Witch's Wardrobe* for every skill level—I can't wait to try some of these patterns (fairy dress, I'm looking at you!). And don't miss the magical side info—scarves for voice magic, securing your magic with buttons, kitchen witchery, and more!"
—**NATALIE ZAMAN,** coauthor of *Social Media Spellbook*